RICHARD COEUR DE LION

broadview editions
series editor: Martin R. Boyne

RICHARD COEUR DE LION

edited and translated by Katherine H. Terrell

broadview editions

BROADVIEW PRESS – www.broadviewpress.com
Peterborough, Ontario, Canada

Founded in 1985, Broadview Press remains a wholly independent publishing house.
Broadview's focus is on academic publishing; our titles are accessible to university and college
students as well as scholars and general readers. With over 600 titles in print, Broadview has
become a leading international publisher in the humanities, with world-wide distribution.
Broadview is committed to environmentally responsible publishing and fair business practices.

The interior of this book is printed on 100% recycled paper.

PERMANENT   100%

Ancient
Forest
Friendly™

Library and Archives Canada Cataloguing in Publication

Richard Coeur de Lion (Romance). English
    Richard Coeur de Lion / edited and translated by
Katherine H. Terrell.

Translated from Middle English.
Includes bibliographical references.
ISBN 978-1-55481-278-3 (softcover)

    I. Terrell, Katherine H., editor, translator II. Title.
III. Title: Richard Coeur de Lion (Romance). English

PR2065.R4A38 2019   821'.1   C2018-906206-1

Broadview Editions
The Broadview Editions series is an effort to represent the ever-evolving canon of texts in the
disciplines of literary studies, history, philosophy, and political theory. A distinguishing feature
of the series is the inclusion of primary source documents contemporaneous with the work.

Advisory editor for this volume: Colleen Humbert

Broadview Press handles its own distribution in North America:
PO Box 1243, Peterborough, Ontario K9J 7H5, Canada
555 Riverwalk Parkway, Tonawanda, NY 14150, USA
Tel: (705) 743-8990; Fax: (705) 743-8353
email: customerservice@broadviewpress.com

Distribution is handled by Eurospan Group in the UK, Europe, Central Asia, Middle
East, Africa, India, Southeast Asia, Central America, South America, and the Caribbean.
Distribution is handled by Footprint Books in Australia and New Zealand.

Broadview Press acknowledges the financial support of the Government
of Canada for our publishing activities.

Canada

Typesetting by Aldo Fierro
Cover design by Aldo Fierro

PRINTED IN CANADA

Contents

Acknowledgements

I am grateful to Suzanne Conklin Akbari for first introducing me to *Richard Coeur de Lion* in a graduate seminar at the University of Toronto, and to my friend and fellow student in that seminar, Suzanne M. Yeager, for encouraging me to develop the selected translation that I had made for my students' use into a full translation and edition. My students at Hamilton College have helped to develop my thinking about the poem. I am grateful to Hamilton College for research support and to Clare Hall, University of Cambridge, for the fellowship that allowed me to work with the manuscript housed in Gonville and Caius College. I am also indebted to Peter Larkin, whose 2015 edition for TEAMS has made my work considerably lighter. Merilee Atos, Martin Boyne, Colleen Humbert, and Marjorie Mather at Broadview Press have my gratitude for their patience and aid in shepherding the work to completion.

Permission for use of the following materials for the appendices to this edition has been generously granted:

Ailes, Marianne, and Malcolm Barber, editors; Marianne Ailes, translator. Excerpt from *The History of the Holy War: Ambroise's Estoire De La Guerre Sainte: I. Text; II.* Rochester, NY: Boydell Press, 2003. Reprinted with the permission of Boydell & Brewer Ltd.

Appleby, John T., editor. Excerpt from *The Chronicle of Richard of Devizes of the Time of King Richard the First.* London: Nelson and Sons, 1963. Reprinted with the permission of John Tate Mitchell on behalf of the Estate of John T. Appleby.

Babcock, Emily Atwater, and A.C. Krey. Excerpt from *A History of Deeds Done Beyond the Sea*, by William of Tyre. New York: Columbia UP, 1943. Reprinted with the permission of Columbia University Press, and Letitia E. Basford on behalf of the Estate of A.C. Krey.

Barber, Malcolm, and Keith Bate, translators. Excerpt from *Letters from the East: Crusaders, Pilgrims and Settlers in the 12th–13th Centuries; Crusade Texts in Translation.* Copyright

Bird, Jessalynn, Edward Peters, and James M. Powell, editors. "Pope Gregory VIII's Call for a Crusade," from *Crusade and Christendom: Annotated Documents in Translation from Innocent III to the Fall of Acre, 1187–1291*. University of Pennsylvania Press, 2013. Reprinted with the permission of the University of Pennsylvania Press.

Chibnall, Marjorie, editor. Excerpt from *The Ecclesiastical History* by Orderic Vitalis. Oxford: Oxford University Press, 1975. Reprinted with the permission of Oxford University Press.

Chibnall, Marjorie, translator. Excerpt from *Memoirs of the Papal Court* by John of Salisbury. London: Nelson and Sons, 1956.

Edbury, Peter, editor and translator. Excerpt from *The Conquest of Jerusalem and the Third Crusade: Sources in Translation*; Crusade Texts in Translation. Copyright © 1999, Routledge. Reprinted with the permission of Taylor & Francis Books UK.

Faletra, Michael, editor and translator. Excerpt from *The History of the Kings of Britain*, by Geoffrey of Monmouth. Peterborough, ON: Broadview Press, 2008.

Levine, Robert, editor and translator. Excerpt from *The Deeds of God through the Franks: A Translation of Guibert of Nogent's 'Gesta Dei per Francos.'* Rochester, NY: Boydell Press, 1997. Reprinted with the permission of Boydell & Brewer Ltd.

Levine, Robert, translator. Excerpt from *A Thirteenth-Century Minstrel's Chronicle (Récits d'un ménstrel de Reims): A Translation and Introduction*; Studies in French Civilization 4. Lewiston: Edwin Mellon Press, 1990. Reprinted with the permission of The Edwin Mellon Press.

Nicholson, Helen J., editor and translator. Excerpt from *The Chronicle of the Third Crusade: The Itinerarium Peregrinorum et Gesta Regis Ricardi*; Crusade Texts in Translation. Copyright © 2011, Routledge. Reprinted with the permission of Taylor & Francis Books UK.

Introduction

The anonymous Middle English romance of *Richard Coeur de Lion* transforms Richard I (1157–99)—a French-speaking king who spent only six months out of his ten-year reign in England, and who is said to have joked that he would sell London if he could only find a buyer[1]—into a national hero for England. It does so by blending fact and fiction, history and legend, chronicle and romance into a tale of adventure centred upon a Richard who is superhuman in his bravery, cleverness, and martial skill, even if his penchant for cannibalism challenges traditional notions of the heroic.

The romance focuses upon Richard's campaign in the Third Crusade, in which he battles to retake Jerusalem and the surrounding territory from Saladin (Salâh al-Dîn), the Sultan of Egypt and Syria. This much is factual: Richard was indeed a leading figure in the Third Crusade (1189–92), and—as in the poem—he conquered first the island of Cyprus, and then the coastal cities of Acre, Jaffa, Ascalon, and Darum. He nearly achieved his goal of capturing Jerusalem, coming within sight of the city before being forced to retreat. The poem enhances Richard's role in these victories and invents others, while streamlining the course of history and downplaying other participants' roles in the Crusade. Throughout, it contrasts Richard's fearless dedication to the cause of Christianity with the weakness and treachery of both his allies and his enemies, inventing numerous episodes as showcases for Richard's single-minded heroism.

Modern readers may well see a dark side to Richard's heroism, particularly in the gusto with which Richard ordains the slaughter of thousands (including civilians and captives) and in his enthusiastic cannibalism of his enemies. Part of what makes Richard's general bloodthirstiness so unsettling is that the poem never openly questions either its morality or its efficacy: rather, Richard's violence enables both his own greatness and that of

---

1 William of Newburgh, quoted by Gillingham, *Richard I* 118; also Richard of Devizes 9.

England.[1] Envisioning cross-cultural relations primarily in terms of power and conquest, the poem extols the English at the expense of almost everyone else, including other Christians (the Germans, Greeks, and French) as well as Muslims (known in the poem as Saracens, a pejorative term that could be applied to any non-Christian).[2] Indeed, Richard's spectacular violence seems to guarantee a uniquely close association between the English and the Christian God.

Richard Coeur de Lion is part of a larger medieval tradition of crusade literature that regards Muslim occupation of the Christian Holy Land as a source of shame and pollution and that sees the only remedy as the conversion or death of the Muslim inhabitants. The poem's vision of unremitting hostility between Christians and Muslims simplifies a more complex historical reality but participates in a popular literary tradition that portrays the conflict as one of good versus evil.

Genre, Audience, and Sources

Richard Coeur de Lion (hereafter *RCL*) is often identified as one of a number of Middle English poems known as "Crusade romances." The term "romance" has a rather different resonance for modern students than it did for a medieval audience. Originally, the French word *romanz* simply meant a work in a vernacular language rather than Latin; over time, it came to denote a genre that recounted the amorous and/or chivalric adventures of noble characters in a long-ago or far-away landscape. In Crusade romances, as the name implies, that landscape is typically the Middle East. Mary Hamel defines the genre as one "in which a Christian military power, because it is Christian, is called upon to confront and overcome in battle a non-Christian invader or usurper in another country—because it is not Christian" (177). Religion is the most important marker of difference, and the desire for conquest drives the narrative.

RCL, however, is more fact-based than most Crusade romances. The seven extant manuscripts, all dating from the fourteenth and fifteenth centuries, preserve both an older version

---

1 Suzanne M. Yeager finds that while Richard's violence fits within the standards of medieval warfare, the poem consistently increases the scale of his violence in comparison with chronicle accounts and attributes it to divine will (61–62).

2 See Tolan, *Saracens* 126–28, for the origins of the term.

of the poem—which scholars have labelled the *b* version—and a later, more expansive retelling, labelled the *a* version (which is the basis for this translation; for more detail, see the Note on the Text, p. 29). John Finlayson has argued that the original *b* version should be considered a "historical epic ... to which some fictional elements have been added" (*Richard* 160–61). He makes the case that in the manuscripts, *RCL* "[p]redominantly ... appears in contexts which suggest that it was viewed as 'historical' and heroic, not 'romantic' and fantastic, both in the B and A versions" (165). The poem can productively be compared to the French genre of *chanson de geste* ("song of heroic deeds"); indeed, the genres of *chanson de geste* and romance were always less clearly distinguished in England than in France (Furrow). *RCL* itself uses "jeste" (5) and "romaunce" (7) interchangeably in its opening lines, and while the poet compares Richard to other famous heroes of "romaunce" (7–20), the characters he lists—Roland, Alexander, Charlemagne, Arthur, Achilles, and their companions—are all characters who are also familiar from *chanson de geste* and chronicles. If a difference between the genres is significant at all, it is merely one of focus. Heather Blurton observes that "whereas twelfth-century *chanson de geste* is a genre about the articulation of religious difference, the project of *RCL* is to reorient this discourse toward an articulation of national difference" (128). Fracturing Christendom into quarrelling nations, the poem sometimes seems to celebrate English exceptionalism at the expense of the crusading ideal that urged Christians to unite against a common enemy (see Ambrisco; Blurton 128–31; Turville-Petre 122–24). Yet, as Lee Manion has observed, the poem is also deeply interested in the details of crusade policy and leadership, which depended upon "the creation of communities across regional and linguistic divides" (20). It seems clear that the poet envisioned *RCL* as a heightened version of actual historical events, and it was probably taken that way by its original audience.

The audience of Middle English romance seems to have been composed mainly of "the prosperous middle classes and the provincial gentry who had the money to buy books and the education to read them" (Putter, "Historical" 6). However, it is also demonstrable that romances were known to members of the court, and they were likely heard—if not necessarily read—by people farther down the social scale as well. As the "principal secular literature of entertainment" (Pearsall 15) of the Middle Ages, romances seem to have had a large and diverse audience.

The *a* version's invention of Richard's two main knights, Sir Fulk D'Oilly and Sir Thomas Multoun, may provide a more detailed clue to its original audience. In the poem, these two knights emerge pre-eminent from Richard's tournament at Salisbury and go on to lead two divisions of Richard's army, while he himself leads the third. Although no knights by these names are mentioned in the historical records of Richard's campaigns, the names appear to link the poem to the D'Oyly and Multon families of Lincolnshire, important baronial families in the fourteenth century that were connected both to each other and to other high-ranking families, including that of the earls of Warwick (Finalyson, "Legendary"). The Warwick family, in turn, was connected to William Longespee, Earl of Salisbury, a hero of the Fourth Crusade who also makes a heroic, if ahistorical, appearance in *RCL*.[1] The *a* version's poet may well have invented these illustrious ancestral figures for patrons in the D'Oyly, Multon, and Warwick families who wished to raise their prestige by claiming descent from crusading heroes.

The poem's sources likely include a lost Anglo-Norman original, but outside of the poem's own references to a French source (lines 21, 5098, and 7008), there is no definitive evidence for one (see Loomis). It is more certain that the poet was familiar with some of the historical chronicles that recount Richard's role in the Crusade. Ambroise's Anglo-Norman *Estoire de la Guerre Sainte* (*History of the Holy War*) and Roger of Howden's Latin *Chronica*, both from the late twelfth century, as well as Richard de Templo's Latin *Itinerarium Peregrinorum et Gesta Regis Ricardi*, from the early thirteenth century, all have enough in common with the poem that they may well have been used as source material (see the Appendices for excerpts from all of these chronicles, and see Finlayson, "*Richard*" 176–77, and Yeager 52). Ambroise and Howden were both participants in the Third Crusade; Ambroise was probably a member of Richard's army, while Howden was a parson and royal clerk who travelled in Richard's retinue for a year of his campaign (from August 1190 to August 1191). Numerous episodes in the poem—even some that seem fantastic—ultimately derive from chronicle accounts. To give only one example, in lines 2458–2606, Richard and his fleet, on their way to Acre, encounter an immense Saracen supply ship whose sailors claim to be French. The English see through the deception and ram the ship, sinking it and killing all but thirty sailors, whom they take

---

1 Finlayson details the familial connections in "Legendary" 304–05.

captive. It is said that Acre never could have been captured had the ship reached its destination. These details are all to be found in the chronicles; the only exaggeration is Richard's outsized role in the combat. The poem also draws upon the considerable body of legend that had, by the fourteenth century, built up around Richard and his family. See Appendix E for several examples.

Nationalism, Cannibalism, and Religion

Much of the scholarship on *Richard Coeur de Lion* has tried to explain how the poem can simultaneously portray Richard as a cannibal and as a heroic figure. The problem here is that cannibalism is more typically regarded as a firm taboo, something that one cannot engage in and remain fully human; cannibals tend to be regarded as monsters, as barbarous others excluded from the civilized world and from full participation in humanity. From classical antiquity onwards, depictions of cannibalism in literature and ethnography mark otherness and provide a rationale for colonization; yet cannibalism takes on a particular resonance in the literature of the Crusades. Heather Blurton notes that the characterization of Saracens as cannibals was "the most important 'othering' mechanism of the *chanson de geste* form" (120–21) serving to dehumanize the Saracens and justify their slaughter or forced conversion.

However, there is always a certain irony in these depictions of Saracen cannibals, for the best-documented cannibalism of the Crusades occurred, during the First Crusade, among Christian soldiers driven to desperation by famine (see Appendix C1). Geraldine Heng identifies this cannibalism as the source of a long-lasting cultural trauma:

> it is virtually impossible for moderns to grasp the precise horror and dimensions of abhorrence, the trauma to the cultural imaginary of medieval Christendom caused by crusader cannibalism of the Muslim enemy. The crusaders were represented by their Pope as pilgrims enjoined to rescue from infidel pollution the sacred places of the Holy Land, not to visit the contagion of heathen pollution upon themselves. (*Empire* 25–26)

So potent was this trauma, Heng argues, that the romance genre itself developed "as a form of cultural rescue in the aftermath of the First Crusade," turning to "cultural fantasy" in order that "what is unthinkable and unsayable by other means, might surface into discussion" (2). Accordingly, Heng suggests that Richard's joyful cannibalism recasts the trauma of the First Crusade as a joke, using the power of humor to render the transgressive acceptable while rewriting historical failure as literary success (73–78).

Other scholars see the trauma of the First Crusade as less influential—and, indeed, as less traumatic. Jay Rubenstein notes that even at the time of the First Crusade, "we cannot presume that all of the warriors felt an unbearable trauma at what must have been sometimes willful, aggressive, deliberate cannibalism" (549). Further, he suggests that contemporaries recognized "cannibalism not as an aberration from the ethos of holy war but as an aspect of it" (530), one that was justified by the crusaders' unique status as God's warriors and the consequent demonization of their opponents (551). Blurton, analyzing the literary representation of cannibalism from the tenth through the fourteenth centuries, finds "the lines of literary influence between crusader cannibalism and *chanson de geste* harder to trace" than Heng; instead, she argues that *RCL* "appropriates for its English protagonists the structural position that belonged to the Saracen in *chanson de geste*. This reworking of generic form becomes the basis for the romance's politics of asserting a model of English dominance in a post-crusading Europe" (121). In other words, Blurton finds that in *RCL*, Richard takes actions that are more typical for Saracens in Crusade romances; as a result, the English rather than the Saracens emerge as the newly threatening power, in a poem that is more about asserting dominance than recouping trauma. The question of the extent to which the cannibalism of the First Crusade influences the poem's portrayal of Richard is still a matter of debate.

However, it seems clear that *RCL* portrays Richard's cannibalism as a key aspect of his greatness as an English king: the poem transforms this paradigmatic indicator of barbarity into a marker of national distinction. More than anything else, Richard's willingness to engage in extreme violence is what sets the English apart from their fellow Christians—particularly the French, whose main function in the poem is to serve as foils to the English. Whereas Richard and his commanders cavalierly slaughter entire cities full of Saracens who refuse to convert, the French king Philip ignores Richard's command that he do the same; the Saracens from whom Philip accepts ransom then turn against him and have to be reconquered by Richard. Philip's complaint that "I never liked to slay men" (4687) epitomizes this national difference: as Alan Ambrisco quips, "The English are cannibalistic and barbaric; the French, to their deep discredit, are neither" (516). While Richard is the only character in the poem who actually engages in cannibalism, he himself suggests that his "English Christian" soldiers could sustain themselves indefinitely in the Holy Land by feasting upon their enemies (3549): the English, uniquely in the poem, are viewed as hardy enough to derive strength from unthinkable acts.

This English exceptionalism depends not only upon denigration of the poem's French characters but also upon a wholesale recasting of historical Anglo-French relations. Richard I spoke no English and was French in language, culture, and outlook; his roles as Duke of Aquitaine and Duke of Normandy (among others) appear to have been as important to him as that of King of England. The poem's hostility to the French may be explained partly by the fact that fourteenth-century English monarchs reigned over a territory that was much reduced from the Angevin Empire that Richard commanded, which encompassed about half of modern-day France as well as England. Richard's successor, his younger brother John I (r. 1199–1216), was a disastrous ruler who lost most of these continental possessions, ensuring that future English monarchs would be based in England. As early as 1295—not quite a century after Richard's death—Edward I (r. 1272–1307) was rallying nationalist sentiment in a summons to Parliament by claiming that it was "the detestable purpose" of the French king "to wipe out the English tongue altogether from the face of the earth"; by the mid-fourteenth century, with the two nations embroiled in the Hundred Years' War, it had become commonplace to define English and French identities as fundamentally opposed.[1] Indeed, Suzanne Yeager suggests that RCL was intended to encourage its English audience's support for the Hundred Years' War by promulgating the view "that the French were not only unworthy allies of England, but also enemies of God" (76).

The poem retroactively writes this hostility into the historical record. For example, in order to maintain "the illusion that

---

1 Ambrisco usefully summarizes the shift in Anglo-French relations between the twelfth and fifteenth centuries (511–15). For a more detailed account of Richard I's Angevin Empire, see Gillingham, *Richard I*. See Yeager 74–75 for a review of the scholarship on the anti-French rhetoric of the fourteenth and fifteenth centuries (which increasingly invoked crusade rhetoric against the French).

Richard was solely a king of England," it explains the conflict between Richard and Philip as mere personal enmity, rather than acknowledge that it was rooted in "political disputes over French territories" (Ambrisco 516). Most glaringly, in what Heng terms "a strategic act of forgetting" (*Empire* 107), the poem rewrites Richard's genealogy. Richard's actual mother, Eleanor of Aquitaine—a fascinating and powerful figure who had been queen of France before she became queen of England, and from whom Richard inherited the Duchy of Aquitaine and many of his cultural sensibilities—is erased in the *a* version, along with the rest of Richard's continental ancestors.[1] In Eleanor's place, the poet creates the mysterious and possibly demonic figure of Cassodorien, the daughter of the king of Antioch. In the xenophobic world of *RCL*, a diabolical origin is apparently preferable to descent from a former queen of France. Based on an ancestral legend that the historical Richard boasted about, this unusual genealogy adds to Richard's air of supernatural prowess (see Appendix E). Suzanne Akbari notes that the transposition from Eleanor to Cassodorien "produces a Richard whose alien nature is not French, but Oriental" ("Hunger" 205), providing Richard with a latent Saracen identity that helps to account for his savagery, even as it separates him from his French heritage. Here, Richard's Saracen ancestry substitutes for the inheritance rights that he historically claimed by virtue of his great-grandfather's involvement in the First Crusade and helps to literalize the common assertion that the Holy Land was the rightful heritage of Christendom (Yeager 73; see Appendix B).

Throughout the poem, Richard's strange eating habits—first the lion-heart episode that gives him his name, and later his cannibalism—help to establish his reputation as a fearsome military leader. Richard's eating of the lion's heart stages a precise blend of civilization and savagery: eating the heart still warm, without bread but neatly dipped in salt, he prompts the German king to exclaim, "This is a devil and no man" (1112), but also to assert that "He may be called, rightly, / The christened king of most renown, / Strong Richard Coeur de Lion!" (1116–18). Nicola McDonald observes that the *RCL* poet is especially concerned with questions of eating, noting that "[n]o matter where we look

---

1 The *b* version, by contrast, omits any discussion of Richard's ancestry at the beginning but does include a brief (11-line) episode following line 2040, based on historical events, in which Eleanor brings Berengaria of Navarre to Messina to be Richard's wife.

in *Richard* we are likely to find food—or, in its absence, hunger" ("Eating" 131). Richard first consumes human flesh unknowingly, in response to hunger: recovering from a grave illness, he has a great longing for pork, the food of home.[1] When his men are unable to find any pork in this Muslim country, they order that a Saracen prisoner be killed, cooked, and served to the King, who is instantly healed. (See Appendix C3a for another example of healing cannibalism.) When he later demands to be served the head of the pig, and thus realizes what (or whom) he has eaten, Richard's reaction is telling:

> When the King saw his dark face,
> His black beard, and his white teeth,
> And how his lips grinned wide,
> The King cried, "What devil is this?"
> And began to laugh as if he were mad. (3211–15)

Richard's reaction shows none of the revulsion that we might expect from someone who has unwittingly engaged in cannibalism. Instead, he *laughs*. This demotion to food source clearly dehumanizes the Saracen enemies, especially as their flesh is equated with that of swine: traditionally unclean animals in Islam, which medieval Christians knew Muslims were forbidden to eat. However, the grisly emphasis on the human features of the slain prisoner refuses to allow the audience to forget that this is indeed a *man* whom Richard has devoured. Whether eating a lion's heart or a Saracen's body, Richard enacts the old adage that "you are what you eat," becoming ever fiercer as he absorbs not only the flesh but also the ferocity of his opponents (Akbari, "Hunger" 208; McDonald, "Eating" 139; Yeager 55–56).

Richard also sees strategic potential in cannibalism, and he welcomes this culinary innovation as a solution to the problem of famine that so often plagued crusaders in the Middle East. He exclaims,

> What, is Saracens' flesh this good,
> And I never knew it until now?
> By God's death and his resurrection,
> We shall never die for hunger

---

1 Akbari notes that, because of Richard's Saracen heritage, this meal "is, paradoxically, food from home" that not only heals him but also seems to heighten his Saracen identity ("Hunger" 209).

> While we may, in any assault,
> Slay Saracens, take their flesh,
> Boil them and roast them and bake them,
> And gnaw their flesh to the bones.
> Now that I have proved it once,
> Before hunger makes me wretched,
> I and my folk shall eat more! (3216–26)

Richard's gleeful and highly pragmatic response essentially treats the Saracen enemies as livestock: beasts to be slaughtered for the consumption of his armies. The fact that he envisions this slaughter as occurring within an "assault" further links his military and culinary ambitions: putting the expected death toll of his campaign to good use, Richard will ensure that his armies literally feed upon conquest.

Richard is attuned to the symbolic as well as the practical potential of cannibalism, and the second episode involves a carefully orchestrated element of political theater played out for Saladin's ambassadors. He orders the execution of the highest-ranked Saracen prisoners and has their heads cooked, labelled with their names, and served both to the messengers and to himself; Richard laughs heartily at the messengers' horror as he enjoys his own meal and pretends to be unaware that their customs differ from his. As Heng observes, "the very act of eating your enemy is also a potent demonstration of political power.... In the realm of the political, what after all is cannibalism but a hideously somatic literalization of the language of military conquest, which encompasses how successful conquerors swallow up and absorb unto themselves the land and possessions of the defeated?" (*Empire* 31). Swearing that "We will not return to England / Until we've eaten every one!" (3561–62), Richard succeeds in making his point: the Saracen messengers return and report the events at great length (also replaying them for the audience, in case anyone missed the details), arguing that Richard is "a devil, without fail" (3664) who will "eat our children and us" (3669) if Saladin does not make peace. Richard shows himself to be wholeheartedly dedicated to simultaneously annihilating and assimilating the entirety of the Saracen world, subsuming it both literally and metaphorically into the English Christian body and state.

While Richard's reputation for savagery helps his military campaign, it also, paradoxically, seems to ensure his favor with God. Various scholars have suggested that Richard's eating of the Saracens parallels a central ritual of the Catholic faith: the sacrament of the Eucharist.[1] At a crucial point during the celebration of mass, the priest would consecrate bread and wine, transforming it, according to church doctrine, literally and entirely into the material flesh and blood of Christ (known as the Eucharist or the Host). Believers participated in this ritual either by taking communion—literally ingesting Christ's body and blood—or, more commonly, by witnessing the elevation of the consecrated Eucharist that the priest would then ingest on behalf of the congregation.[2] Believers who took part in this ritual were thereby bound together in a shared Christian body. Richard's eating seems to function similarly, but here again the nation takes precedence over the ideal of a united Christendom: Akbari notes that "Just as the priest consumes the Host on behalf of the spiritual community, so Richard as king consumes the [Saracen] flesh on behalf of the national community. Through Richard, the English become empowered to consume the world of the Saracens, if only in a metaphorical sense" ("Hunger" 214). Yeager furthers the argument: "Through Richard the potentially polluting Saracen body has the opposite effect: it heals and strengthens the king and unifies his people. In this role, Richard proves God's favor of him: the English king becomes at once mediating priest to Christian crusaders and scourge to his adversaries" (59). Throughout the poem, Eucharistic theology seems to hover in the background, enhancing the symbolism of Richard's eating and helping to establish what the poem sees as his divine right to the holy city of Jerusalem (Yeager 76–77).

The deferral of England's projected conquest of Jerusalem—first for the three-year, three-month, and three-day truce that Richard concludes with Saladin, and then indefinitely, due to Richard's untimely death—means that *RCL* ends with unfinished business: the constraints of history disallow the happy ending that's more typical of a medieval romance. Nevertheless, Richard remains a larger-than-life figure, and the poem's sensational blend of fact and fiction asserting English political, military, and religious dominance guaranteed the poem's popularity for at least two centuries. *RCL*'s original audience may well have been drawn to its enthusiastic embrace of violence on behalf of a victorious

---

1   See, especially, Akbari, "Hunger"; McDonald, "Eating"; Yeager.
2   For details of medieval Eucharistic theology and practice, see Rubin.

and divinely supported English king; modern readers may be more intrigued by the convergence of religion, race, and nation in this multilayered poem, which freely transgresses taboos as it reimagines English history.

Appendices

In the appendices, I have gathered a wide array of historical and literary texts that bear on the poem. As background to the crusading movement, I begin with the calls to crusade of two popes: Urban II in 1095, who launched the First Crusade, and Gregory VIII in 1187, who instigated the Third. Since the poem's scenes of cannibalism have become such a focus of recent scholarship, I then provide brief selections from nine chroniclers and one poem, spanning the twelfth century, that recount the cannibalism that took place during the First Crusade; two fourteenth-century selections that make clear the connections between cannibalism and the celebration of the Eucharist; and two contemporary literary depictions of cannibalistic acts. I then turn to excerpts from Richard I's own letters and from several chronicles that comment upon Richard's character and relate his exploits on crusade. This section could easily be expanded, as the poem relies so heavily on chronicle sources; however, most of these chronicles are widely available in translation, so I encourage interested readers to delve into them further. Finally, I offer a selection of legendary material that was in circulation before and during the time of the poem's composition. Richard's family seems to have inspired an unusual number of rumours and legends, not all of which were complimentary. Some of these have been credited with inspiring the poem's depiction of Richard's peculiar ancestry and quasi-supernatural prowess. I also include some background on the poem's most common slur against the English: that they have tails.

While most of this contextual material can be found elsewhere, it is widely scattered and sometimes out of print. I hope that students will find it useful to have it gathered in one place. The majority of the texts are drawn from others' editions, for which I am grateful for the permission to reprint here, but the translations from Middle English sources are my own. The rest of the material in the Appendices appears in its original form.

Richard I: A Brief Chronology

1122	Eleanor of Aquitaine born.
1133	5 March: Henry Plantagenet born.
1137	Eleanor marries King Louis VII of France.
1147–49	Eleanor accompanies Louis on the Second Crusade.
1152	March: Marriage of Eleanor and Louis VII is annulled. May: Eleanor marries Henry Plantagenet.
1154	December: Henry Plantagenet is crowned King Henry II of England.
1157	8 September: Richard is born at Oxford to Henry II and Eleanor of Aquitaine.
1169	Designated heir of Poitou and Aquitaine and betrothed to Alice, daughter of Louis VII.
1173	Joins his mother and his brothers Henry and Geoffrey in an unsuccessful rebellion against Henry II.
1174	Henry and his sons are reconciled and Eleanor is imprisoned in England.
1174–83	Henry sends Richard to subdue rebels in Aquitaine.
1180	Louis VII dies; his son King Philip II of France (Philip Augustus) is crowned.
1183	Richard's older brother Henry dies; Richard becomes heir to the throne.
1186	Geoffrey (Henry II's third son and Richard's younger brother) dies.
1186–88	Conflict between Henry II and Philip II.
1187	Saladin captures Jerusalem. Richard takes the cross (pledging himself as a crusader).
1188	Does homage to Philip II and allies with him against Henry II.
1189	4 July: Henry II agrees to do homage to Philip II for his French possessions and recognizes Richard as his heir. 6 July: Henry II dies. 20 July: Richard becomes Duke of Normandy. 13 August: Arrives in England and sets about raising money for his crusade. 13 September: Crowned King Richard I of England. Jews are barred from the coronation and riots ensue. 12 December: Returns to France; he and Philip swear allegiance to one another.

1190	March: Massacre of Jews at York.
	4 July: Richard and Philip depart (by separate routes) for the Holy Land.
	22 September: Richard arrives in Messina, Sicily.
	October: Captures Messina.
1191	March: Philip attempts to ally with Tancred of Sicily against Richard; Richard and Philip quarrel.
	Philip releases Richard from his engagement to his sister Alice.
	Queen Eleanor brings Berengaria of Navarre to marry Richard.
	1–12 May: Richard reaches Cyprus, quickly conquers it, and marries Berengaria.
	7 June: Captures a Saracen supply ship.
	June–July: Richard and Philip lay siege to Acre.
	12 July: Acre surrenders; the Crusaders arrange a truce with Saladin.
	31 July: Philip leaves Acre to return to France.
	20 August: Orders the execution of nearly 3,000 Muslim prisoners.
	7 September: Wins a major victory at Arsuf.
	10 September: Takes possession of Jaffa and fortifies the city.
	31 October: Sets off for Jerusalem, intending to capture it.
1192	January: Richard's army is forced to retreat.
	22 May: Captures Darum.
	29 May: Messengers brings news that Richard's younger brother John, with the support of Philip, is plotting against him.
	6 June: Sets out for Jerusalem again; captures a large Saracen caravan.
	28–31 July: Saladin attacks and besieges Jaffa; Richard recovers the city.
	2 September: Saladin and Richard conclude a three-year truce.
	9 October: Departs for England, but is shipwrecked on the Istrian coast; he and his men disguise themselves as pilgrims and travel by land.
	December: Captured by Duke Leopold in Vienna, then handed over to the Emperor Henry VI and imprisoned.
1193	4 March: Saladin dies.

1194	February: England pays an enormous ransom to Henry VI and Richard is released.
	13 March: Richard arrives in England and resumes control.
	12 May: Returns to Normandy.
1194–96	Recaptures territory from Philip.
1196	January: Philip and Richard conclude a peace treaty at Louviers.
1197–98	Continuing struggles over territories in France.
1199	6 April: Dies, aged 41, at Chalus-Chabrol in Aquitaine while suppressing a rebellion of barons.

A Note on the Text

Richard Coeur de Lion survives in seven manuscripts, dated from the 1330s to the late 1400s, and in two early printed editions by Wynkyn de Worde, dated 1509 and 1528. The poem seems to have been very popular, as none of the manuscripts seems to have been a source for any of the others; this suggests that there must have been many copies in circulation. Similarly, the fact that de Worde published a second edition of the poem implies that the first edition sold well, attesting to its continuing popularity well into the sixteenth century. The extant versions of *RCL* fall roughly into two groupings, which scholars have labelled the *a* and *b* groups (see Brunner). Somewhat confusingly, the *b* version of the poem is the earlier one. There are significant differences among the *b* texts: the earliest (c. 1331–40) and least fantastic version, which is one of many romances in the well-known Auchinleck Manuscript (Edinburgh, NLS Advocates' 19.2.1), is incomplete, but it may well be the closest to a lost Anglo-Norman original. The later *a* version has been expanded by about 1,200 lines, mainly consisting of fabulous legendary material. For example, whereas the *b* version mentions Richard's actual mother, Eleanor of Aquitaine, the *a* version opens with an account of Richard's descent from a mysterious and possibly demonic mother (thereby explaining Richard's own supernatural prowess). The *a* version also contains an extended episode in which Richard fights in disguise at a pre-Crusade tournament; it creates two fictional knights—Thomas Multoun and Fulk D'Oilly—as Richard's chief companions; and it includes an ahistorical battle with Saladin, complicated by his gift to Richard of a demonic horse. In addition, it expands the *b* version's single episode of cannibalism (which itself occurs in only one *b* manuscript) to two instances of Richard eating his Muslim opponents.[1] So far, only the longer *a* version has been accessible in modern editions; it is the basis of most scholarship on the poem and is the source of this translation.

In translating *RCL*, I have followed the two modern editions of the *a* version in taking the Cambridge, Gonville and Caius College 175/96 manuscript as the base text, supplementing its

---

1 Among the five *b* texts, cannibalism occurs only in MS London, BL Egerton 2862.

gaps (it is missing leaves at three points) with readings from de Worde's 1509 printed edition. Karl Brunner's 1913 edition has become largely inaccessible to students, both because it has long been out of print and because its introduction and notes are in German. It has recently been updated by Peter Larkin, whose 2015 edition, with its copious explanatory and textual notes, will supply many of the needs of modern scholars, graduates, and advanced undergraduates who have a working knowledge of Middle English.

This volume offers the first Modern English translation of the full text of *Richard Coeur de Lion* and is intended for a broader audience. Throughout, I have tried to follow the Middle English closely, so as to facilitate comparison between this translation and Larkin's Middle English edition. The section breaks throughout the translation, however, follow those of the manuscript. At times I have rearranged the word order for the sake of clarity, but these rearrangements rarely extend beyond two or three lines. Similarly, I have sacrificed rhyme in favour of accurately rendering the sense of the original: while at times the Middle English rhymes could translate naturally to Modern English, more often at least one of the rhyming words requires translation, and the available rhymes would stray too far from the sense of the passage. Therefore, I have deliberately steered clear of rhyme at some points in order to avoid the awkwardness of a partly rhyming translation. I hope that whatever is lost in poetic effect will be made up for by ease of understanding. The rhyming couplets of the original text may be readily appreciated even by students who are new to the language. In Appendix A, I have included four passages of the original text, transcribed directly from the Cambridge, Gonville and Caius College 175/96 manuscript, for comparison.

I have endeavoured to strike a balance between keeping the footnotes to a minimum and explaining everything necessary for students who may have little knowledge of the historical and religious context of the poem. At times, rather than replicate earlier scholarship, I direct interested readers to Larkin's edition for fuller information. I follow Larkin's identification of place names and have modernized those whose identification seems secure; where there is doubt, I leave the manuscript's original spelling. The poem differs rather dramatically from the historical record of Richard's life, although it also corresponds to the chronicle accounts in sometimes surprising ways. In the notes, I have mentioned divergences from history only when they're particularly interesting or have obvious implications for interpreting the poem. Readers should not take the lack of a note as evidence of the poem's historical accuracy.

RICHARD COEUR DE LION

Lord Jesus, King of Glory,
What grace and victory
You sent to King Richard,
Who was never found to be a coward!
It is very good to hear tales   5
Of his prowess and his conquests.
Men make many new romances
Of good knights, strong and true;
Both in England and in France
Men read of their deeds in romances: 10
Of Roland, and of Oliver,
And of all Charlemagne's twelve peers,
Of Alexander, and of Charlemagne,
Of King Arthur and of Gawain,
How they were good and courteous knights;   15
Men read in rhyme of Turpin,
And of Oger Daneys, and of Troy,
About the war there in olden times:
Of Hector, and of Achilles,
And of the folk they slew in that combat.[1]   20
But these poems are written in French books:
Uneducated men don't understand them,
For uneducated men don't know French—
Barely one among a hundred.
And nevertheless, with good cheer,   25
I understand that many of them
Would like to hear of the noble deeds
Of the valiant knights of England.
Therefore I will now tell you
Of a king, valiant in deeds: 30
King Richard, the best warrior
That men may find in any tale.
Now may God grant a good end
To all who hear this speech!
        Lords, listen now   35
How King Richard was begotten and born.
His father was called King Henry;[2]
In his time, certainly,
As I find in my story,

---

1 This list includes many of the major heroes of medieval romance. See
   Appendix D1 for a chronicle account that makes a similar comparison.
2 King Henry II (r. 1154–89).

Saint Thomas was slain 40
At Canterbury at the altar,
Where many miracles are done.[1]
When he was twenty winters old
He was a very bold king.
He would have no wife, I understand, 45
Even if he found one very wealthy.[2]
Nevertheless his barons advised him
That he should agree to wed a wife.
Hastily he sent his messengers
Into many diverse lands, 50
So that the fairest women alive
They should bring him for a wife.
Messengers were all prepared;
They went to ships that very night.
Right away they drew up sails; 55
The wind served them well enough.
When they came to the middle of the sea
They had no wind at all—
Therefore they were very woeful.
Another ship they encountered there, 60
Such a one as they never saw before.
It was all white as walrus-bone,
And every nail engraved with gold;
The prow was made of pure gold,
The mast was of ivory, 65
The sail all made of samite,
And the ropes of twisted silk,
As white as any milk.
That noble ship was all over
Spread about with cloths of gold, 70
And its spar and its windlass
Were truly made of azure.
In that ship were set
Knights and ladies of great prowess;
And a lady was therein ·75
Bright as the sun through a glass.
Its men went to stand on deck,

---

1 Thomas Beckett, Archbishop of Canterbury, was murdered in
  Canterbury Cathedral in 1170, following a dispute with Henry.
2 In 1152, at the age of 19, Henry married Eleanor of Aquitaine (c.
  1122–1204). See Appendix E2.

And brought the other ship to their hands,
And prayed them to stay
And to tell their plans;   80
And they granted very readily
To tell everything at their will.
"Such wide lands we have traversed,
For King Henry has sent us
To seek a queen for him,   85
The fairest that might be found."
A king rose up from a chair,
With the words they spoke there—
The chair was carbuncle stone,
Such a one as they had never seen—   90
And two dukes beside him,
Noble men of much pride,
And each one welcomed the messengers.
Into that ship they went then;
Thirty knights, without lie,   95
Truly were in that company.
They went into that rich ship
Like messengers that had been sent.
Knights and ladies came to them,
Seven score, and more I think,   100
Welcomed them all at once.
They set up trestles, and laid a board—
Spread with cloth of silk—
And the King himself commanded
That his daughter be fetched forth   105
And set in a chair before them.
Trumpets began to blow;
She was fetched forth at once
With twenty knights all about,
And even more noble ladies;   110
They all proceeded to kneel to her,
And ask her what she wished to be done.
They ate and drank and made merry
As the King himself commanded.
When they had eaten,   115
They did not forget to speak of adventures.
The King told how, in his mind,
He had had a vision—
In the land that he came from—
That he should go into England;   120

And his daughter, who was dear to him,
Should go together with him.
"In this manner we have prepared ourselves
To go directly into that land."
Then answered a messenger—   125
His name was Bernager—
"We will not seek any further:
She shall be brought to my lord.
When he sees her with his own eyes,
He will be well recompensed."   130
The wind arose out of the northeast
And served them extremely well.
They arrived at the Tower;
The knights went swiftly to land.
The messengers had told the King   135
Of the lady, fair and noble—
In the Tower where he lay,
They told him of that lady white as a flower.
King Henry prepared himself
With earl, baron, and many a knight,   140
To go and see the lady,
For he was courteous and well-mannered.
The damsel was led onto land,
And cloths of gold spread before her,
And her father together with her,   145
With an excellent crown of gold,
And the messengers on every side,
And minstrels with great pride.
King Henry arrived in haste
And fairly greeted that unknown king,   150
And that fair lady also:
"You are all welcome to me!"
To Westminster they went together,
The lords and ladies that were there.
Trumpets began to blow;   155
They went in to dinner right away.
Knights served there in good style;
There's no need to tell what they had.
And after dinner, in haste,
Spoke King Henry, our king,   160
To the other king that sat there,
"Dear sire, what is your name?"
"My name, he said, is Corbaryng;

<u>I am the King of Antioch,"</u>[1]
And he told him, in his wisdom,   165
That he came there because of a vision.
"For truly, Sire, I tell you,
I would otherwise have brought a greater company,
Many more, without fail,
And more ships with provisions."   170
Then he asked that lady bright,
"What are you called, my sweet one?"
"Cassodorien, without lying,"[2]
Thus she answered the King.
"Damsel," he said, "bright and clear,   175
Will you stay here, and be my Queen?"
She answered with calm words,
"Sir, I am subject to my father's will."
Her father granted then quite soon
That all Henry's will should be done,   180
And she should be swiftly wed
As Queen unto the King's bed;
And prayed him, for his courtesy,
That it must be done privately.
    The wedding was done that night;   185
Many a knight danced there,
And there was much joy among them.
In the morning a priest sang Mass;
Before the elevation of the Host[3]
The Queen fell down in a swoon.   190
The people wondered and were afraid.
She was led into a chamber, and
She said, "Because I am thus afflicted
I never dare to see the sacrament."
Her father took his leave the next day;   195
He would tarry there no longer.
The King lived with his Queen;

---

1 Antioch, in modern-day Turkey, was a city of particular strategic
  importance during the Crusades, changing hands numerous times.
  Corbaryng is a fictional character.
2 Cassodorien is a fictional character who, here, replaces Richard's
  actual mother, Eleanor of Aquitaine (see Appendix E2). Her name
  may derive from *cassidoine*, Old French for the jewel chalcedony.
3 This is the crucial point in the Catholic Mass when the priest
  consecrates the Host and, according to Catholic belief, transforms
  it from bread and wine into the body and blood of Christ.

They had children between them,
Two boys and a girl,
Truly, as the book tells us. 200
The first was called Richard, indeed,
Of whom this romance is made;
Truly the other was called John, and
The third his sister Topaz.[1]
Thus they lived together 205
Until the fifteenth year.
One day, before the cross,
As the King stood at Mass;
There came an earl of great power:
"Sire," he said, "How may this be, 210
That my lady the Queen
Never dares to see the sacrament?
Give us leave to make her stay
From the beginning of the Gospel
Till the Mass has been sung and said, 215
And you shall see a curious trick."
With good will, the King allowed him
To hold her still with strength:
"Neither for joy nor for woe
Allow her to go from the church." 220
And when the bell began to ring,
When the priest should consecrate the Host,
She wished to go out of the church.
The earl, for good, said, "Nay,
Lady, you shall remain here 225
Whatever may happen."
She took her daughter in her hand,
and would not abandon her son John;
She went right out through the roof,
Openly before all their sight. 230
John fell from her in that place,
And broke his thigh on the ground.
And with her daughter she fled away,
And never was seen again.[2]
The King wondered at that thing, 235

---

1 Henry and Eleanor had eight children, of whom Richard was the third
   and John (r. 1199–1216) the youngest. Topaz is a fictional character.
2 For the probable source of this episode, see Appendix E1.
   Broughton, *Legends* 78–86 lists other analogues.

That she made such an ending.
Because love had treated him that way,
He would never after come or go there.
He ordained, after his death,
His son Richard to be king.   240
Thus was Richard, certainly,
Crowned after King Harry:
That was in his fifteenth year.[1]
He was a man of great power;
He gave himself to deeds of arms,   245
As it behooves kings and knights to do.
He became so strong and so valiant,
That no man had any might compared with him.
In every place he took honour
As a noble king and conqueror.   250
          The first year that he was king
He held a tournament at Salisbury
And commanded every man to be there,
Both with shield and with spear,
Earls and barons, every one—   255
Not one stayed at home.
On pain of forfeiting life and land,
They wouldn't stay for anything.[2]
This was announced, I understand,
Throughout all of England.   260
All wanted to look, and view
The best knights that might be.
They all came there at his will,
To fulfill his commandment.
The jousters were set far apart;   265
They ran together without delay.
King Richard began to disguise himself,
In a remarkable stratagem.[3]
He came out of a valley
In order to watch the tournament   270

---

1 When he became king in 1189, Richard was 32.
2 The historical Richard never held such a tournament, but a three-
   day-long tournament is a common trope of romance. See Weston.
3 Disguise is another romance trope. For example, see *Ipomedon* and
   Sir Gowther: in each, the hero appears at a three-day tournament in
   a disguise of black, red, and white. For earlier French examples, see
   the *Prose Lancelot* and Chrétien de Troyes's *Cligés*.

Disguised as a knight-errant.
His attire was opulent:
Entirely coal-black
Was his horse, without blemish.
A raven stood upon the crest of his helmet,   275
That gaped like it was mad,
And about its neck hung a bell,
For this reason, as I shall tell:
The nature of the raven is
To be in adversity, truly;   280
The significance of the bell is
To dwell with Holy Church
And to grieve and annoy those
Who do not have the right beliefs.
He bore a lance that was great and strong: 285
It was fourteen feet long,
And it was big and sturdy,
Twenty-one inches around.
The first knight that he met there
He greeted him very eagerly   290
With a blow to the shield;
He threw down his horse in the field,
And the knight fell to the ground,

not only a king in name, but also in action Nearly dead in that place.
The next knight that he met there,   295
He gave him a great stroke
On the gorget[1] with the head of his lance,
So that he broke his neck in two:
He and his horse fell to the ground
And both died there in that place.   300
King Richard stayed and waited to see
If any more would ride to him.
Trumpets began to blow,
And knights jousted at that time.
Another knight, good and hardy,   305
Sat on a steed as red as blood,
He armed and well prepared himself
In all that was proper for such a knight.
He took a lance that was great and long,
That was heavy and strong,   310
And said he would ride to Richard,

---

1 A piece of armour for the neck.

If he dared to face him.
Trumpets began to blow then:
Thereby many men knew
That all the noble knights that were there 315
Should continue jousting.
King Richard was aware of him
And bore a spear against him,
And encountered him in the field.
He bore away half his shield, 320
Together with his breastplate,
And also his visor, neckpiece,
And other pieces of armour.
The knight repented that he came there!
King Richard waited, and watched, 325
And thought to rest himself in the field,
To see if there were any other knight or squire
Who would ride against him.
He saw that none would come, so
On his way he rode forth 330
Into a wood, out of their sight,
And dressed himself in another disguise.
He rode upon a steed as red as blood,
As was all the attire that he wore,
Horse and shield, armour and man, 335
So that no man should know him.
Upon his crest was a red hound,
Whose tail hung to the ground:
That was a symbol of
Bringing down the heathen men, 340
And slaying them for God's love,
And placing Christian men above them.
Still he stayed and waited there;
He planned to ride to them again.
He rode all about the throng, 345
He observed from inside and outside.
He saw a baron beside him,
And began to ride toward him.
He gave his spear to a squire;
He would not bear it against the baron. 350
He took out a mace,
Thinking to set a great stroke
On his helmet, that was so strong:
Sparks shot out from that blow.

The baron turned him aside,   355
And said, "Fellow, ride forth,
Go and play with your peers!
Come here no more, I pray you!
And certainly, if you do,
You shall have a knock or two!"   360
King Richard wondered in his mind
That the baron thought his stroke was nothing,
So he came again by another way,
And thought to repay him better.
He stood up in his stirrups,   365
And smote him with wrathful spirit:
He set his stroke on his iron helmet,
But that other still sat in his saddle.
Hastily, without more words,
He took his mace, which was made   370
Of cast brass, in his hands.
He wondered who this man was.
<u>Such a stroke he gave Richard</u>
<u>That Richard's feet went out of his stirrups.</u>
Despite his armour and padded jacket,   375
His mail coat and quilted tunic,
He had never before endured a stroke
That caused him half as much trouble.
He began swiftly to ride away
Out of the crowd there beside.   380
To himself he said,
"I want no more of such strokes!"
He went down to a well,
And using his helmet drank his fill,
And he watered his steed also.   385
He put on <u>a third disguise:</u>
All his attire was milk-white;
Even his horse was dressed in silk.
Upon his shoulder was a red cross,
That symbolized God's death   390
And fighting with his enemies
In order to win the Cross, if he might.[1]
Upon his head a white dove

---

1 The cross upon which Jesus Christ was crucified, which had been
captured in 1187, at the Battle of Hattin; its recovery was a goal of
the Third Crusade. See Appendix B1.

Symbolized the Holy Spirit:
To be bold enough to win the prize   395
And destroy God's enemies.
Then another noble knight
Prepared himself to meet King Richard:
His name was Fulk D'Oilly.[1]
The King loved him for his fame.   400
He gave him a stroke
To serve him well with all his might.
He smote him on his helmet,
A great blow without restraint:
It sunk in to his cheekbone.   405
Sir Fulk advised him to go forth,
To stay no longer in jeopardy
If any blow should befall.
The King saw that he felt no pain,
And he thought to give him more,   410
So he struck him another blow:
He laid his mace upon his head,
Striking that blow with good will.
The baron thought he would stop him,
And with his heavy mace of steel   415
There he gave the King his share,
So that he rent his helmet asunder,
And he fell over his saddle
And lost his stirrups:
He'd never had such a stroke before.   420
He was so stunned by that blow
That he nearly lost his life,
And because of that stroke he was given
He didn't know whether it was day or night.
When he recovered from his faint   425
He withdrew to his palace.
Then he hastily commanded
Heralds to make an announcement
That every man should make his way
Home to his own friends.   430

---

1 Fulk D'Oilly and Thomas Multoun (line 433) are largely fictional
   creations but are linked to the Multon and D'Oyly familes of
   Lincolnshire, who were related by marriage and were important in
   the twelfth to fourteenth centuries; their prominence in the romance
   may provide a clue to its patronage. See Finlayson, "Legendary."

The King immediately sent
A messenger in secret
To Sir Multoun,
Who was a noble baron,
And to Sir Fulk D'Oilly,   435
To call them to him at once,
And let them not delay in any way,
Until they both were there.
The messenger went his way,
And said the King had sent after them   440
Eagerly for them to come to him,
Without delay.
The knights hurried and were glad:
They went readily to the King,
And greeted him courteously.   445
He took them and set them beside him,
And spoke to them with noble words:
"You are now welcome to me!"
He took one by either hand,
And guided them into a chamber.   450
Richard said, "My two dear comrades,
Tell me truly, I pray you,
In these jousts, good friends,
Which knight was he who rode the best charge,
And which one best knew the skill   455
To guide his lance well,
To strike down his opponents with blows?
Which of them won renown,
And who broke the sturdiest lance?"
Multoun said, "One in black attire   460
Came riding over the fallow field:
Everyone who was there beheld him,
How he rode as if he were insane;
He paused a time, and waited.
On his crest sat a black raven,   465
And he didn't take either side.
He bore a strong and sturdy lance:
It was fourteen feet long,
And twenty-one inches around.
He asked all the company   470
If anyone dared to come and test
His might, for his sweetheart's love,
Against a knight errant. Now here

A young knight, a strong squire,
He grasped a lance and bestrode a steed,   475
And rode to that knight errant.
The knight errant met with him:
He struck such a blow on his shield
That he overthrew horse and man.
But there was no man who knew him.   480
Trumpets blew, heralds cried out,
And everyone else was afraid
To joust against him with lance.
Another one took a chance:
A hearty knight, bold and fierce,   485
Grasped a lance with great rage.
'Now he has felled one of us!
We'll never be worthy to be called men
Since he has done us this dishonour,
If he gets out of here alive   490
Without so much as a knock!'
He rode forth out of the company
With a long lance, strong and sturdy.
In the middle of the charge they came together;
The knight errant struck in the middle of his shield.   495
A wondrous thing happened to our knight:
The knight errant struck him down
Off his steed with anger, and broke his neck.
The third knight began to speak:
'This is a devil, and no man,   ← superhuman   500
That strikes down and slays our people!
Whether I live or whether I die,
I shall fight against him if I may!'
The knight errant, with great ferocity,
Struck our knight so hard that   505
His shield was broken in two pieces;
He broke his shoulder with his lance,
And threw him over his horse's back
So that he fell down, and broke his arm—
He did him no more harm.   510
The knight errant then turned again
And waited motionlessly to see
Who dared to joust against him again.
They were so sorely afraid of him
That no one dared to joust with him again,   515
Lest he might take their lives,

And when he saw that no more came,
He rode back where he had come from.
　　　After the black knight another came:
All the people took notice.　　　　　　　　　　520
His horse, and his attire was red:
He seemed very like a devil.
A red hound was placed on his helmet, above.
He came to seek and to challenge
Whether any would dare to joust with him.　　　525
When he was aware that none would
Challenge him with a lance,
He rode right down the line of men.
The devil hang him wherever he may be!
I don't know what the devil he had against me!　　530
He entrusted his lance to a squire
And beheld me with a grim look,
And smote me so with his mace
That had I not had the grace of Jesus Christ
My neck would have snapped in two.　　　　　535
I told him to go forth on his way,
And deal with fools like himself.
Again he came by another way,
And gave me a worse blow than that,
But still I sat in my saddle.　　　　　　　　　540
Then many a mother's son said,
'Alas for Sir Thomas Multoun,
That he is stuck wrongfully!'
My mace I grasped with good will,
And I smote him so that everyone saw it—　　　545
He was almost knocked off his horse.
When I had given him one stoke,
And would have blessed him better,
He wouldn't wait for any more:
He swiftly began to ride away."　　　　　　　550
When Multoun had told his tale,
Fulk D'Oilly, the baron bold,
Said to King Richard,
"Afterward there came a third,
In attire white as snow—　　　　　　　　　555
High and low folk all beheld him.
In his shield was a cross red as blood,
And a white dove stood on his helmet.
He paused, and beheld us eagerly,

To see if there was any knight so valourous,   560
Any man so hardy, and strong of bone,
That would dare to joust with him once.
There was no one so brave and fierce
That dared then to joust with him.
He quickly went down the line of men,   565
Until at the last he came to me.
Truly, Sir King," said Sir Fulk,
"I believe that knight was an evil spirit.
With his mace on my helmet
He set such a blow with his right hand,   570
With fierce wrath and bitter force,
That my brain was nearly all dazed.
I spoke to him with few words:
'Ride forth now, you wood-devil,
And play with your peers!   575
If you come again in this manner,
I'll teach you to be wise.'
Afterwards he began to seek more combat.
He gave me a worse stroke yet,
And I greeted him with my mace   580
So that he lost both of his stirrups,
And rode, stunned, out of the company,
And back again under the boughs."
King Richard sat very still and laughed,
And said, "Friends, certainly   585
Don't take it hard, for it was I!
When you were gathered all together,   ¹
I came as a knight errant, in this manner,
To test which of you was the strongest
And who could best repay strokes.   590
Lords," he said, "don't you know
What I've decided in my mind?
We three, without more knights,
Shall travel to the Holy Land,
In disguise as pilgrims,   595
To secretly inspect the Holy Land.
I want you to swear an oath to me
To let no man know what we've taken on,
Neither for joy nor for woe,
Until we have come and gone."   600
They granted his request
Without any contention,

To live and die with him,
And never cease for love nor for fear.
On the Bible they lay their hands,   605
To stand by that pledge,
And all three of them kissed the others,
In order to be truly sworn.
Trumpets blew and sounded out,
And they went to dinner right away.   610
And by the end of the twentieth day
They were ready to go,
With staffs, wallets, and cloaks
Like pilgrims wear in pagan lands.[1]
     Now these three knights very thoroughly   615
Prepared themselves to travel.
They set sail, the wind was good,
And they sailed over the salt-flood
Into Flanders, I tell you.
Richard and his two companions   620
Went forth, in a glad mood,
Through many lands, far and near,
Until they came to Brindisi,
Which is an excellent coast.
There they found a noble ship   625
Ready to sail to Cyprus.
The sail was raised, the ship was strong,
And they were a long time at sea.
And at the last, I understand,
They landed at Famagusta.   630
There they dwelled for forty days,
In order to learn the laws of the land,
And afterwards they went back to sea,
Towards the rich city of Acre,
And so from there to Macedonia,   635
And to the city of Babylon,
And from there to Cesare;
They learned about Nineveh,
And the city of Jerusalem,
And went to the city of Bethlehem,   640
And to the city of Sudan Turry,

---

1 This trip is fictional, though Richard did disguise himself as a
   pilgrim when returning from the Crusade. See Gillingham, *Richard
   the Lionheart*.

And also to Ebedy,
And to the Castle Orgulous,
And to the city of Aperyous,
To Jaffa, and to Safrane,   645
To Taboret, and to Archane.
Thus they visited the Holy Land,
To see how they might win it to their possession,
And they took themselves homeward,
To England with all their might.   650
When they had passed the Greeks' sea,
The three pilgrims stopped in Germany,
Before they might go on.
That caused much woe for them![1]
I shall tell all of you that are here,   655
So listen, all of you, to what happened!
    They prepared a goose for their dinner
In a tavern where they were.
King Richard stoked the fire,
And Thomas turned the spit,   660
And Fulk D'Oilly prepared the gravy.
They dearly paid for that goose!
When they had drunk well, at last,
A minstrel came in,
And said, "Good men, truly,   665
Would you like any minstrelsy?"
Richard commanded him to go away:
That was the cause of much woe.
The minstrel considered this,
And said, "You are ungracious men,   670
And if I can, I'll make you regret
That you gave me neither food nor drink!
For noble men should give
Of their food, wine, and ale
To minstrels that travel about: 675
For fame comes from minstrels."

---

1   The historical Richard was captured by Leopold V, Duke of Austria
    (r. 1177–94) and then handed over to the Holy Roman Emperor
    Henry VI (r. 1191–97) on his way home from the Crusade. See
    Gillingham, *Richard I* 217–40, for a full account. In the poem, the
    capture occurs before the Crusade, and Modard and his daughter
    Margery are fictional characters. Bradford G. Broughton discusses
    the legends surrounding Richard's capture (*Legends* 111–15).

He was English, and knew them well
By their speech, and sight, and skin and complexion.
He went forth at that time
To a castle that was nearby,   680
And told the King everything:
That men were come to the city,
Strong men, bold and proud:
They were without peer in the world.
King Richard of England was the one man,   685
Fulk D'Oilly was another,
And the third was Thomas Multoun,
Noble knights of renown.
They were disguised in pilgrims' attire,
So that no man should rightly know them.   690
The King said to him, "Certainly,
If what you've told is true,
You shall have your reward
And choose a rich town for yourself."
The King commanded his knights   695
To arm themselves very strongly,
"And go and take all three of them,
And quickly bring them to me!"
The knights went forth together,
And captured the pilgrims as they sat at dinner.   700
They were brought before the King,
And he asked them immediately:
"Pilgrims," he said, "where do you come from?"
"We're from England," they said.
"What's your name, fellow?" said the King.   705
"Richard," he said, "without lying."
"What's your name?" he asked the older man.
"Fulk D'Oilly," he answered.
"And what of you, grey-hair?" he said.
"Thomas Multoun," he answered.   710
The King asked them all three
What they were doing in his country.
"I say to you, truly,
You seem to be spies!
You've seen my land up and down: 715
I believe you're plotting to do some treason,
Forasmuch as you, Sir King,
And your barons, truly,
Don't seem to be dressed as such.

Therefore you shall, according to law and right,   720
Be placed in a strong prison,
Because you're plotting to do treason."
King Richard said, "As I may thrive,
You do wrongly, it seems to me,
To imprison by night or day   725
Pilgrims who are passing through.
Sir King, for your courtesy,
Do no villainy to us pilgrims!
For God's love that we have sought,
Let us go, and don't trouble us   730
Because of misfortunes that may happen
In foreign lands where you travel."
Right away the King commanded
That they should be thrown in prison.
I understand that the porter   735
Took King Richard by the hand,
And both of his companions with him.
They had no more mercy there,
Until the next morning.
The King's son came, to his misfortune.   740
Wardrew was his name:
He was a knight of great fame.
He was great, and strong, and fierce:
In all that land he had no peer.
"Porter," he said, "I pray you   745
To let me see the prisoners!"
The porter said, "Sir, at your will,
Early or late, loud or still."[1]
He brought all three of them forth.
Richard came first, and   750
Wardrew spoke to him then:
"Are you Richard, the bold man,
As men say in every land?
Do you dare to withstand a blow from my hand,
If tomorrow I allow you   755
To give me one, too?"[2]
Immediately King Richard

---

1 These formulaic poetic phrases mean "always."
2 The exchange of blows is a common romance and folklore motif;
   Broughton discusses analogues in *Legends* 120–23. Richard's use of
   wax to cheat at the game, while clever, is most unchivalrous.

Agreed to that bargain.
The King's son, fierce and proud,
Gave Richard a clout on the ear   760
So that fire sprang out of his eyes.
Richard thought he did him wrong,
And he swore an oath by St. Martin:
"Tomorrow I shall repay him!"
The King's son with goodwill   765
Ordered that they should have their fill
Of food and drink,
That they would eat of the best,
So that Richard might not fail
To strike his blow from feebleness.   770
And he ordered that they should rest in beds,
So that Richard would be ready to repay him.
The King's son was courteous:
That night he made them very comfortable.
In the morning when it was day   775
Richard arose, as I tell you.
He took wax, clear and bright,
And he soon had a fire prepared,
And by the fire he coated his hands in wax,
Lengthwise and crosswise, you may be sure,   780
A straw's breadth thick and more,
For he planned to strike painfully
With the hand that he had prepared
To make the repayment that he had promised.
The King's son came in then,   785
To keep his pledge like a true man,
And he stood before Richard,
And spoke to him with courage and wrath:
"Strike," he said, "with all your power,
As you are a valiant knight!   790
And if I stoop or fall,
May I never again bear a shield."
Richard struck with his hand under his cheek;
Whoever saw it said truly
That he tore away the flesh and skin   795
So that he fell down in a deadly faint.
Richard broke his cheekbone in two;
He fell down as dead as a stone.
A knight hastened to the King,
And told him this news,   800

super human abilities →

That Richard had slain his son.
"Alas," he said, "Now I have none!"
With that word he fell to the ground.
Like a man wrapped in woe,
He fainted for sorrow at their feet. 805
His knights picked him up at once
And said, "Sir, don't think that way!
It can't change what's happened."
The King then spoke in haste
To the knights that stood nearby, 810
"Tell me quickly of this affair,
In what manner he died."
Every one of them stayed quiet;
They couldn't tell for sorrow.
When the Queen heard the noise she came in. 815
"Alas," she said, "how may this be?
What is this sorrow and this commotion?
Who has caused you all this grief?"
"Lady," he said, "don't you know,
Your fair son has been killed! 820
Since I was first born,
I've never felt such sorrow!
All of my joy is turned to woe,
And I will slay myself for grief!"
When the Queen understood, 825
She nearly went mad with sorrow.
She tore her veil and her hair.
"Alas!" she said, "What shall I do?"
She scratched herself in the face,
Like a woman in a rage. 830
Her face was covered in blood;
She tore the robe that she wore
And wrung her hands, lamenting that she was born.
"In what manner has my son been lost?"
The King said, "I tell you, 835
This knight standing here told it to me.
Now tell me truly," said the King then,
"In what manner this death happened,
And, unless you tell the truth,
You shall die a terrible death!" 840
The knight called the jailer,
And commanded him to stand near,
To bear witness to his speech

About how he was slain.
The jailer said, "Yesterday, in the morning,   845
Your son came, to his misfortune,
To the prison door with me.
He wanted to see the pilgrims,
And I fetched them forth right away:
Richard came first.   850
Wardrew asked, without delay,
If Richard dared to withstand a blow,
And he himself would withstand another,
For he was a true knight of this land.
And Richard said, 'By this light,   855
Smite on, sir, with all your power!'
Wardrew struck Richard so
That he nearly overpowered him.
'Richard,' he said, 'now I ask you
To give me another blow tomorrow!'   860
They departed in this way.
In the morning Richard arose,
And your son soon came again,
And Richard struck him back,
As was the agreement between them.   865
Richard struck him, to say truly,
So that his cheek-bone burst in two,
And he fell down dead as a stone.
As I am sworn to you here,
This is the manner in which it happened!"   870
The King said angrily,
"They shall still live in prison—
Lock fetters on them tightly!
For their wicked deeds,
And because he has slain my son,   875
He shall die, by just law."
The porter went, as he was sent,
To do his lord's commandment.
That day they had nothing to eat,
Nor might they get any drink.   880
      The King's daughter was in her chamber,
With her maidens of honour:
Margery was her name.
She loved Richard with all her heart.
At midday, before noon,   885
She went swiftly to the prison,

Along with three of her maidens.
"Jailer," she said, "Let me see
The prisoners—quickly, now!"
Readily he said, "Certainly."   890
He fetched forth Richard right away.
Fairly he greeted that lovely lady,
And said to her, with gracious heart,
"What do you desire, lady, with me?"
When she saw him with her own two eyes,   895
She cast her love upon him then,
And said, "Richard, except for God above,
You're the one I love most of all!"
"Alas," he said in that place.
"I am unjustly imprisoned!   900
What might my love do for you?
I'm a poor prisoner, as you may see.
This is the second day together
That I've had neither food nor drink!"
The lady took pity on him,   905
And said that it should be amended.
She commanded the jailer
To bring food and drink to him there:
"And take the fetters off of him,
I command you, for my sake.   910
And after supper, in the evening,
Bring him to my chamber,
Dressed as a squire—
I shall look after him there.
By Jesus Christ and Saint Simon,   915
You shall have your reward!"
At evening, the porter didn't forget.
He brought Richard to her chamber.
He dwelled with that lady,
And amused himself with her as he wished.   920
Until the seventh day, truly,
He came and went very privately.
Then he was spied by a knight
As he came to her chamber one night.
Discreetly he told the King   925
That his young daughter had been seduced.
The King asked him immediately,
"Who, then, has done this deed?"
"Richard," he said, "that traitor!

He has done this dishonour. 930
Sir, by my Christianity,
I saw when he came and went."
    The King grieved painfully in his heart,
He spoke no more to him,
But immediately, without fail, 935
He sent after his councillors:
Earls, barons, and wise clerics,
To tell them of these woeful deeds.
The messengers went for right away,
And his councillors came directly: 940
By the time it was the fourteenth day,
They had arrived, as I tell you.
All of them greeted the King,
Truly, without lying.
"Lords," he said, "welcome to you all!" 945
They went forth into a hall,
And the King seated himself among them.
"I shall tell you without delay
Why I have sent after you:
To give judgement to a traitor 950
Who has done a great treason to me—
King Richard, who is in my prison."
He told them all, in his own words,
How Richard had slain his son,
And also seduced his daughter. 955
"I would be very glad if he were dead!
But now it has been ordained
That men should not put a king to death."
A bold baron spoke to him:
"How did King Richard come to be in prison? 960
He is regarded as such a noble king that
No one dares to do anything to him!"
The King told him in every particular
How he had found him in disguise,
And two other barons with him, 965
Noble men of great renown.
"I took them, for suspicion,
In this way to my prison."
He took his leave of every one,
And commanded them to go into a chamber 970
In order to take their counsel, and
Decide what might be the best plan.

Three days and more
They stayed there and debated,
And quarrelled vigorously, like they were mad,   975
With great anger and fierce temper.
Some wanted to bring him to trial,
And others said it was against the law.
In this way, because of their quarrelling,
They couldn't agree for anything.   980
The wisest said, "Truly,
We can give him no judgement!"
They said thus to the King,
Truly, without any lying.
A knight spoke to the King: 985
"Sire, don't grieve at all,
For Sir Eldred, truly,
Can tell you what is best,
For he is a wise man for giving advice:
He has condemned many to death."   990
The King commanded, without delay,
That he be fetched before him.
He was brought before the King,
Who asked him, in these words:
"Can you tell me, in any manner,   995
How I may be avenged on King Richard?"
He answered with generous heart:
"This is what I advise you.
You know well, it is against the law
To hang and draw a king.   1000
You shall do this, by my advice.
Immediately take your lion,
And withhold his meat so that
He doesn't eat for three days.
Then have Richard brought into a room,   1005
And let the lion go there, too.
In this manner he shall be slain.
That way you do nothing against the law:
The lion shall slay him there,
And you'll be avenged on your foe."   1010
Margery heard that advice,
That Richard should die through treason,
And she soon sent after him
To warn him of that judgement.
When he came to the chamber,   1015

"Welcome!" she said, "my sweetheart!
My lord, following advice, has ordained
That you'll be put to death on the third day.
You shall be put into a room,
And a lion shall be let in with you,   1020
One who is sorely hungry;
Then I know well, you'll live no more!
But, dear sweetheart," she said then,
"Tonight we will flee from this land,
With gold, and silver, and great treasure,   1025
Enough to last forevermore."
Richard said, "I understand
That it would be against the law of the land,
To go away without permission;
I will not so grieve the King.   1030
I'm not worried about the lion;
I have an idea about how to slay him.
By late morning, on the third day,
I'll give you his heart as plunder."
He asked for silk kerchiefs,   1035
Forty of them, white as milk.
"Bring them to the prison
A little before evening."
When it came to the time,
The maiden took her way to the prison,   1040
And a noble knight with her.
Their supper was all ready.
Richard commanded his two companions
To come to their supper,
"And you, sir porter, also—   1045
The lady commands you to."
That night they were glad enough,
And afterwards they went to their chamber:
Richard and that sweet one
Dwelled together all that night.   1050
In the morning, when it was day,
Richard prayed her to go on her way.
"No," she said, "by God above,
I shall die here for your love!
I will stay here right now,   1055
Although death may await me.
Certainly, I shall not go from here;
I will take the grace that God will send!"

Richard said, "Noble lady,
Unless you quickly go from me, 1060
You shall grieve me so painfully
That I shall love you no more!"
Then again she said "No!
Sweetheart, now have a good day!
May God, who died upon the Cross, 1065
Save you if it be His will!"
He took the kerchiefs in his hand;
He wound them about his arms.
He thought, with that same strategy,
To slay the lion with some guile. 1070
He stood all alone in a tunic,
Awaiting the fierce, crazy lion.
　　　With that the jailer came in,
And two others together with him,
And the lion among them. 1075
His claws were both sharp and long.
They unlocked the chamber door,
And led the lion to him.
Richard cried, "Help, Jesus!"
The lion made a great onslaught, 1080
And would have torn him all to pieces;
King Richard then dodged to the side,
And struck the lion upon the breast,
So that the lion turned all about.
The lion was hungry and feeble, 1085
And beat his tail all about against the walls,
In order to seem bold;
He spread out all his claws,
And cried loudly, and gaped wide.
King Richard thought to himself at that time 1090
What was best to do, and started towards him.
He thrust his arm in at his throat, and
Ripped out the heart with his hand, and
Lungs, and liver, and all he found.
The lion fell dead to the earth; 1095
Richard had neither blemish nor wound. ✳
He kneeled down right there
And thanked Jesus for His grace,
Who had kept him from shame and harm.
He took the heart, still warm, 1100
And brought it into the hall,

Before the King and all his men.
The King sat at dinner on the dais,
With dukes and earls, proud in the company.
The saltcellar stood on the table.   1105
Richard pressed out all the blood,
And wet the heart in the salt—
The King and all his men looked on—
Without bread he ate the heart.
The King wondered, and said soon,   1110
"Indeed, as well as I can understand,
This is a devil and no man,
Who has slain my strong lion,
Drawn the heart out of his body,
And has eaten it with good will!   1115
He may be called, rightly,
The christened king of most renown,
Strong Richard Coeur de Lion!"[1]
      Now we'll let this be,
And instead speak of the King.   1120
In care and mourning he leads his life,
And often he calls himself a wretch, and
Curses the time that he was born,
Because of his son that was lost,
And his daughter that was seduced,   1125
And his lion that was slain.
Earls and barons came to him,
And his Queen did also,
And asked him what was wrong.
"You know well," he said, "my situation,   1130
And why I live in terrible grief:
For Richard, the bold traitor,
Has caused me so much woe.
I may not have him put to death;
Therefore I will, for his sake,   1135
Take ransom for his life,
For he has defiled my daughter
Contrary to the rules of marriage.
In every church in which priests sing,

---

1   For other examples of the origin of Richard's moniker, see
     Broughton, *Legends* 115–19. R.S. Loomis gives examples from
     medieval art in "Richard Coeur de Lion and the Pas Saladin in
     Medieval Art," *PMLA*, vol. 30, 1915, pp. 509–28.

Or say Mass, in which bells ring,   1140
There are two chalices therein;
One of these shall be brought to me,
And if there's more than that,
Half of that shall come to me, too.
When I have been paid that fee,   1145
Then Richard shall be released.
And my daughter, for her outrage,
Shall lose her inheritance.
Thus," he said, "it shall be done."
The barons readily agreed to this.   1150
Afterwards they sent for King Richard
To hear their judgement.
King Richard came into the hall,
And greeted the King, and all his men.
Then the King said, "Truly,   1155
We have ordained, through judgement,
That you shall pay ransom
For yourself and your two barons.
From every church in your land
You shall deliver wealth to me: 1160
Wherever there are two chalices inside,
One shall be brought to me,
And if there are more than two,
Half of that shall come to me, too.
From throughout your land, know it well,   1165
I will have half the wealth.
When you have thus made your payment,
I give you leave to go your way,
And to take my daughter with you, too,
Whom I never wish to see again."   1170
King Richard said, "As you have laid it out,
I hold myself bound to that agreement."
King Richard, courteous and noble,
Said, "Who will travel for me
To my chancellor in England,   1175
So that my ransom may be paid here?
Whoever does it, without fail,
I shall reward him well for his labor."
A noble knight stood up:
"I will take your message very well."   1180
King Richard had a letter written—
A noble clerk penned it—

And therein made mention,
More and less, of the ransom.
"Appeal well, I tell you,   1185
To both of my two archbishops,
And also to my chancellor,
To obey the letter in every way.
Be sure that the letter doesn't fail;
It will certainly be worth their while."   1190
He set his seal on the letter,
And the knight took it without delay,
Prepared himself, and made ready
To travel over the sea.
When he was brought over the sea,   1195
He didn't forget to go his way:
He hastened immediately to London,
And there he found every one of them.
He took the letter, as I tell you,
To the two archbishops,   1200
And directed them to read it intently,
For it was sent out of great need.
The Chancellor broke the wax,
And he soon knew what it said.
The letter was read among them all,   1205
About what should happen therefore:
How King Richard, because of treason,
Awaited ransom in Germany.
He had slain the King's son,
And also seduced his daughter,   1210
And also slain his lion:
He had done all of these harms.
They asked clerks to go forth,
To every church far and near,
So that it would be accomplished swiftly,   1215
And the treasure brought to them.
"Messenger," then he said,
"You shall wait here, and you shall have
Five bishops to ride with you,
And five barons, certainly,   1220
And enough other people with you;
There shall be no insufficiency in us."
From every church, greater and lesser,
They gathered up the treasure,
And went over the sea,   1225

In order to make the fair present.
When they came to the city,
They greeted the rich king,
And said, as they were instructed,
"Sire, the ransom is brought here: 1230
Take it all, as is your will, and
Let these men go, as is right."
The King said, "I give them leave to go:
I shall grieve for them no more."
He took his daughter by the hand,   1235
And commanded her to quickly leave his land.
The Queen saw what would befall,   ·
And proceeded to call her daughter to her chamber,
And said, "You shall dwell with me
Until King Richard sends for you,   1240
As a king does for his queen.
So I advise that it shall be."
        King Richard, and his two companions,
Took their leave, and departed
Home again to England.   1245
Thanks to Jesus Christ,
They came to the City of London.
Richard's earls, and his noble barons,
Thanked God very readily,
That they saw their lord alive.   1250
His two companions travelled home,
And their friends were glad of their coming.
They bathed their bodies, that were sore
Because of the trouble they had experienced.
Thus they dwelled for half a year,   1255
Among their powerful friends,
Until they were strong enough to travel.
The King commanded throughout the land
That there would be a Parliament at London:
None denied his command   1260
Who wanted to save their lives,
And their children, and their wives.
At his summons, to London
Came earl, bishop, and baron,
Abbots, priors, knights, squires,   1265
Burgesses, and many young retainers,
Sergeants, and every freeholder,
To learn the King's command.

Before that time, a great country
That lay beyond the Greeks' sea,[1]   1270
Acre, Syria, and many lands[2]
Were in the hands of Christians—
Along with the Cross that Christ was killed upon,
Who redeemed us all from evil;
And the whole country of Bethlehem,   1275
And the towns of Jerusalem,
Of Nazareth, and of Jericho,
And all Galilee, too.
Each traveller and each pilgrim
Who wanted to go there at that time   1280
Might pass, with good will,
Without ransom or any payment
Either of silver or of gold,
To every place that he wished.
He would find no one to abuse him   1285
Or lay violent hands on him.
Duke Myloun of Syria,[3]
A bold baron, was lord of that place.
He held that land in defiance of the Sultan,
And defended it well with spear and shield.   1290
He, and the brave Earl Renaud,[4]
Frequently gave the Sultan very hard assault,
And very often in plain battle
They slew knights and a great many foot soldiers
Of the misbelieving Saracens:[5]   1295
The Sultan was very aggrieved.
Now listen to an outrageous treason

---

1 The eastern part of the Mediterranean Sea.
2 The following lines lay out the extent of the crusader kingdoms
   following the First Crusade. See Appendix B2.
3 Probably Guy of Lusignan, son of Baldwin V and King of
   Jerusalem (r. 1186–92). See Larkin, n. 1287.
4 Probably Reynald of Châtillon, Prince of Antioch (c. 1125–87).
5 A pejorative term that denoted some combination of pagan,
   Muslim, and/or Arab, three categories that often were not
   clearly distinguished in medieval Europe. The Saracens of *RCL*,
   for example, are both Muslims (in the sense that they follow
   Muhammad) and pagans (in that they worship multiple gods). See
   Tolan, *Saracens*.

Of the Earl Roys, who was among them,[1]
In whom Myloun had great trust:
And he was a false and fickle traitor.   1300
The Sultan privately sent to him
And promised him land and revenue
To betray the Christian army.
When he had victory over them, he would pay
Many thousands of pounds of gold: 1305
The Earl agreed at that time.
Another traitor, Marquis Montferrat,[2]
Also knew of that agreement.
He had part of the gold that the Earl took,
And afterwards he forsook Christianity.[3]   1310
Thus through the treason of Earl Roys
Syria and the Holy Cross were lost.
The Earl Renaud was cut down
All to pieces, so says our tale.
The Duke Myloun was given his life,   1315
And fled from the land with his wife—
He was the heir of Syria,
King Baldwin's son, I understand—
So that no man ever knew
Where he went, or in what land,   1320
So that his fame, and pity of him,
Spread throughout all of Christendom.
      A holy Pope named Urban,
Called to every Christian man,
And absolved them of their sins,   1325
And agreed that all who would go there
And avenge Jesus against his foes

---

1 Karl Brunner (52, 471) suggests that Earl Roys may refer to
   Reginald of Kerak or Count Raymond II of Tripoli, who was
   (perhaps unfairly) accused of treachery following the disastrous
   Battle of Hattin (4 July 1187). See also Larkin, n. 1298.
2 Conrad, Marquis of Montferrat (c. 1140–92) and briefly King
   of Jerusalem in 1192. Richard supported his own vassal, Guy of
   Lusignan—an alternative candidate—in the political struggle
   for the kingship of Jerusalem, while King Philip II of France (r.
   1180–1223) supported Conrad. Conrad was elected king but was
   assassinated soon thereafter.
3 He did not, although he did cooperate with Muslims when it was
   politically expedient to do so.

<u>Would attain Paradise.</u>[1]
The King of France, without fail,
Journeyed there with plentiful provisions, and   1330
The Duke of Blois, the Duke of Burgundy,
The Duke of Austria, and the Duke of Soissons,
The Emperor of Germany,
And the good knights of Brittany,
The Earl of Flanders, the Earl of Cologne,   1335
The Earl of Artois, and the Earl of Boulogne.[2]
Many folk had already gone there,
Who had nearly lost their lives
In great war and painful hunger,
As you may hear afterwards.   1340
     In harvest time, after the Nativity,[3]
King Richard with great solemnity
Held a royal feast at Westminster
With bishops, earls, honest barons,
Abbots, knights, and strong squires.   1345
And after dinner among them
The King stood up and proceeded to say,
"My dear friends, I pray you,
Be in peace, and listen to what I say,
Earls and barons, great and small,   1350
Bishops, abbots, learned and unlearned!
All of Christendom may well be afraid!
Pope Urban has sent to us
His Bull[4] and his commandment,
About how the Sultan has begun a war: 1355
He has won the town of Acre
Through Earl Roys and his treachery,
<u>And all the Kingdom of Syria.</u>
<u>Jerusalem and the Cross have been lost,</u>
And <u>Bethlehem, where Jesus Christ was born.</u>   1360
Christian knights are being drawn and hanged:

---

1 The poet seems to conflate Pope Urban II (r. 1088–99), who called
    the First Crusade, with Pope Gregory VIII (r. 1087), who called
    the Third. See Appendix B for their speeches.
2 This list blends real and fictitious crusaders.
3 The Nativity of the Virgin Mary, 8 September.
4 An official document issued by a Pope. Urban II did not actually is-
    sue such a Bull, though he did deliver an influential speech calling
    for a crusade. See Appendix B1.

The Saracens have now slain
Christian men, children, husbands and wives.[1]
Therefore that lord, the Pope of Rome,
Is vexed and aggrieved   1365
That Christendom is thus being destroyed. ✳
He sends messages to every Christian king,
And asks them in the name of God
To go there, with great armies,
In order to bring down the Saracens' arrogance.   1370
Therefore I myself intend
To journey there, to win the Cross ⎤
And great fame with sword-strokes. ⎦
Now friends, what do you intend?
Will you go? Say yea or nay!"   1375
Earls, barons, knights, and all that company
Said, "We are agreed as one
To journey with you, Richard, our lord!"
The King said, "Friends, many thanks!
Listen why: it is to our honour   1380
To set out and grant the Pope's request
As other Christian kings have done.
The King of France has set out.
I advise that east, west, north, and south,
Throughout England we announce   1385
And make a true crusade."
Many people have taken the Cross;[2]
They came to King Richard
On horse and foot, well equipped.
Two hundred ships were provisioned well   1390
With flour, mail coats, swords, and knives:
Thirteen ships were laden with beehives.
He had made a very strong tower

---

1 In fact, Saladin's conquest of Jerusalem was accomplished with
   little bloodshed: he allowed the city's occupants to ransom them-
   selves on generous terms (although several thousand of the poorest
   were sold into slavery). While formerly Muslim sites were returned
   to Islamic use, the Church of the Holy Sepulchre—the site most
   sacred to Christians—was entrusted to the Greek Orthodox
   Church. See Claster 194.

2 To "take the Cross" was to commit oneself to participation in the
   Crusade. The phrase derives from Christ's command: "If any man
   will come after me, let him deny himself, and take up his cross, and
   follow me" (Matt. 16.24).

Of great timbers and long planks,
Made ingeniously by his engineers: 1395
Three ships were laden with it.
Another ship was laden
With a siege engine called Robynet—
It was Richard's own mangonel[1]—
And all the tackle that went with it.   1400
When they were all readily prepared
To set forth out of the harbour,
Jesus sent them a very good wind,
To bear them over the salt sea.
King Richard said to his shipmen,   1405
"Friends, do as I instruct you!
And Master Alan Trenchemer,[2]
Wherever you go, far or near,
If you meet on any sea
Ships from any other land,   1410
If they're Christian men, on your life
Don't take any goods from them—
And if you meet with any Saracens,
Be sure that you leave none of them alive!
Ship, vessel, or galley,   1415
All I give you to be your prey.
But at the city of Marseille
You must remain a while
And leave your ship at anchor,
Waiting for me and my army.   1420
For my valiant knights and I
Will quickly travel through Germany
To speak with Modard, the King,
To find out why, and for what reason,
He held me in prison.   1425
Unless he yields my treasure again,
That he took from me with falsehood,
I shall give him his retribution."
    Thus King Richard, as you may hear,
Became God's own pilgrim,   1430
✳ Against God's opponents.

---

1 A type of catapult.
2 Alan Trenchemer is a historical figure: he captained the ship
   that brought Richard to England from his captivity in Germany
   following the Crusade.

The archbishop Sir Baldwin
Went before, with fine knights,
By Brindisi and by Constantinople,
And at last, afterward,   1435
There came the bold King Richard.[1]
King Richard led three companies
Into the heathen lands for God's sake: *
He himself would be in the vanguard,
With hardy men of great prowess.   1440
Fulk D'Oilly led the other,
And Thomas the third, certainly.
Every company that he led with him
Had forty thousand men, good at need—
None were therein but mighty men   1445
Who were well proved in war and fight.
King Richard called his justices:
"Look that you do as I have ordered:
Keep my land with reason and justice,
And be sure to hang and draw any traitors.   1450
In my stead the Bishop of York,
My Chancellor, shall be here.
I desire that you follow his will
To govern with right and reason,
So that I hear of no strife hereafter,   1455
As you value your own life!
And in the name of Almighty God,
Rule the poor with justice!"
Thereto they each held up their hand,
Swearing to lead all England with right.   1460
Bishops gave them their blessing,
And prayed for them in church and town,
And prayed for Jesus Christ to aid them,
And for Heaven to give them their reward.
    Now King Richard has passed over the sea;   1465
Right away he divided his army in three,
Because he didn't wish to trouble people,
Or to destroy their goods,
Or take anything without payment.
The King commanded, as I tell you,   1470
Each company to stay ten miles from the other:

---

1 The following episode (lines 1437–1666) appears only in the *a*
version of the poem and has no parallel in the historical record.

Thus he ordained at this time.
In the middle company he would ride himself,
With one company on either side.
They went forth without delay,   1475
To the city of Cologne.
The High Mayor of that city
Commanded, as I shall tell you,
That no man should sell them a fowl,
For anything that they might do.   1480
The steward told Richard, the King,
Of that news right away,
That he couldn't buy any fowl,
Neither for love nor for fear.
"Modard, the King, forbids it,   1485
For he hates you above everything.
He well knows that you have sworn
To pay for everything you take.
You won't take anything by force,
Therefore, he truly believes   1490
That you shall have no food at all:
Thus he thinks to slay your men."
King Richard answered as he thought:
"That shall not stop us.
Now, steward, I exhort you,   1495
Buy us a great many vessels,
Dishes, cups, and saucers,
Bowls, trays, and platters,
Vats, tuns, and kegs,
And prepare our meal without delay,   1500
Whether you will boil or roast;
And the poor men also, God help you,
That you find in the town,
Have them come at my summons."
When the meal was prepared and ready,   1505
The King ordered a knight
To go to the mayor,
For he is courteous and noble.
The mayor came, as I have said,
And the table and cloth were laid.   1510
Right away they were seated at table,
And a fair meal was set before them.
King Richard asked at once,
"Sir Mayor, my lord, where is the King?"

"Sire," he said, "At Worms,   1515
Truly, without lie,
And also my lady the Queen.
On the third day you shall see him,
And Margery, his gracious daughter,
Who will be glad of your coming."   1520
They washed, as was the custom in that land,
And then a messenger came riding
Upon a steed as white as milk;
His trappings were of crimson silk,
With five hundred ringing bells   1525
Fair to see, as I understand.
He dismounted from his horse,
And fairly greeted King Richard, indeed:
"The King's daughter, who is so gracious,
Greets you well by me.   1530
Before you go to bed, she will come
With a hundred knights and more."
King Richard answered at once:
"Welcome," he said, "more than anything!"
He made the messenger comfortable,   1535
With a glad face and merry cheer,
And gave him a cloth of gold,
For he was very dear to him.
They came to him that same night,
Those knights and that beautiful lady.   1540
When King Richard saw her,
He said, "Welcome, sweetheart."
Each of them began to kiss the other,
And made great joy and bliss.
Then they sojourned until it was day,   1545
And went on their way in the morning.
At midday, before noon,
The came to a worthy city,
That was named Marburg.
There the King wished to remain.   1550
His marshal quickly came to him:
"Sire," he said, "How shall we proceed?
With the fowl that we bought yesterday?
For I'm not able to get any livestock."
Richard answered with generous heart: 1555
"There is great plenty of fruit here,
Figs, and raisins in baskets,

And nuts will do very well for us,
And throw in some wax, too,
And also mix in some tallow and grease,   1560
And thus you may make our food,
Since you can't get any other."
They remained there all that night;
In the morning they resolved
To go to the city of Carpentras,   1565
Where King Modard himself was.
He might not flee any farther from them:
Throughout the land Richard had sought him.
King Richard proceeded to take his lodging;
There he began to avenge Modard's arrogance   1570
And his great wrong against the right,
On account of the goose that he had prepared.
King Modard knows that Richard has come.
He well believes that he will be captured
And be imprisoned forever,   1575
"Unless my daughter will help me!"
She came to him where he sat.
"What now, father, how is that?"
"Certainly, daughter, I will be shamed;
Unless you help, I will be dishonoured!"   1580
"Certainly, sire," she said then,
"As I am a gentlewoman,
If you will have a humble heart,
King Richard will do you nothing but good.
Just grant him, with good will,   1585
What he asks, and fulfill his request,
And put yourself completely at his mercy,
And you shall be kissed, by Our Lady![1]
The two of you, who have been so angry,
Will be very pleasantly reconciled—   1590
And also my lady, the Queen—
You shall all be good friends."
She took her father and went with him
To King Richard, as I tell you,
And also earls and more barons,   1595
And sixty knights together.
King Richard saw how they came,

---

1 The Virgin Mary, Jesus' mother. The ritual of a kiss would signify
  reconciliation.

And he took the way toward them.
King Modard knelt before him,
And greeted King Richard very eloquently,   1600
And said, "Sire, I am at your service."
Said Richard, "I want nothing but what's reasonable.
Provided that you return my treasure,
I shall love you forevermore,
Love you and be your friend."   1605
King Modard said, "My gracious son,
I will swear upon a book,
That which I took from you is ready:
All of your treasure is ready
If you will have it, and much more   1610
I shall give you, to make my peace."
King Richard took him in his arms,
And kissed him very many times:
They were friends and made merriment.
The same day King Modard   1615
Ate, indeed, with King Richard.
         And after the meal, right away,
King Richard spoke with joyful words
To the King who sat near him:
"You are welcome, certainly!   1620
Sire, I pray you, for your love,
For your help to travel with me
To heathen lands, without fail,
To give battle for God's love."
The King granted everything in peace: 1625
All the people of his land would travel with him,
"And I myself will go, too."
"No," said Richard, "I don't want that:
You are too old to contend in battle,
But I pray that you will give me   1630
A hundred knights, stalwart to stand,
And the best in all your land,
And the squires who serve them;
And enough provisions, all prepared,
To last for a year."   1635
The King granted that it would be so.
"Another thing I shall give you,
That may help you while you live:
Two rich rings of gold:
The stones therein are very powerful.   1640

From here to the land of India,
You shall find none better:
For whoever has that one stone,
May never be drowned by water.
The other stone, whoever bears it,   1645
May never be injured by fire."[1]
"Sire," said Richard, "many thanks!"
His knights were all readily prepared,
Sergeants of arms and squires,
Packhorses and warhorses,   1650
And armour and other provisions.
King Richard went with his equipment,
And they rode to Marseille,
With his armies on both sides:
Fulk D'Oilly, Thomas Multoun,   1655
Dukes, earls, and many barons.
Richard's official, Robert of Leicester—
In all England none was his better—
And also Robert de Turnham;[2]
Great English people came with him.   1660
They found their fleet all ready,
Loaded with armour, food, and drink.
They boarded—arms, men, and steeds—
Along with stores to feed all of their folk.
They all boarded by the sea shore   1665
To travel to the Holy Land.
The wind was both good and strong,
And drove them over to Messina.
Before the gates of the Gryphons,[3]
King Richard pitched his pavilions.   1670
He found the King of France there,
In pavilions square and round;
They each kissed the other,
And became sworn brothers,
To travel into the Holy Land,   1675
To avenge Jesus, as I understand.

---

1 Magical rings are a well-known folklore motif; unfortunately, the
   poem never mentions them again.

2 Both are historical figures who accompanied Richard on crusade.

3 An insulting name for the Greeks, based on the gryphon, or
   griffin, a mythical beast with the head and wings of an eagle and
   the body of a lion.

The King of France thought of a treason
Against King Richard, without delay.[1]
To King Tancred he sent a writ
That afterward turned him away from reason;   1680
He said that King Richard, with his strength,
Would drive him out of his land.
Tancred, who was King of Apulia,
Said "Alas!" about this writ.
Right away he sent a messenger   1685
To his son, named Roger,
Who was the King of Sicily,
Asking him to come to him,
Together with his barons,
Earls, and lords of renown.   1690
And when they had come, every one,
The King spoke to them right away,
And told them how the King of France
Had warned him of a quarrel:
How King Richard had come from afar   1695
With great strength, to make war against him.
King Roger struck with his glove
To call for silence, and spoke first:
"Mercy, my father: at this time
King Richard is a pilgrim, and has taken the Cross   1700
As a Crusader to the Holy Land;
That writ lies, as I understand.
I dare to swear for King Richard
That no harm will come to you from him.
But send a messenger to him,   1705
Asking that he come to you here:
He will come to you very gladly,
And will inform you of his plans."
The King was pleased with that advice,
And sent after King Richard, without fail.   1710
In the morning he came to him, indeed,
Into the rich city of Reggio.
He found Tancred in his hall,
Among all his earls and barons.
They each greeted the other very pleasantly,   1715

---

1   There was a good deal of intrigue among Richard, Philip, and
    Tancred (c. 1075–1112) at Messina, but this episode is fictional.
    See Tyerman 441–43; Gillingham, *Richard I* 132–43.

With mild and gracious words.
Then Tancred said to King Richard,
"Lo, Sir King, by Saint Leonard,
It has come to my knowledge
By a legitimate writ from a friend   1720
That you have come, with great power,
To deprive me of my lands here.
You would do better to be a pilgrim
And slay many a pagan
Than to grieve a Christian king   1725
Who has never done you any harm!"
King Richard grew all ashamed,
And sorely troubled by his words,
And said, "Tancred, you have the wrong idea
To think such things of me,   1730
And bear such a rage against me,
To think that I would harm you with treason,
And suspect me of such treachery!
I bear the Cross upon my flesh!
I will only dwell here for a day;   1735
Tomorrow I will go my way.
And I pray you, King Tancred,
To bring no evil upon me;
For many a man thinks to injure another,
And the weight falls upon his own head;   1740
For whoever plots to injure me,
He shall not escape unharmed."
"Sir," said Tancred, "Don't be angry about this.
Look, here is the letter, indeed,
That the King of France sent me   1745
The other day in this place."
King Richard saw and understood
The King of France would do him no good.
King Richard and King Tancred kissed,
And were the best of friends   1750
That might be in any land;
Praised be Jesus Christ's providence!
King Richard went away very peacefully,
And endured the French king's will.
He unlocked his treasury,   1755
And bought beasts for his stores.
He purchased both salted and fresh meat,
Three thousand oxen and cows,

Swine and sheep, so many
That no man could count them.   1760
He bought twenty thousand quarters of
Wheat and beans, I find,
And so much fish, fowl, and venison
That I can't count it all.
The King of France, without doubt,   1765
Camped in the city of Messina,
And King Richard outside the wall,
Below the House of the Hospitallers.[1]
The English men went into the market,
And often took hard blows: 1770
The French and the Gryphons openly
Slew our English knights there.
King Richard heard of that discord,
And complained to the King of France,
And he answered that he wasn't the keeper   1775
Of the tailed Englishmen.[2]
"Chase the Gryphons, if you can,
Because you'll get no justice from me."
King Richard said, "Since it is so,
I know well what I have to do.   1780
I shall avenge them myself so well
That all the world shall speak of it!"   *
Christmas is a time to be honoured,
And King Richard kept it with great festivity.
All his earls and barons   1785
Were set in their pavilions
And served with great plenty
Of food and drink and every delicacy.
Then a knight arrived in great haste;
He could barely catch his breath.   1790
He fell to his knees, and he said,
"Mercy, Richard, for Virgin Mary's sake!
My brother lies slain in the town
By the French and the Gryphons,

---

1 After the 1099 conquest of Jerusalem in the First Crusade, the
   Hospitallers (the Order of Knights of the Hospital of Saint John of
   Jerusalem) evolved from a group that was dedicated to caring for
   pilgrims into a religious and military order charged with defending
   the Holy Land. See Tyerman 253–57.
2 "Tailed" was a common slur for the English: see Appendix E3.

And with him lie slain fifteen   1795
Of your knights, good and bold.
Today and yesterday, I've counted
Thirty-six that they have slain!
Your Englishmen quickly lose their good fortune!
Good sire, take heed,   1800
Avenge us, sire, manfully,
Or we shall hastily
Flee from this peril, I think,
And return again to England!"
King Richard was furious and fierce at heart,   1805
And began to stare as if he were mad.
He smote the table with his foot,
So that it immediately crashed to earth,
And swore he would quickly be avenged.
He would not change course because of the Christmas fast.   1810
The High Day of Christmas
They armed themselves, the greater and lesser.[1]
King Richard went in front,
The Earl of Salisbury afterward,
That was called at that time   1815
Sir William Longespée.[2]
The Earl of Leicester and the Earl of Hertford
Very properly followed their lord;
Earls, barons, and squires,
Bowmen and crossbowmen,   1820
Hastened with King Richard
To be avenged on the French and Gryphons.
The folk of that city quickly perceived
That the Englishmen would do them harm.
They hastily shut the gate   1825
With bars that they found there,
And quickly ran onto the walls
And shot with bows and catapults,
And called to our men, without fail,

---

1 In response to conflicts between his men and the local citizens,
   Richard sacked Messina on 4 October 1189.
2 William Longespée, third Earl of Salisbury (c. 1176–1226), was
   an illegitimate son of Henry II. He seems to have been close to his
   half-brother John, but not to Richard. He did not go on crusade,
   although his son, William Longespée II (c. 1212–50), would go on
   crusade twice in the 1240s (*ODNB* 385–90). See also Lloyd.

"Go home, dogs, with your tails;   1830
For all your boasting and all your pride,
Men shall thrust up your arses!"
Thus they behaved badly and spoke evilly;
All that day they vexed King Richard.
That day our king by no account   1835
Could achieve anything in battle.
At night, King Richard and his barons
Went to their pavilions.
Whoever slept or whoever woke,
King Richard took no rest that night.   1840
In the morning, he sent for his councillors
Of the ports, the master mariners.
"Lords," he said, "you are with me:
Your council ought to be secret.
We should all strive to avenge ourselves   1845
With ingenuity and with strength,
On the French and Gryphons
That have insulted our people.
I have a siege tower, I understand,
Made of English timber,   1850
With six stories full of turrets,
Well adorned with embrasures:
Therein I and many a knight
Shall take the fight to the French.
That siege engine shall have a nom de guerre: 1855
It shall be called the Mate-Gryphon.[1]
Mariners, arm your ships,
And raise your spirits.
Assail them by the waterside,
And we'll do so by land, without fail.   1860
Joy will never come to me
Until I be avenged upon them!"
Thereto man might hear the cry,
"Help, God and Saint Mary!"
The mariners went swiftly   1865
With ship and with galley,
With oars, poles, and sails also,
They advanced towards them.

---

1 An actual engine used in the sacking of Messina, its name trans-
   lates to "Kill-Greek" or, in Tyerman's rougher translation, "Kill
   the locals" (442).

The knights erected the siege tower
Upon a hill before the city.   1870
The King of France saw all this,
And said, "Have no fear
Of all these English cowards,
For they are nothing but fools.
But raise up your catapult,   1875
And cast at their siege engine,
And shoot them with crossbows,
To terrify the tailed dogs."
Now listen about Richard, our king,
How he caused all of his folk at dawn   1880
To bear shields and hurdles
Right before the city wall.
At once he ordered his host to shout,
So that men might hear it in the sky,
"Now let the French fools come,   1885
And give battle to the tailed ones!"
The French men all armed themselves,
And ran in haste onto the walls,
And the English began the assault.
There began a strong battle: 1890
The English shot with crossbows and bows,
And felled and slew the French and Gryphons.
The galleys came to the city,
And had nearly won entry;
They had so mined under the wall   1895
That many Gryphons tumbled down.
With hooked arrows and crossbow bolts,
They felled them out of the towers,
And broke both their legs and arms,
And also their necks: it was no loss!   1900
The French men came to the battle
And cast wildfire[1] out of the tower,
With which I know, truly, indeed,
They burnt and slew many Englishmen.
And the English defended themselves well   1905
With good swords of shining steel,
And slew so great a number of them

---

1 Wildfire, also known as Greek fire, was an incendiary substance
   that burned easily and was difficult to extinguish; it was used as a
   weapon of war.

That many folk lay there in heaps;
And at the land gate, King Richard
Continued his assault equally hard.   1910
And he took command in such a manly way ✻
That he never left behind one of his men.
He looked beside and saw a knight
Waiting, who beckoned him with a glove.
King Richard came, and he spoke to him   1915
In English, making claims stout and bold.
"Ah, lord," he said, "Truly I now see
A thing that makes my heart light.
Here," he said, "is a gate by itself,
That has no guard at all.   1920
The folk there have gone to the water tower
In order to give assistance,
And there we may, without resistance,
Now enter, truly."
Then King Richard was joyful,   1925
And he boldly went towards the gate.
Many knights, bold in deeds,
Urged their steeds after him.
King Richard entered without fear,
And a great fellowship followed him.   1930
He placed his banner upon the wall,
And many a Gryphon beheld it.
Like a greyhound released from a leash,
King Richard struck in the thick of combat.
With his good sword our king   1935
Cut through the middle of seven chains
That had been drawn for great fear
Within and without the gates.
He won the portcullis and gates,
Which were pulled up to let every man come in.   1940
Men might see French and Gryphons
Suffer shame in every street and lane;
Some ran into houses in haste,
And tightly barred the doors and windows.
Our Englishmen with big crowbars   1945
Broke them open with great vigour.
All those who stood against them
Passed through death's hand.
They broke open coffers and took treasure:
Gold and silver and cloths,   1950

Jewels, stones, and spices,
And all that they found in treasuries.
There was no one of English blood
Who didn't have as much gold
As he could carry   1955
To ship or pavilion, I swear;
And ever King Richard cried,
"Slay down every French coward,
And teach them that in battle
You have no tails!"   1960
The King of France came riding
Against Richard, our king,
Dismounted his horse and fell on his knees
And asked for mercy, for God's body,
For the crown and the love   1965
Of Jesus Christ, King above,
And for the voyage and for the Cross,
That they should be in agreement, and take honour,
And he would pledge
That those who had done amiss   1970
To Richard or to his people
Should amend all the injury.
King Richard had great pity
For the King of France, on his knees,
And alighted—so says the book—   1975
And took him up in his arms
And said it would be peace henceforth.
And Richard yielded the town to him,
And bade him not to be angry then,
Although he had avenged himself on his foes   1980
Who had killed his good knights,
And also reviled him.
The King of France proceeded to speak
And asked Richard to be his soul's physician,
And to return the treasure   1985
That he had taken from every man,
Or else he might not, with God's good will,
Be able to reach Jerusalem.
King Richard said, "With all your treasure
You could not amend the dishonour   1990
And the wrongs they have done to me;
And Sire, you also did wrong
When you sent to King Tancred

To slander me with your lying.
We have sworn to take our way to Jerusalem.   1995
Whoever violates our pilgrimage is damned,
Or whoever makes any discord
Between the two of us in this way."
When that strife was ended,
There came two Justices of France   2000
Riding upon two steeds,
And they began to chide King Richard.
The one was called Margarite,
The other Sir Hugh Impetite.
They annoyed him very severely,   2005
Called him "tailed," and slandered him.
King Richard held a strong truncheon,
And he drew near to them.
He gave Margarite a blow
On the head above the eye: 2010
The skull broke with that blow,
His right eye flew out easily,   ✳
And he quickly fell down dead.
Hugh of Impetite was aghast,
And rode away without fail,   2015
And Richard soon came up behind him
And gave him such a stroke on the head
That he thought he would be dead.
Threes and fours[1] he gave him there
And said, "Sir, thus shall you learn   2020
To slander your superior.
Go complain now to your French king!"
An archbishop came very soon;
He fell to his knees and begged a favour.
He asked mercy of King Richard,   2025
That he would cease there
And do no more harm
To the people, for God's love.
King Richard granted him this,
And withdrew all his men to their pavilions.   2030
To this day men may hear speech
About how the English were avenged there.
All the time that they were there
They might easily buy their goods;

---

1 Refers to rolls of dice.

There was no man so bold 2035
As to speak one evil word against them.
King Richard dwelled there in peace and rest
From the High Feast of Christmas
Until after Lent,
And then he went on his way.[1] 2040
In the month of March the King of France
Boarded ship without delay.
When he was gone, soon afterward
Came the bold King Richard.
He wished to travel towards Acre 2045
With great stores of silver and gold.[2]
Four ships were loaded, I find,
All sailing toward Cyprus,
Filled completely with treasure,
And soon a sorrowful event befell. 2050
A great tempest arose suddenly,
Which lasted five days, truly.
It broke their masts and their oars,
And their rigging, greater and lesser,
Anchor, bowsprit and rudder, 2055
Ropes, cords, one and other;
And they were on the point of sinking
As they came toward Limassol.
The three ships, right away,
All broke up against the stone. 2060
They were all torn to pieces;
The folk aboard were not easily saved.

---

1 Following this line, the *b* group manuscripts (apart from the
Auchinleck MS) all include 11 lines recounting how Richard's
mother, Eleanor, brought Berengaria of Navarre (c. 1165–1230)
to be his wife. This is based on an historical episode; on 30 March
1191, Eleanor did bring Berengaria to Messina, and entrusted
her to the care of Richard's sister Joan; after three days, Eleanor
returned to Normandy. See Gillingham, *Richard the Lionheart* 160.
For the text of these lines see Larkin, n. 2040.

2 The *b* group manuscripts here insert six lines telling how Joan and
Berengaria arrived before Richard. This, too, is a historical detail:
their ship barely escaped the shipwreck that destroyed two other
vessels. See Gillingham, *Richard I* 144–54, for an account of the
following events. For the text of these lines see Larkin, n. 2046.
RCL's account of the conquest of Cyprus follows the historical
record in its broad outlines, though the details are fictionalized.

The fourth ship dwelled behind;
The sailors restrained it with difficulty;
And that ship was left in the deep   2065
So that the people on land might weep:
For the Gryphons, with sharp words,
Some with axes and some with swords,
Made great slaughter of our English,
And stripped the living all naked.   2070
They killed sixteen hundred of them,
And brought five hundred into prison,
And also sixty score,
As naked as their mothers bore them.
They were glad of the ships' breaking.   2075
The Justices of Cyprus ran very quickly
And hauled up many coffers
Full of silver and of gold,
Dishes, cups, brooches, and rings,
Cups of gold, and other rich things.   2080
No man, by north or south,
Could compute what it was worth.
And all that treasure was carried
Wherever the Emperor wished.[1]
The third day afterward,   2085
The wind came driving King Richard
With all his great ships
And his sailing galleys,
To a ship that stood in the deep.
The gentlemen therein wept,   2090
And when they saw Richard, the King,
Their weeping all turned to laughing.
They welcomed him with great honour,
And told him of the breaking of their ships,
And the robbery of his treasure,   2095
And all that other dishonour.
Then King Richard grew extremely angry,
And he swore a great oath
By Jesus Christ, Our Saviour:

---

1 Isaac Ducus Comnenus, who had ruled Cyprus since 1184; he
   belonged to the family that had previously ruled the Byzantine empire,
   of which Cyprus was no longer a part. In a letter Richard refers to him
   as "the tyrant who—revering neither God nor man—had usurped the
   name of emperor" (quoted in Gillingham, *Richard I* 153–54).

The Emperor would pay for it dearly.   2100
He called Sir Steven and William,
And also Robert de Turnham,
Three noble barons of England,
Wise of speech and bold of deeds:
"Now go and tell the Emperor   2105
To return my treasure again,
Or I swear by Saint Denys,
I will have double three times of his;
And to release my men out of prison,
And pay ransom for that deed,   2110
Or I warn him severely,
I will do him great harm,
Both with spear and with lance.
Immediately I shall take vengeance!"
The messengers went forth right away   2115
to do their lord's commandment,
And graciously said their message.
The Emperor began to rage,
He gnashed his teeth and breathed rapidly,
And threw a knife at Sir Robert.   2120
He dodged away with a leap,
And it lodged in a door a hand's breadth deep!
And afterward he cried, just as uncourteously,
"Out, tailed ones! Out of my palace!
Now go, and tell your tailed king   2125
That I owe him nothing!
I am very glad of his loss,
And I will give him no other answer,
And tomorrow he shall find me
At the harbor to do him sorrow,   2130
And work as much destruction for him
As for his men that I have captured!"
The messengers left very quickly,
And were glad of their escape.
The Emperor's steward, with honour,   2135
Said thus unto the Emperor:
"Sir," he said, "You have done wrong!
You have almost slain a knight
That is the messenger of a king,
The best under the shining sun.   2140
You have enough treasure for yourself.
Return his treasure to him or you'll get great injury,

For he is a Crusader and pilgrim,
As are all the men who are with him.
Let him make his pilgrimage,   2145
And keep yourself from damage."
The Emperor's eyes twinkled,
And he smiled like an evil traitor.[1]
He drew his knife out of its sheath,
Intending to do the steward harm,   2150
And called him, without fail,
And said he would tell him a secret.
The steward set himself down on his knees
To converse with the Emperor,
And the faithless Emperor   2155
Carved off his nose by the gristle
And said, "Traitor, thief, steward,
Go complain to the tailed English one!
And if he come on my land,
I shall do him such disgrace—   2160
Killing him and all his living men—
Unless he hastily turn back again!"
The steward seized his nose—
Truly, his face was ruined—
And quickly ran out of the castle.   2165
He took leave of no man!
He cried mercy of the messengers,
That for Mary's love in that time,
They should tell their lord
Of that dishonour, from beginning to end: 2170
"And hasten again to this land,
And I shall yield into your hands
The keys of every tower
That the false Emperor owns:
And I shall bring him tonight   2175
The Emperor's beautiful daughter,
And also a hundred knights,
Stout in battle, strong in combat,
Against that false Emperor
That has done this dishonour to us."   2180
The messengers hurried quickly
Until they came to King Richard.

---

1 There is not a clear source for the following fictional episode; see
   Larkin nn. 2147–62 for analogues.

They found King Richard playing
At chess in his galley.
The Earl of Richmond played with him, 2185
And Richard won all that he wagered.
The messengers told all the dishonour
That the Emperor did to them,
And the outrage he did to his steward,
In contempt of King Richard, 2190
And about the steward offering
His pledge and his assistance.
Then King Richard answered—
In deed a lion, in thought a leopard—
"I am glad of your words! 2195
Let us go quickly to that land!"
A great cry arose suddenly;
Many a bolt was shot from bow.
The bowmen and the crossbowmen
Armed themselves for whatever might happen, 2200
And shot bolts and arrows
As thick as hailstones.
The folk of the country ran away
And were eager to retreat and flee.
The barons and good knights 2205
Afterward came right away
With their lord King Richard,
Who was never found a coward.
King Richard, I understand,
Before he went out of England, 2210
Had an axe made for the occasion,
In order to break the Saracens' bones.
The head was crafted very well:
Therein were twenty pounds of steel.
And when he came into Cyprus, 2215
He took the axe in his hand.
All that he hit he beat to pieces.
The Gryphons hastened away quickly;
Nevertheless, he cut many of them to bits,
And thereby put a stop to their reproaches! 2220
And when he came to the prison,
Right then with his axe he smote
Doors, bars, and iron chains,
And delivered his men out of trouble.
He commanded them all to be clothed; 2225

He was furious over their humiliation,
And swore by Jesus, Our Saviour,
That the false emperor should pay for it dearly.
King Richard ordered all the burgesses of the town
To be slain without ransom.   2230
Their treasure and their jewels
He seized as his own property.
News came to the emperor
That King Richard was in Limassol,
And had put his barons to death.   2235
No wonder that he was woeful!
He sent immediately, without fail,
After all his council,
That they should come to him at once
To avenge him on his enemy.   2240
His host had arrived by midnight,
And was ready to fight in the morning.
Listen now, about the steward!
He came at night to King Richard,
And the Emperor's daughter with him.[1]   2245
She greeted King Richard in amity and accord;
The steward fell to his knees and began to weep,
And said, "King Richard, God keep you!"
The steward said, "I am ruined for your sake!
Gentle lord, avenge me!   2250
I deliver unto you, noble knight,
The Emperor's beautiful daughter,
And I also surrender to you the keys
Of every castle in his power.
A hundred knights I promised you: 2255
Behold, they're here, all prepared.
That shall aid and succor you
Against that false Emperor!
You shall be both lord and sire
Of his empire before tomorrow.   2260
And sweet sir, without fail,
My counsel is still of use to you.
I shall lead you by a coast
Secretly against his army;
You shall take him in his pavilion.   2265

---

1 In reality, it was Guy of Lusignan who captured Isaac's daughter;
   this prompted Isaac's surrender on 1 June 1190.

Then reflect upon the great injury
That he has done you before this!
It doesn't matter if you slay him!"
King Richard greatly thanked
The steward for his counsel,   2270
And swore by God, his Saviour,
That his nose should be bought very dearly.
Ten hundred steeds, good and sturdy,
King Richard had arrayed in trappings.
An English knight, stout in arms   2275
And strong in fight, leaped on every one,
And the steward, in faith,
Led them by the moonlight
So near the Emperor's pavilion
That they heard the sound of the trumpets—   2280
It was before dawn.
The steward said to Richard, the King:
"Look here, Richard, vigorously assail
The pavilion with the golden heron.
Therein lies the Emperor.   2285
Avenge this dishonour!"
Then Richard was as eager to fight
As ever a bird was to fly.
He rode forth upon his steed:
A very great troop followed him.   2290
He held his axe drawn in his hand;
He has slain many Gryphons.
The watchmen of that host spied that,
And began to cry out very loudly:
"To arms, lords, all and some!   2295
We are betrayed and taken!
In an evil time our Emperor
Robbed King Richard of his treasure,
For he is here among us,
And slays men outright, by Jesus!"   2300
The English knights, for the occasion,
Chopped the Gryphons' bodies and bones.
They cut the cords and felled down
Many a rich pavilion.
And squire and knight ever cried,   2305
"Smite! Lay on! Slay outright!
Yield the treasure back again
That you took from King Richard!

You are worthy of such a reward,
To lie and bleed with many wounds!"   2310
In the Emperor's pavilion, King Richard
Dismounted; so did the steward.
And the Emperor had fled away,
By himself alone; before it was day,
That false coward had fled.   2315
King Richard sought him intently:
He found his clothes and his treasure,
But he had fled, that vile traitor.
Long before the day began to dawn,
Twenty thousand Gryphons were slain.   2320
The Emperor's pavilion was made
Of silk, sendal, and silk woven with gold:
There was no such thing in the world,
Nor anything nearly so rich.
King Richard won great honour,   2325
And ordered that they should be brought to ship.
At Acre no pavilions of such excellence
Were to be found.
Cups of gold, great and small,
He won there, without number.   2330
Many coffers great and small
He found there, well hammered.
King Richard found two steeds,
One called Favel and the other Lyard.
Their peer was not to be found in the world: 2335
There was no dromedary nor camel,
War-horse or Arabian steed,
That ran so swiftly, without fail.
One of those should not be sold
For a thousand pounds all counted out.   2340
All that his men had lost before,
They now had sevenfold in return.
The news came to the Emperor
That his daughter was taken,
And that his high steward   2345
Had delivered her to King Richard.
By that he knew well, truly,
That he had done badly.
He called two messengers at once,
And ordered them to go to King Richard,   2350
"And say that I, your Emperor and King,

Sends God's greeting to him.
I will yield to him and give him homage annually,
And I will hold all my land under him,
Provided that he will, for charity,   2355
Leave me in peace hereafter."
The messengers went forth right away,
And said as their lord commanded.
King Richard answered them:
"I grant well that it be so.   2360
Go and tell your Emperor
That he did great dishonour
When he robbed pilgrims
Who were going to fight the pagans.
Let him return my treasure to me   2365
If he will be my retainer,
And also tell your Emperor
That he must amend the dishonour
That he did to his steward
In contempt of King Richard.   2370
And tell him to come early tomorrow
And beg my pardon with remorse,
And do homage to me annually,
And else, I swear by my crown,
He shall never have a foot of land   2375
Out of my hand ever after."
The messengers by one accord
Told this to their lord the Emperor.
Then the Emperor was very woeful
That he must do this deed.   2380
He came to King Richard in the morning;
He had much sorrow in his heart.
He fell to his knees—so says the book—
And took King Richard by both feet,
And cried mercy with good will,   2385
And he forgave him his hostility.
He swore an oath of fealty, and did homage,
Before all his baronage.
That day they were at one accord,
And ate together at the same table;   2390
In great solace and much joy
They were together all that day,
And when it drew toward evening,
The Emperor took his leave

And went toward his lodging; 2395
He was not at all content in his heart.
He held himself a foul coward
That he did homage to King Richard,
And thought how he might avenge himself.
He rode forth right away 2400
To a city that was called Buffavento.
By daylight he arrived, truly.
There he found many a great lord,
The richest men of his empire.
The Emperor complained to them 2405
Of the shame and dishonour
That King Richard did to him
Through the help of his steward.
A noble baron stood up,
Rich with castles and towns: 2410
He was the uncle of the steward
Whose face the Emperor had ruined.
"Sir," he said, "you are misinformed;
You are worried about nothing.
Without grounds for conviction and judgement 2415
You have disgraced your good steward
That should, as he well could,
Have helped and saved us now!
Through your malicious will,
You would treat us the same way; 2420
And I say these bold words:
I will not hold with such a lord
To fight against King Richard,
The best king under the shining sun.
Neither will any of my baronage 2425
Ever do you homage."
All the others said as one
That Richard was their legitimate lord,
And the Emperor, for his villainy,
Well deserved to die. 2430
The Emperor saw and understood
That his barons wished him no good;
He went to another town and stayed there:
He had much care in his heart.
Meanwhile, the High Steward 2435
Consulted with King Richard.
He said that he bitterly regretted

That the Emperor was so forlorn.
They sought him everywhere,
And found him in the city of Pyse.   2440
And certainly, King Richard
Would not attempt to protect him,
For he had broken his oath.
He had no pity for him,
But ordered a sergeant to bind   2445
His hands fast behind him,
And cast him into a galley,
And led him into Syria,
And swore by Him who made moon and stars
That he should learn to fight against the Saracens.   2450
When all this war was ended,
King Richard established peace in that land.
The Earl of Leicester, truly,
Through the advice of his barons,
He made steward of that land,   2455
To govern the realm for him.[1]
They held a great feast afterward.
King Richard had his ships prepared:
He would go toward Acre,
With great stores of silver and gold,   2460
With two hundred ships, I find,
Sailing forward with the wind,
And afterward fifty galleys
In order to guard his fleet.
And as the bold King Richard   2465
Came sailing towards Acre,
And had sailed with the wind at will
For ten days, fair and calm,
The eleventh day they sailed through a tempest.
That night and day they had no rest.   2470
And as they were in great peril,
They saw an immense ship
That was so heavily loaded
That it could hardly sail at all.[2]
It was going towards the Saracens,   2475

---

1 Actually, Richard made Richard of Camville and Robert of
   Turnham the stewards of Cyprus.
2 Most of the details of the following episode are to be found in the
   Chronicles. See Gillingham, *Richard I* 157–58; Nicholson 195–99.

Loaded with grain and with wine,
With wildfire and other provisions.
King Richard saw the ship, without fail;
He called in haste to Allen Trenchemer,
And ordered him to sail near them,   2480
And ask where they were from
And what goods they had on board.
Allen quickly began to row
To that ship, with plenty of men,
And asked who they were,   2485
And what goods they carried.
Immediately their translator stood up
And answered Alan Trenchemer:
"We're with the King of France, without fail;
We bring these provisions from Apulia.   2490
We've lain in the sea for a month;
We're trying to get to Acre."
"Wind up sail!" said Alan then,
"And we'll sail forth with light winds!"
"No! By St. Thomas of India,   2495
We must follow behind!
For we are so heavily laden,
We may hardly sail at all."
Then Allen soon said,
"I hear only one of you speak.   2500
Let all stand up together
So that we might hear more,
And afterwards know your language,
For we will not believe just one man."
"Certainly," said the translator,   2505
"You may not speak with any more here.
They came through a tempest last night;
They're all lying down and taking their rest."
"Certainly," said good Allen then,
"I will say to King Richard   2510
That you are all Saracens,
Loaded with grain and wine!"
The Saracens stood up all ready,
And said, "Fellow, go do your best!
We wouldn't give two flies   2515
For King Richard and his galleys!"
Then Trenchemer rowed hard
Until he came to King Richard,

And swore to him by Saint John
That they were Saracens, every one.   2520
Then said our renowned king,
Called Richard Coeur de Lion,
"I am glad of your words;
Let's see you arm quickly!
You steer my galley, Trenchemer;   2525
I want to test that scoundrel.
I shall strike them with my axe;
No Saracen shall escape me!"
Right away his axe was brought to him,
And he didn't forget his other armour.   2530
Plenty of sailors came to him.
King Richard ordered them to row fast:
"Row on, quickly! Whoever is timid,
May he be drowned in evil water!"
They rowed hard and sung as they did so,   2535
With "heave-ho" and "rummeloo!"
        The galley went along as fast
As a bolt flies from the crossbow;
And as the ship came with the wind,
Its bow, hitting the Saracen ship,   2540
Broke a large piece off of the back,
Which fell into the sea, I understand.
Then the Saracens had armed themselves well
Both in iron and in steel;
They stood on board and fought hard   2545
Against the bold King Richard.
And King Richard and his knights
Slew the Saracens down outright.
And as they began to cause them woe,
Always more and more stood up,   2550
And struck upon them, at the time,
Stern strokes with hard stones
Out of the topcastle on high,
So that Richard was never so near his death.
Then seven galleys came behind,   2555
Quickly sailing to the ship,
And barons and knights stood on board
To help King Richard fight.
A strong battle began there,
Between them and the heathen men,   2560
With swords, spears, and sharp missiles.

Arrows and bolts flew between them
As thickly, without cease,
As hail after a thunderclap,
And in the battle that was so fierce,   2565
King Richard came into the Saracen ship.
When he had come on in haste,
He placed his back against the mast.
Whoever he reached with his axe,
He hastily received his death.   2570
Some he hit on the helmet
So that he cleaved them to the chin,
And some to the waist,
And some to the ship's deck.
Some he struck in the neck   2575
So that head and helmet flew into the sea.
For no armour withstood his axe,
No more than wax withstands a knife.
The Saracens, I tell you,
Said he was a devil of Hell,   2580
And they leaped overboard
And drowned in the sea that day.
Sixteen hundred were killed,
Apart from thirty Saracens the King ordered held
In order that they should be witnesses   2585
Of this battle at Acre.
The King found in their ship, without fail,
Many stores and ample provisions,
Many barrels full of Greek fire,
And many thousand Turkish bows,   2590
And hooked arrows and crossbow bolts.
They found a great number of barrels
Of wheat and wine—there was great abundance—
And gold and silver, and every delicacy.
He didn't get half the treasure   2595
That was found in the ship,
For so much was sunk in the sea
Before half of those goods were unloaded.
All Christianity was advanced:
For if the ship had crossed the sea   2600
And reached Acre before King Richard,
Acre wouldn't have been won
For a hundred years afterward,
Despite all the Christian men under the sun!

Thus King Richard won the ship,   2605
Through God's help and Saint Edmund.
    King Richard afterwards right away
Took himself to Acre,[1]
And as he sailed toward Syria,
He was warned by a spy   2610
How the folk of heathen religion
Had drawn a great chain
Across the harbor of proud Acre,
Which was fastened to two pillars
So that no ship should enter in,   2615
Nor any leave that were within.
Therefore, for seven years and more,
All the Christian kings remained there,
And suffered the pain of great hunger
Because of the hindrance of that same chain.   2620
When King Richard heard that news,
His heart began to leap for joy.
He swore and said in his thought,
That this chain would not help them at all.
He took a very strong galley,   2625
And Trenchemer, so says the book,
Steered the galley very straight,
Right through the middle of the harbor.
Whether the sailors were calm or angry,
He made them both sail and row.   2630
The galley went as swiftly
As a bird in the air,
And King Richard, who was so good,
Stood in the bow with his axe.
And when he came to the chain,   2635
With his axe he struck it in two,
So that all the barons, truly,
Said it was a noble stroke,
And for joy of this deed,
The cups went swiftly around   2640
With good wine, spiced wine, and clary,
And they sailed toward the city of Acre.
King Richard from his galley
Cast wildfire into the sky,

---

1 On the historical siege of Acre, see Gillingham, *Richard I* 155–71. A
   good deal of this portion of the poem is fictionalized.

And Greek fire into the sea,[1]   2645
As if sea and sky were all on fire.
Trumpets sang out in his galley,
And drums and Saracen horns:
Men might hear it into the sky.
The whole sea burned with Greek fire.   2650
He had wondrous siege engines for throwing bolts,
Catapults of great ingenuity,
Crossbows, bows, and siege machines,
In order to win the Holy Land.
Clearly surpassing all the others,   2655
He made a mill of great power
To stand in the middle of a ship,
Such as no man in the land ever saw.
It had four sails,
Yellow and green, red and blue,   2660
With canvas laid well all about.
It shone within and also without:
All within it was full of fire
From torches made with very clear wax;
Crosswise and lengthwise,   2665
Stones were hung with strings of wire,
Stones that never did any good:
They never ground wheat nor grain,
But rubbed away like they were mad;
Out of the millstone's hole red blood ran.   2670
Before the trough one stood
All covered in blood:
He had great horns upon his head,
And the Saracens had great fear of him.
For it was within the night   2675
That they were terrified by that sight,
And by the rubbing of the stones:
They believed that it ground men's bones,
And said he was the devil of Hell,
Who was come to kill them.   2680
A little before the light of day,
They had been completely driven away.
      After that marvel, King Richard
Went into that land, without fail.
The King of France came toward him   2685

---

1 See note to line 1902.

And took him in his arms
And kissed him with great honour,
And so did many an emperor.
All the kings of Christianity
That had been there a long time   2690
And lingered there seven years in suffering,
Received King Richard with honour.
The Archbishop of Pisa
Pledged his service to King Richard,
And led him, as you may see,   2695
Into a pavilion privately,
And told him a doleful tale
Of evil occurrences and much wickedness.
"King Richard," he said, "look here!
The siege has lasted seven years,   2700
But it may not be defended from you!
We have suffered much sorrow!
For we had no castle
That offered us any protection,
Unless we made a wide and deep moat   2705
To keep ourselves within it,
With barbicans, for the occasion,
Built high of hard stones.
And when our moat was made,
Saladin the Sultan was glad,   2710
And came against us with a great company,
And beset us all about,
And with him Marquis Montferrat,[1]
Who believes in Muhammad and Termagant.[2]
He was once a Christian king;   2715
He causes us more shame and deceitful guile
Than the Sultan and all his host.
Father, Son, and Holy Ghost,
Grant him the grace of worldly shame,

---

1 See note to line 1307. Montferrat never converted to Islam, but his
   willingness to negotiate with Saladin made certain of his contem-
   poraries distrust him. See Gillingham, *Richard I* 158, 162, 183–84.
2 Muhammad was popularly (and erroneously) believed to be a god
   of the Muslims, rather than a prophet; Termagant is a fictitious
   deity frequently mentioned in romance as another Muslim god. On
   medieval Christian misunderstandings of and slurs against Islam,
   see Tolan, *Saracens*.

He who is named Marquis Montferrat! 2720
Our first battle, certainly,
Was very fierce and deadly.
Our Christian knights fought well,
And slew down the Saracens outright.
Our Christians had the victory: 2725
The Saracens fled with woe and cry.
We slew many of them then,
And they many of us, also:
And I shall tell about the fate
That befell many a man, alas! 2730
As we put the Saracens to death,
It befell that a noble steed
Broke away from a pagan;
Our Christian men rushed after him.
The Saracens saw that they came, 2735
And fled aside, all and some,
And came upon us with great prowess,
And slew many a Christian man outright,
So that we lost before we knew it
The best men under Christ: 2740
The Earl of Ferrers of England
(There was no bolder man of might),
And the Emperor of Germany,
And Janin, the Earl of Plain Spain.
Eleven thousand of our company 2745
Were slain without pity!
Therefore the Sultan was glad,
And in the morning he made a new assault.
He ordered all the corpses
Of the men and horses taken, 2750
And cast into the water of our well,
In order to poison and kill us.
He never did a worse deed
To Christian men, by any account.
Through that poison and the stench, 2755
Forty thousand took their death.
Soon after the new year, to hide nothing,
A third predicament afflicted us.
A ship came sailing in the sea
Loaded with plenty of wheat, 2760
With wildfire and bright arms,
To help the Saracens in battle.

The Christians planned, without fail,
That they would assail the ship:
And so they did, to our harm!   2765
The wind blew with great rage;
The Saracens drew up their sails,
And sailed over our folk, without fail,
So that sixty score were lost
Of the best men ever born!   2770
This was the beginning of the tribulation
That we have suffered these seven years,
And yet, Sir King, you shall hear of more
That has grieved us very painfully.
    On Saint James's Eve,¹ truly,   2775
The Saracens went out of Acre
Fully a mile beyond the city,
And pitched pavilions round and wide,
And dwelled there a long time:
And it was all to deceive us.   2780
Our Christian men, who were brave,
Earl, baron, squire, and knight,
Saw that the Saracens had riches,
While all of our goods were scarce,
And thought to win for ourselves   2785
Some of that treasure and that wealth.
Fifty thousand armed themselves well,
Both in iron and in steel,
And went forth to battle.
The Saracens saw them coming,   2790
And quickly rushed aside,
And our men hastily came after
And proceeded to ride with great speed
Until they came to their pavilions.
They found no armed warriors therein,   2795
And believed that they had fled for fear.
They found white bread and wine,
Gold, silver, and brocades,
Vessels of silver, cups of gold,
More than they could carry.   2800
Some stood and some sat down,
And ate and drank great abundance,
And after they ate they took their swords

---

1   25 July 1191.

And cut down all the new pavilions,
Then loaded their horses with provisions   2805
As foolish men would, without fail!
They tossed gold and silver into bags,
And tied them with their belts.
When every man had his load,
They started for home, without delay.   2810
The Saracens well saw their going,
And came quickly flying after—
In short, a great swarm of them—
And beset our host all about.
They cast down their bags   2815
And fought strongly against the Saracens,
And there they lost fifteen thousand
Noble men, bold and brave.
This case grieved us so sorely
That we thought we were lost;   2820
But God Almighty, Heaven's King,
Soon sent us some assistance:
The brave Earl of Champagne,[1]
And good knights of Bretayne,
And Ranulf de Glanville,[2]   2825
And John de Nesle and his brother Miles,[3]
And Baldwin, a very merry cleric,
The Archbishop of Canterbury,
And with him came his nephew,
A baron of great virtue,   2830
Hubert Walter of England,[4]
To stand against the Saracens,
Along with many knights of Hungary
And many other nobles.
Then we held fierce battle,   2835
But a difficult situation befell us, without fail.

---

1 Henry II, Count of Champagne (1166–97) was a nephew of both
   Richard and Philip; he joined the Third Crusade and became
   King of Jerusalem in 1192 when he married the widow of Conrad
   Montferrat soon after his assassination.
2 Justiciar under Henry II and Richard until 1190, Ranulf de
   Glanville accompanied Richard on crusade and died at Acre.
3 Probably Jean de Nesle, a leader of the Fourth Crusade.
4 Hubert Walter (also called Hubert Gautier), Bishop of Salisbury
   and from 1193 Archbishop of Canterbury and Richard's Justiciar,
   travelled with Richard on crusade and became a leader of the
   English contingent at Acre.

At Michaelmas,[1] it must be told,
The weather began to grow cold.
Then both rain and hail fell,
And snow five feet deep, without fail.   2840
Thunder, lightning, and severe weather
Killed our people through hunger.
Between hunger and the cold winds,
We lost sixty thousand of our folk!
Then we slew our good horses,   2845
Boiled them and ate the tough guts.
The flesh was served out with dignity:
No man had plenty of it.
We carved the head all to pieces,
And cooked it on the coals;   2850
We boiled the blood in water:
We thought that meat was very good!
Men sold a quarter of wheat
For sixty pounds of florins counted out!
Men sold an ox for forty pounds,   2855
Even if it was barely grown,
A swine went for a hundred florins,
A goose for half a mark of fine gold,
And for two hens
Men gave fifteen shillings in pennies;   2860
For a hen's egg, eleven pennies,
And for a pear, six or seven,
And for an apple, six pennies;
And thus our folk began to grow thin,
And died for hunger and for woe.   2865
The wealthy men made a plan, then,
To allot a rich share
To barons and to poor knights.
They gave twelve pennies to every one,
And six to others that were not rich,   2870
And four to the common men;
Thus the wealthy shared out alms.
Therewith the greater and lesser
Bought themselves horse and donkey meat.
They might have nothing else,   2875
For neither French nor English currency.
I have here told you, Sir King,

---

1   29 September 1191.

All the story of our men,
And of the damage to Acre's company.
But blessed be the Holy Ghost, 2880
And Mary that bore Jesus,
That you have come among us!
Through your help we hope to promptly
Strike down the Saracens' host!"
King Richard wept with both his eyes, 2885
And thus he said to him, truly:
"Sir Bishop, pray for us,
That sweet Jesus might send me the power
To destroy all His foes,
So that they annoy us no more!" 2890
King Richard took leave and leaped on his steed,
And rode out of that fellowship.
He rode about the moat
Toward Acre, certainly,
Until he came to the hospital 2895
Of Saint John, as I find in this tale.
There he ordered his pavilion to be pitched,
And raised his Mate-Gryphon,
Which was a very fine siege tower
With which to assault many Saracens, 2900
So that he might see into Acre.
He had thirteen ships full of bees.
When the engine was well constructed,
They set a mangonel inside it,
And he commanded his men right away 2905
To bring up many beehives,
And to beat on drums and blow trumpets,
And to make an assault all at once.
King Richard ordered a great many beehives
To be cast into the city of Acre. 2910
It was hot in the summertime,
And the bees burst out on every side.
They were annoyed and full of rage,
And they did the Saracens great injury,
For they stung them in the face, 2915
So that they all began to struggle,
And hid themselves in deep cellars,
So that none of them dared to come near;
And they said that King Richard was very shrewd
When his flies bit so well! 2920

King Richard had another siege engine erected,
That was called Robynet:
A strong engine for the occasion,
Which cast hard stones into Acre.
King Richard, the conqueror,   2925
Called his miner in haste,
And commanded him to mine up to the tower
That is called Maudyt Colour.[1]
He swore an oath by Saint Simon
That unless it were brought down   2930
To the outermost wall by noon,
He would chop him up in small pieces.
The miners began to mine fast;
The engineers cast bees and stones.
The Saracens all armed themselves,   2935
And ran to the wall right away.
They dressed themselves in white sheets
For the biting of his flies,
And said, "This man does us great harm,
When he will both throw and mine.   2940
We never saw a king begin so:
It's very doubtful that we will win!"
King Richard stood in his Mate-Gryphon,
And saw their deeds in the town:
And wherever the Saracens flew,   2945
Archers saw and shot at them,
And crossbowmen, too, with piercing bolts
Shot through legs and arms, heads and hearts.
The French men with great nobleness
Helped to mine that same day,   2950
So that the outermost wall was cast down
And many a Saracen quickly slain.
That day King Richard triumphed so well
That he was held a conqueror:
For he had more success that day before noon   2955
Than the others had done in seven years.
        The Saracens might not endure.
They fled into the high tower
And lit torches about the wall
So that men could see it all around.   2960

---

1   In siege warfare it was a common practice to dig under and thus
    literally "undermine" the foundations of walls to bring them down.

The torches cast a great light;
That signified that a new attack
Had come from England,
One which they could not withstand
Unless Saladin, the Sultan, 2965
Came to help with many men.
Saladin was ten miles away,
And saw the torches burning brightly.
They gathered their folk together,
As thick as rain falls in wet weather. 2970
They assembled on a plain
Beside Acre, on a mountain.
Sixty thousand foot soldiers, I find,
He ordered to bind bunches of hay,
To go before them quickly 2975
And fill up the Christians' moat.
So they have agreed on a plan
To put the Christian men to death.
Afterwards came barons and knights,
A hundred thousand strong in combat. 2980
They came in battle order as was their custom,
With banners of red sendal
Cleverly painted with three gryphons,
And a fair band of azure.
Soon after there came riding just as many 2985
Of bold barons, in noble armour.
Their battle standards and their pennons
Were skillfully crafted of green sendal,
And on each one was a dragon
Fighting with a lion.[1] 2990
The first were red, and these were green.
Then came the third battalion all together:
Five and sixty thousand knights,
Clothed in indigo and well armed.
Afterwards came, white as snow, 2995
A row of fifty thousand.
There among them was Sir Saladin,

---

1 The heraldic symbol of the dragon probably symbolizes the devil
   here, while the lion refers to the three lions in the Royal Arms of
   England—or, more generally, to the conflict between East and
   West. See the later references to Richard's (5708) and Saladin's
   (5768) arms.

And his nephew, Myrayn-Momelyn.[1]
Their white banners, without fail,
Showed three Saracen heads of sable,   3000
Which were noble and large.
They had both shields and targes of whalebone.
No man could count that host:
They beset the Christians all about.
The foot soldiers cast in bundles of hay   3005
To make a ready way for the horsemen,
And completely filled the moat
So that all the host might enter in.
The Saracens nearly won entry,
But God Almighty saw that.   3010
The cry arose in the Christian host:
"Onward, lords! To arms, now![2]
Unless we have better defense,
We are lost, by Saint Saviour!"
Then men might see that many brave men   3015
Hastily ran for their arms
And went quickly to the moat,
And swiftly defended themselves.
There many noble heads
Were quickly severed from their bodies;   3020
Many shields were shorn in two,
And many steeds stabbed also.
And many a knight lost his weapons,
And many a steed dragged its entrails,
And many a bold man, without fail,   3025
Was slain in that battle.
King Richard was ill then,
And all of Christendom felt great woe![3]
He might not stir out of his bed,
Even if his pavilion had been on fire.   3030
Therefore the King of France announced

---

1 Larkin notes that "the name given to the nephew of Saladin is likely
   a corruption of *Amir al-Mu'minin*, which means 'Leader of the
   Faithful,' another title of the Caliph" (n. 2998).
2 This line is in French in the original: "Susé seynours, has armes tost!"
3 Richard and Philip were both ill during the siege of Acre; see
   Gillingham, *Richard I* 160. The *Itinerarium* notes that this illness was
   "due to the unfamiliar climate of that region, which did not agree with
   his natural constitution" (Nicholson 204). See Appendix D4b for a
   contemporary account of Richard's illness the following summer.

Throughout the Christian company
That no man should, for fear of death,
Pass outside of the moat,
But keep themselves all within   3035
So that the Saracens should not defeat them.
And those Saracens who had been
Captured and brought in,
They were to be quickly put to death:
Ransom did them no good!   3040
    I may tell you the reason
That King Richard was so ill:
For the exertion of travel by sea
And the foul air of that country,
And unnatural cold and heat,   3045
And food and drink that he found there,
Which was not wholesome for his body,
As was the food in England.
Richard ordered his men to seek
For some wise clerk and trustworthy physician,   3050
Either Christian or Saracen,
To examine his urine.[1]
And every man gave his opinion,
But there was no man so wise
That he might cease his sorrow,   3055
Nor release him from his pains.
The English folk were sorry,
For their lord lay in great anguish;
So was all the Christian host,
Because Richard lay so badly ill.   3060
The Christian host prayed on their knees
To the Father, the Son, and the Holy Ghost,
By day and night with good will:
"Give King Richard relief!"
For love of His dear Mother,   3065
Her Son granted their prayer.
Through His grace and His virtue,
Richard emerged from his fever.
He had no appetite for food,
Not for wine, nor water, nor any liquor,   3070
But he longed for pork.

---

1 Examination of the patient's urine was a well-known diagnostic
   procedure.

But though his men should be hanged,
They might not in that country
For gold, nor silver, nor any money,
Find, take, or get any pork   3075
That King Richard might eat.[1]
    An old knight was with King Richard;
When he learned of that news,
That the King's condition was so,
He spoke to the steward privately: 3080
"Our lord king is badly sick, indeed,
And he longs for pork,
And you may find none for sale:
May no man be so foolhardy as to tell him!
If you did, he might die!   3085
Now, it behooves you to do as I say,
So that he knows nothing of it.
Take a Saracen young and fat.
In haste let the scoundrel be slain,
Cut open, and skinned,   3090
And boiled very quickly
With seasoning, and spices,
And with saffron of good colour.
When the King smells the scent thereof,
As long as his fever has broken,   3095
He will have a good appetite for it.
When he has had a good taste,
And eaten a good meal,
And drunk a mouthful of the broth,
Slept afterwards, and sweated a drop,   3100
Through God's might, and my counsel,
Soon he will be refreshed and healthy."
To say the truth in few words,
The heathen rogue was soon slain and boiled;
It was brought forth before the King.[2]   3105

---

1 Because Islam forbids the eating of pork, it would indeed be
   difficult to find it for sale in a Muslim country. The *RCL* poet
   seems to be aware of this prohibition, which makes the subsequent
   substitution of a Muslim's body for a pig's (and Richard's inability
   to tell them apart) a particularly pointed insult.
2 For other examples of cannibalism in the Chronicles of the
   First Crusade and in medieval literary and religious sources, see
   Appendix C.

His men said, "Lord, we have found pork;
Eat, and drink the sweet broth.
Through God's grace it shall be your remedy."
A knight carved before King Richard;
He ate faster than he might carve.   3110
The King ate the flesh, and gnawed the bones,
And drank well afterward, for the occasion.
And when he had eaten enough,
His folk turned away and laughed.
He lay still, and drew in his arms;   3115
His chamberlain wrapped him up warmly.
He lay, and slept, and sweated a while,
And became healthy and sound.
King Richard dressed himself, and arose,
And walked about in the courtyard;   3120
He showed himself to all the people,
And both the learned and uneducated were glad,
And thanked Jesus and Mary
That he was healed of his malady.
The Saracens worked day and night   3125
With all their might to win the moat.
They felled down the barbicans,
And had nearly entered the common.
When King Richard heard of this,
He spoke and behaved as a madman: 3130
"Arm me in my armour,
For the love of Christ our Creator!
I have a great desire to fight
Against the hounds that will do us outrage.
Now that I find myself healthy and well,   3135
This day I shall prove my might,
If I am as strong as I'm accustomed to be,
And if I can deal strokes
As I was wont to do in England.
If I have my axe in my hand,   3140
All that I meet shall feel me,
And I shall deal out such punishment to them
That they shall have their eternal reward
For the love of their Muhammad!"
He was armed as was proper,   3145
As were his foot soldiers, squires, and knights,
And the Christians all together.
It was a wonder to see that host!

To tell the truth, and conceal nothing,
There were twice as many heathens. 3150
His Templars[1] went before, along with
His Gascoignes[2] and his Hospitallers.
　　Our king rode among the Saracens,
And some he cleaved to the saddle.
He hit a king over the shield 3155
So that head and helmet flew into the field.
He brought such a stroke to another
That all his armour didn't help him.
He split the fourth down to the saddle,
And all that he smote flew to the earth. 3160
The Christian fellowship was merry
Over King Richard and his deeds,
For no armour withstood his axe
Any more than wax withstands a knife.
When the Sultan saw that he was so strong, 3165
He said the devil was among them,
For King Richard slew them outright.
The Sultan withdrew with all his host,
And flew quickly with his barons
Into a town men call Gaza. 3170
But certainly, all the rearguard
Was slain by King Richard.
The Saracens who were in Acre
Were vexed and full of care
When they saw the Sultan flee, 3175
And King Richard slay outright.
Thus all the day until nighttime,
They and the Christians continued the fight.
At evening, when the sun had set,
Every man withdrew to his shelter. 3180
The Christians, both rich and poor,
Went within the moat
To rest, for they were weary.
King Richard commanded

1　The Templars (or Knights Templar) originated in 1119 as a religious
　　and military order dedicated to the protection of pilgrims to the Holy
　　Land. The order expanded into a prominent charity throughout
　　Europe, and it grew in wealth and power. See Tyerman 253–57.
2　Gascoignes are men from Gascony; Richard was Duke of Gascony,
　　so these are his liege men.

Trusty folk to guard the borders   3185
While the others lay and slept.
The Saracens who were outside
Were so terrified of King Richard,
For he had won the victory,
That they rode away and quickly ran   3190
That night, to flee and to hide.
None of them dared to wait for him
Within ten miles' distance.
When King Richard had rested a while,
A knight unlaced his armour   3195
In order to comfort and relax him.
He was brought bread soaked in wine.
"Bring the head of that same swine
That I ate before," he commanded the cook,
"For I am weak, and faint, and distraught. 3200
I am now afraid of my illness;
Serve me my supper right away!"
The cook said, "I don't have that head."
Then said the King, "So God me save,
Unless I see the head of that swine,   3205
Truly, you'll lose yours!"
The cook saw that there was nothing else to do;
He fetched the head, and let him see.
He fell to his knees, and cried,
"Behold, here is the head! My lord, have mercy!" 3210
When the King saw his dark face,
His black beard, and his white teeth,
And how his lips grinned wide,
The King cried, "What devil is this?"
And began to laugh as if he were mad.   3215
"What, is Saracens' flesh this good,
And I never knew it until now?
By God's death and his resurrection,
We shall never die for hunger
While we may, in any assault,   3220
Slay Saracens, take their flesh,
Boil them and roast them and bake them,
And gnaw their flesh to the bones.
Now that I have proved it once,
Before hunger makes me wretched,   3225
I and my folk shall eat more!"
In the morning, without fail,

They began to assail the city.
The Saracens might not endure;
They fled into the high tower,   3230
And cried truce and parliament
To King Richard, who was so noble,
And also to the King of France,
And begged mercy without delay.[1]
Immediately their translator stood up,   3235
And cried out in a voice loud and clear:
"Hear me," he said, "Noble lords,
I bring you good tidings
That Saladin sends you through me.
He wishes that Acre and Jerusalem   3240
Be surrendered into your hands,
And all the land of Syria
To the River Jordan's clear waters,
For ten thousand bezants[2] a year.
And if you don't wish to do so,   3245
You may have peace forevermore,
Provided you make Marquis Montferrat,
Of great power, King of Syria;
For he is the strongest man, certainly,
In Christendom or Heathenness."   3250
Then King Richard answered,
"You lie," he said, "vile coward!
In each gathering and every company,
The Marquis is a false traitor and lies.
He has whitened Saladin's hand with silver,   3255
Bribed him to be King of Syria,
And by the King in Trinity,[3]
The traitor shall never be that!
He was a Christian in my father's day,
And since then he has renounced his religion   3260
And has become a Saracen:
May God give him an evil end!
He is worse than a hound!
He stole sixty thousand pounds

---

1 See Appendix D3 for contemporary accounts of the negotiations
   at Acre.
2 Gold coins.
3 The Christian God, as manifest in three persons: Father, Son, and
   Holy Spirit.

Out of the Hospitallers' hands,   3265
Which my father, who was called
King Henry, sent into this land
To protect Christian men.
I command him to leave this host,
For I swear by the Holy Ghost   3270
And by Mary who bore Jesus,
If I find that traitor among us,
Whether by night or by day,
He shall be drawn with wild horses."
Then the King of France replied   3275
To King Richard without delay,
"Be patient, sir, good friend;[1]
You act unjustly, by Saint Denys,
When you threaten the Marquis,
Who never yet did amiss.   3280
If he has done anything wrong,
He shall amend it at your will.
I am his surety: Lo, here is my glove!
Take it, sire, for my love!"[2]
"No," said King Richard, "By God, my lord,   3285
I shall never make peace with him!
The town of Acre would never have been lost
Except through his false treason.
If he returns my father's treasure
And surrenders Jerusalem with great honour,   3290
Then I will forgive him my wrath,
And never else while I live."
King Philip was distressed at this,
But he dared to speak no more,
For he was always afraid   3295
To receive hard blows from King Richard.
And when the translator heard this,
That the Marquis might not be king,
"Listen," he said, "Good lords,
I bring you other news,   3300
That will be much more to your liking:
If you will let our folk leave in peace,
With life and limb, hand and arm,

---

1 This line is in French in the original: "A sufre, sere, bele amys."
2 King Philip offers his glove as a token of his pledge to be responsi-
   ble for the Marquis.

Without blows and without harm,
We will surrender this town to you,   3305
And also the Holy Cross,[1] with great respect,
And sixty thousand captives, as well,
And a hundred thousand bezants and more,
And you shall also have herein
Rich treasure and great gain,   3310
Sixty thousand helmets and hauberks,
And other riches that you may find:
Enough wheat and other treasure,
To keep your host for seven years and more.
And if you will not accept this offer,   3315
We may keep you out for a long time,
And always one of ours
Will slay ten of yours.
For we have herein, without lie,
Sixty thousand men at defense,   3320
And we pray, for the love of God,
That you will take our offer.
Take the treasure, more and less,
And let us get completely away!"
Then answered King Richard,   3325
"For my part, I grant you this agreement,[2]
As long as you let us come in
It shall be done, all and some."
They let them come in right away.
The Christians took every one of them hostage,   3330
And put them in prison there.
Old and young, highborn and low,
None might leave the city of Acre
Until their ransom was paid,
And the Holy Cross also,   3335
Before they might have peace or pardon.
They found there strong livestock;
That was divided up among the knights.
There was conflict at their entrance:
Richard, our king, took the best treasure.   3340
He gave a great abundance of clothing
To Christian captives in Acre,

---

1 The cross on which Jesus Christ was crucified. It did feature
   prominently in the negotiations at Acre; see Appendix D3.
2 Following this line, the *b* manuscripts have a 10-line passage.

And food and drink and shining arms,
And made them eager to fight,
And took them into his armies   3345
To avenge God against his enemies.
King Richard had captured in Acre
Some Saracens who had come there,
Who were his greatest enemies:
Hardy knights of the highest worth,   3350
The chief lords of Heathenness,
Princes, dukes' sons, and kings,
Emirs and many sultans;
I can't tell their names.
They lay bound fast in prison.   3355
They sent to the Sultan in haste:
"We bear so many great chains
And men torment us to such an extent
That we may neither sit nor lie down;
Unless you buy us out of prison,   3360
And help and rescue us with ransom,
We'll be dead within three days."
The rich Sultan was distressed therefore:
Fully two score of princes and earls,
Emirs, sultans, and many lords,   3365
Said, "We advise you to make accord
With King Richard, who is so bold,
To deliver our children out of prison
So that they won't be hanged or drawn.
King Richard will be glad of treasure,   3370
So that our children may come home healthy.
Load horses and mules, by our advice,
With pure gold and brocades,
In order to ransom our heirs.
Men say that the English love gifts well."   3375
Enough gold for nearly twenty men to carry,
Was loaded onto mules and Arabian horses.
Ten earls all clad in silk,
All old, grey, and not young,
Who were very learned in languages,   3380
Brought the treasure to King Richard.
On their knees they begged him for mercy:
"Our Sultan sends you this treasure,
And will be your friend forevermore,
In exchange for the captives that you have taken.   3385

Let them go with life and limb!
Release them from prison,
And let no man slay or beat them,
For they are all noble vassals,
The sons of kings and emirs, 3390
At this time the most valiant ones
In all of the Saracens' lands,
And the ones our army trusts in the most.
Saladin loves them well, also;
He wishes to lose none of them, 3395
Not for a thousand pounds of gold."
King Richard spoke with mild words,
"God forbid that I take this gold;
Divide each part among yourselves.
I brought more gold and silver with me 3400
In ships and in barges
Than your lord possesses, three times over.
I have no need of his treasure.
But, for your love, I pray you
To stay and dine with me, 3405
And afterward I shall tell you—
In confidence, I shall answer you—
What message you shall take to your lord."
They granted him this with good will.
King Richard privately called his marshal 3410
And met with him alone:
"I shall tell you what you must do.
Go secretly to the prison;
Secretly slay therein
The Saracens of most renown, 3415
Who are come of the richest kin.
And before you strike off their heads,
Be sure that you write every man's name
Upon a scroll of parchment.
Then bear the heads to the kitchen 3420
And cast them into a cauldron,
And tell the cook to boil them well.
And be sure that he removes the hair
From head, and beard, and also from lip.
When we shall sit and eat, 3425
See to it that you don't forget
To serve them in this manner:
Lay every head on a platter, and

Bring it forth hot in your hand,
With his face upward, and the teeth grinning,   3430
And be sure that they aren't raw!
Tie each name tightly above his brow,
What he was called, and of what kin born.
Bring a hot head before me,
And as though I were well pleased with it,   3435
I shall quickly eat it
As though were a tender chick,
To see how the others will like that."
The steward, so the story says,
Immediately did as the King commanded.   3440
At noon, trumpets blew "To the washbasin!" to start the meal.[1]
The messengers knew nothing about
Richard's beliefs, nor his customs.
The King said, "Friends, you are welcome!"
He was companionable to them.   3445
They were placed at a side table:
Salt was set out, but no bread,
Neither water nor wine, white nor red.
The Saracens sat, and began to stare,
And thought, "Alas, how shall we manage?"   3450
King Richard was seated on the dais,
With dukes and earls, proud in the company.
The first course came from the kitchen,
With pipes, and trumpets, and drums.
The steward took very good care   3455
To serve King Richard in a pleasing way,
Lest after dinner he come to harm.
A Saracen's head, all warm,
He brought our King. It was not unlettered:
His name was written on his forehead.   3460
The messengers were served likewise,
With a head between every two.
On the foreheads were written their names:
Therefore they had every grief!
When they saw who they were,   3465
The tears ran out of their eyes;
And when they read the letters,
They feared to be cruelly slain.

---

1 The trumpet blast signals mealtime. The term for the signal, "a
   laver," is in French in the original.

King Richard cast his eyes upon them,
And saw how they began to change their hue. 3470
They sighed grievously for their friends,
Whom they had lost forevermore.
They were of their own kindred:
Thus they well might forbear
To laugh and play! 3475
None of them would get near their meal,
Nor eat a morsel of it.
The King sat and beheld this well.
The knight who would serve the King
Began to carve the head with a sharp knife. 3480
King Richard ate with a good heart;
The Saracens thought he must be mad.
Every man sat still, and poked the other;
They said, "This is the devil's brother,
That slays our men and thus eats them!" 3485
King Richard did not forget them;
He looked about him intently,
With a wrathful face, and stern gaze.
He then urged the messengers:
"For my love, may you all be glad, 3490
And look that you're well at ease!
Why do you not carve your food
And eat vigorously, as I do?
Tell me, why do you look so frightened?"
They sat still and trembled greatly; 3495
They dared neither speak nor look.
They would have crawled into the earth;
They fully expected to be slain.
Not one of them answered a word.
King Richard said, "Take from the table 3500
The meat that you set before them,
And fetch them other food!"
Men humbly brought bread,
Venison, cranes, and good roasts,
Wine, claret, and pleasant drinks; 3505
King Richard urged them all to be happy.
Not one of them desired to eat.
King Richard well understood their thoughts,
And said, "Friends, don't be squeamish.
This is the custom of my house, 3510
To be served first, God knows,

With a Saracen's head all hot;
But I didn't know your custom!
As I am a true Christian king,
You shall therefore be certain   3515
To return again in safe conduct,
For I would not wish, for anything,
That word of me should get around in the world
That I had such discourteous manners
As to do harm to messengers."   3520
When they had eaten, the tablecloth was folded,
And King Richard beheld them:
On their knees they asked permission to go.
There was not one of them all
That had come there as a messenger   3525
Who would not rather have been at home,
With wife, friends, and their kin,
Than have all the wealth in India!
King Richard spoke to an old man:
"Go home, and tell your Sultan   3530
To abate his melancholy,
And say that you have come too late.
Your time was estimated too negligently;
The flesh that men should serve
Me and my company with at noon   3535
Was prepared before you came.
Tell him that it won't work
For you to cut off our food supply—
Bread and wine, flesh and fish, salmon and eel.
None of us shall die for hunger   3540
While we may go into battle
And slay the Saracens outright,
Wash the flesh, and roast the head.
With one Saracen I may well feed
Fully nine, or ten,   3545
Of my good Christian men."
King Richard said, "I guarantee you,
There is no flesh so nourishing
For an English Christian man—
Not partridge nor plover, heron nor swan,   3550
Cow nor ox, sheep nor swine,
As is the flesh of a Saracen!
For he is fat, and also tender,
And my men are lean and slender.

While any Saracen remains alive   3555
Living now in this country,
We shall care nothing about food:
We shall continue on vigorously,
And every day we shall eat
Just as many as we can get.   3560
We will not return to England
Until we've eaten every one!"
The messengers turned home again;
They came and mourned before their lord.
The eldest told the Sultan   3565
That King Richard was a noble man
And said, "Lord, I assure you
That there's no man so fierce in this world!
On our knees we told him our tale,
But our speech didn't help us at all.   3570
He wanted nothing to do with your gold;
He swore he had won better
Rich treasure than you have.
To us he said, 'I give it to you,
Treasure of silver, gold, and fine cloth—   3575
Divide it all among yourselves!'
He asked us to stay to dinner;
We were seated at a table beside him,
And Richard's table stood nearby.
But none of us saw before him   3580
Any bread brought forth, white or leavened,
But only salt, and no other drink.
I saw well the first course that came before him;
I paid close attention.
A knight brought forth from the kitchen   3585
A boiled head of a Saracen!
Without hair, on a broad platter,
His name was written above his eyes
Before the crown of his head;
I won't lie out of fear.   3590
My companions asked whose head it was:
It was the son of the Sultan of Damascus!
As we sat together at the table,
We were served in this manner:
A head between each two.   3595
We thought we'd die for sorrow!
There came between my fellow and me

The son of the King of Nineveh;
The son of the King of Persia went to my neighbour.
The third was the son of the King of Samaria; 3600
The fourth, the son of the King of Egypt.
Then each of us had to wipe his eyes!
The fifth was the son of the King of Africa:
We began to sigh for sorrow.
We thought our hearts would burst! 3605
Lord, you might yet hear a wonder.
Before King Richard a knight swiftly
Carved from the head, and he ate vigorously.
He violently gnawed the flesh with his teeth,
Acting like a mad lion, 3610
With his eyes glaring and fierce.
He spoke, and we beheld him;
We expected to die from terror!
He urged us that we should carve
Our food and eat as he did. 3615
We offered our prayers to Muhammad
That he be our protector from death!
He saw us make terrified faces,
And how we began to tremble from dread!
He ordered his men to remove our meat 3620
And fetch us other food:
They set before us hot white bread,
Geese, swans, cranes, venison
And great abundance of other wild fowl,
White and red wine, spiced wine and clary, 3625
And said, 'You are welcome to me.
Be merry, if it be your will,
Carry on gladly and don't be displeased,
For I knew nothing about your custom.
In my court, this is the sequence of dishes: 3630
My household and I are served first
With hot heads of Saracens!'
We stood in such terror of him and his people
That for fear and grief we thought we'd die.
None of us ate a morsel of bread, 3635
Nor drank any wine, white nor red,
Nor ate any meat, baked nor roasted,
We were so distressed with fear.
After dinner we took our leave,
And he spoke to us with few words: 3640

'You shall go in safe conduct;
No man shall do you harm.'
He sent you a definite answer:
Before we might come there,
The men of noblest kin were slain.   3645
He doesn't care at all whether you carry off
And hide the provisions from all his host.
He says, and his men make boast,
That he shall not leave alive
In all your land a woman or child,   3650
But will slay all that he may find,
And boil the flesh and gnaw them with teeth:
Hunger shall never trouble him!
He will not sail back to England
Until he has completely finished the job!"   3655
For ire Saladin began to tear
His clothes of gold, down to his undergarments.
Kings, princes, and many a nobleman
Said "Alas!" that they had lost
Their noble heirs, born of their bodies,   3660
That were such valiant and strong men.
"Alas!" they cried, "We live too long.
We never heard of such a monster!
It is a devil, without fail.
Alas that this war was begun!   3665
        Now Richard has won Acre.
He intends, if he may go forth,
To win east, west, north, and south,
And eat our children and us!
Lord Saladin, we advise this: 3670
Send to him, and beg him
For those who are still left alive.
If he will let them go,
Give him, since he wants no gold,
Rich bags, for the occasion,   3675
Full of rich precious stones,
Loaded in saddle bags and coffers.
Offer to give him a great
Portion of land if he will agree
To renounce Jesus and Mary,   3680
So that he'll be in peace, and stop the war.
Because he's come from so far,
You don't want him to lose his effort.

Grant him that he may come himself, and choose
The lands that he likes best,   3685
And make him the highest Sultan
After yourself, and the richest king;
Confirm it to him and his offspring.
If he is pleased to do so,
He may swiftly come in peace to you.   3690
Although he has destroyed your folk,
You shall forgo your hostility
And love and kiss him as your brother,
And he shall teach and advise you
To be bold and wise in war, and   3695
To win distinction over all the world.
And so you shall live and be friends,
With joy until your lives' ends."
    Saladin sent King Richard
These presents by his servants,   3700
And begged him for his men
That he held as hostages,
And said that if he would forsake Jesus
And take Muhammad as his lord,
He would make him the King of Syria,   3705
And of Egypt, that rich country,
Of Darras, and of Babylon,
Of Arabia, and of Cesson,
Of Africa, and of Bogye,
And of the land of Alexandria,   3710
Of great Greece, and of Tyre,
And of many a rich empire,
And he would immediately make him the Sultan
Of all India, up to Prester John's realm.[1]
King Richard answered these messengers,   3715
"Fie upon you flatterers,
On you, and on your lord Saladin!
May the devil hang you by a cord!
Go and say to Saladin

---

1 Prester John was a legendary Christian monarch in the Far East who
  was supposed to possess unlimited wealth, lands full of marvels, and a
  particularly pure and virtuous form of Christianity. His legend—bol-
  stered by a popular *Letter* that was attributed to him and that appeared
  c. 1165–70—was widespread during the Crusades, as it held out the
  hope of a powerful Eastern ally against the Muslims. See Brewer.

That he must pay ransom tomorrow   3720
For all his dogs held in hostage,
Or else they shall die violently!
And if I might live a few years,
I won't leave him half a foot
Of all the lands that you've named here,   3725
May God do my soul good!
I will not lose the love of my Lord
For all the lands under Heaven above.
And unless I have the Cross tomorrow,
His men shall die with great sorrow."   3730
They answered at once that
They didn't know what had become of the Cross.
King Richard said then, "Since it is so,
I know well what I have to do.
Your sultan is not so sly as to   3735
Craftily pull the wool over my eyes."
He called his knights right away,
And commanded them to go into Acre:
"And take sixty thousand Saracens
And tie their hands behind them,   3740
And lead them out of the city,
And behead them without pity.
And so shall I teach Saladin
To ask me to believe in Apollo!"[1]
They were brought out of the town,   3745
Except for twenty he held for ransom.
They were led all the way to the place of execution,
And there they heard an angel of Heaven
That said, "Lords, kill! Kill![2]
Spare them not—behead these!"   3750
King Richard heard the angel's voice,
And thanked God and the Holy Cross.
They were beheaded hastily,
And cast into a foul ditch.[3]

---

1 Another pagan deity (this time from the Greek and Roman
   pantheon) that the poem's Saracens are said to worship.
2 The angel's first line is in French: "Seygnyours, tues, tues!"
3 See Appendix D3c for two contemporary accounts (one from each
   side of the conflict) of Richard's killing of hostages at Acre. The
   actual number of hostages put to death seems to have been between
   2,500 and 3,000.

Thus King Richard won Acre, 3755
God grant his soul much bliss![1]
Whoever wants to learn more about his brave deeds,
Listen now, and you may hear.
It's delightful in the month of May
When birds sing their songs;[2] 3760
Flowers bloom on apple and pear trees,
Small birds sing merrily, and
Ladies strew their bowers
With red roses and lily flowers.
There is great joy in meadow and lake, as 3765
Beasts and birds play with their mates.
The damsels hold dances;
Knights play with shield and lance,
Riding in jousts and tournaments.
Many a predicament befalls them, 3770
Many vicissitudes and hard strokes!
So it happened to King Richard.
King Richard invited Philip to a feast.
After dinner, when they were cheerful,
Richard gave gifts in great abundance: 3775
Gold and silver and precious stones,
To heralds and to minstrels;
To drummers and to trumpeters
He gave horses and robes, to uphold his reputation.
Through their praise his renown increased: 3780
They told how he was courteous and generous;
That gathering was entirely noble!
King Richard gave castles and towns
To his earls and barons,
With which to support themselves. 3785
King Richard urged the King of France,
"Give of your gold and your gain

---

1 Richard and Philip took Acre on 12 July 1191, after a siege of only
  one month. Ten days later, Philip announced his intention to
  leave the Holy Land, and he embarked for home on 3 August; his
  presence in the rest of the poem is therefore fictional. On Philip's
  departure, see Gillingham, *Richard I* 162–67. Following Philip's
  departure, Henry of Champagne helped to lead the remaining
  French forces; he enjoyed a much better relationship with Richard,
  although the poem does not reflect this.
2 This springtime scene introduces a fictional episode of conquest
  that lasts through line 4816.

To earl, baron, knight and sergeant of mace!
Generously reward their service:
They toiled for you in battle.   3790
If you have business with them again,
They will be the gladder afterwards
To help you at your need."
King Philip took no heed of this,
But turned a deaf ear   .   3795
And gave him no answer at all:
He took King Richard's words as worthless.
Richard then said to him,
"Let there be peace and accord between us,
By the grace of Jesus Christ, Our Lord,   3800
Who gave us the power to win this town!
Let us prepare to ride forth
To vex Saladin the Sultan,
Seek him out and destroy him.
If he overcomes us in battle,   3805
If need be, we must be secure.
If God chooses that we may live,
And we may escape hither,
And come, alive, within the walls,
Despite Saladin and all his folk,   3810
And the gates are shut well,
We may be certain of strong shelter."
King Richard proceeded to tell Philip,
"I advise that we dwell here no longer.
Let us ride forth to explore the country.   3815
And Philip, do as I teach you.
I shall divide my host in three,
And King Philip, take your army
And divide it into two companies,
And see to it that you do as I tell you.   3820
If you win any town, city, or castle,
Slay all the folk that are therein.
In God's name, I forbid you
To let any live: rich or poor,
Husband or wife, boy or girl,   3825
For any gold, silver, or any reward
That they may offer or give you,

Unless they will accept Christianity!"[1]
Philip understood the words,
But his mood quickly began to change, 3830
Because in his judgement King Richard
Set so little store by him and his men.
Philip was friendly to him;
He used fair words, but spoke falsely,
And thanked him with a glad guise 3835
And said, "Brother, I grant you
To do as you say, certainly,
For you are a wiser man than I,
And know considerably more about war."
Nevertheless he was bitterly grieved. 3840
Out of fear, he and his men did
As King Richard had ordered them,
For fear that he would receive blows.
He divided his men in two companies.
Richard went his way with his host, 3845
Away from him to win plunder.
They parted from each other with love,
But now you may hear of a wonder.
French men are timid and faint,
And Saracens are cunning and crafty, 3850
And ingenious in their deeds.
The French men are covetous.
When they sit at the tavern,
There they are brave and bold
To speak boastful words, 3855
And brag about their deeds.
They're of little worth and foolishly proud:
They can only fight with loud words,
And say that no man is their peer—
But when they come to a dangerous situation, 3860
And see men begin to deal strokes,
Then they quickly turn tail,
And begin to draw in their horns
Like a snail among the thorns.

---

1 Forced conversion to Christianity did occur during the Crusades,
though perhaps not as frequently as *RCL* suggests. See Kadar
42–96.

May a boar retreat from their boasts!¹   3865
Soon King Philip with his host
Besieged a strong city
That was called Taburet.
He surrounded it all about with his host;
The Saracens might go neither in nor out,   3870
Lest they should be cut to pieces.
They showed themselves, armed, on the walls,
And out of turrets and embrasures;
They set up banners and pennons,
And began to defend themselves manfully.   3875
The French expected to die there.
They blew trumpets loudly in boast,
But dared never to shoot or throw
With bow, sling, nor with crossbow
With which to terrify the Saracens,   3880
Nor to attack the city.
But the Chief Emir of the town—
He was named Terryabaute—
Called, "Lord, before you start to attack us,
All the folk of this town   3885
Offer to kneel themselves down
And sorrowfully, with one cry,
To meekly beg you for mercy.
And they will surrender the town to you,
And all the goods that they possess.   3890
Man, woman, and every Saracen
Grants you with a true heart
To each pay a bezant,
Sire, on the condition
That you grant what they desire: 3895
To have their lives and limbs,
Livestock, cattle, and treasure,
And that they will forevermore
Hold this town for your heirs."
Philip took ransom from them: 3900
For reward he spared his foes.
Thus he was at accord with them,
And ordered his folk, upon life and limb,

---

1 The meaning of this line is ambiguous; boars were known as fierce
animals, so it may be ironic, as mere boasts could never frighten
away a boar.

To seize no goods from them,
Not food nor drink, cattle nor cloth.   3905
All of those who were there
Swore a solemn oath to be his men;
And they raised up his banner
On a pole in the highest tower,
With fleur-de-lis of gold and azure.[1]   3910
When they had won this town,
They began to break the siege.
They loaded up in wagons and carts
All their swords and spears, shields and missiles.
King, earls, barons, knights, and squires   3915
Rode royally on elaborately armed steeds.
The foot soldiers went along on their feet;
In such a way they followed the high street,
So that they would not turn aside or become disorderly.
They trumpeted, and displayed their banners   3920
Of silk, sendal, and many flags.
They travelled by the right way to Archane,
And Philip took ransom from them there
Just as he did at the other town,
And let them depart from there in peace—   3925
Except for the poor. He set the rich free.
　　　King Richard proceeded to ride with his host,
And went by another way,
With many an earl and baron
Born of the English nation: 3930
All hardy men and strong of bones,
And well armed for the occasion.
They rode on good, strong steeds.
There were many Gascoignes among them,
As well as men of Lombardy—   3935
Very good and hardy knights—
And folk from the coast of Germany,
And his nephew, Henry of Champagne,[2]
And his official, Robert of Leicester:
Among them all there was no better.   3940
Fulk D'Oilly and Thomas Multoun
Asked to be first in the fight,

1　From the twelfth century on, the Royal Arms of France featured
　the fleur-de-lys (a stylized lily) in gold on a blue field.
2　See note to line 2823.

As was ever yet their custom,
To help their king to prosper well.
From the coast of Brindisi he took with him   3945
A noble baron named Bertram,
And his clergy, and his friars,
And his Templars, and his Hospitallers.
The number was, truly,
A hundred thousand horsemen,   3950
And ten times as many foot soldiers:
Gascoignes, Lombards, and Englishmen.
Fields and plains were all covered
With knights, foot soldiers, and attendants.
King Richard waited and watched,   3955
And arrayed his host in the field,
And to his host he said this:
"We have plenty of folk with us;
I advise that we divide them in three.
One part shall go with me,   3960
Sir Thomas Multoun shall lead
The other—certainly, by all means—
And Fulk D'Oilly shall lead the third.
On penalty of life and limb I now command you
That if you win town, castle, or city,   3965
That you spare no one that is therein.
Slay them all and take their goods,
Unless they agree with mild mood
To be baptized in the font:
Else see to it that you let no one live!"   3970
          King Richard with his company
Went to Sudan Turry;
Thomas, an ingenious knight,
Went with his host to Orglyous,[1]
And Fulk D'Oilly   3975
Went to the city of Ebedy.
Each man besieged his town all around,
So that no Saracen dared to come out,
Because the siege was so strong and tough.
But now let us speak of King Richard,   3980
Who has besieged Sudan Turry.
At the first assault the Saracens

---

1 This fictional name derives from an Old French word, *orgoillos*,
   meaning "proud" or "arrogant."

Wound up their drawbridges in haste,
And barred their gates fast;
They tried to defend themselves.   3985
King Richard ordered his banner to be displayed.
When the Saracens saw it raised,
They were deeply afraid of him.
They began to tremble in terror.
Their mayor—his name was Grandary[1]—   3990
Received advice, and ordered
It announced throughout the city
That every man who might bear arms
Should go to the wall to defend the town.
The armed Saracens leaped forth   3995
Upon the walls to defend the town,
Bold in turrets and in palisades.
Richard drew back a great crossbow with a screw
And shot it straight to a tower,
And it smote through seven Saracens.   4000
The vile dogs fell dead.
But now hear of a clever trick!
King Richard had his folk prepare
To assail half of that town.
When the townsfolk all rushed to that side,   4005
Then King Richard sent his men
To go in on high ladders,
That were cleverly crafted
With iron hooks, good and strong.[2]
They proceeded to hang them on the walls.   4010
Seven men might go in abreast;
Thus men went over the walls,
Three thousand before the Saracens knew it,
While they defended the town.
The Christians came in before they realized: 4015
They shot at them and struck hard,
And great numbers of them fell down,
But when the constable heard tell
That the Christians were coming in,
He took ten thousand prisoner.   4020

---

1 Larkin suggests that his name might translate to "great honour"
(n. 3991).
2 Presumably they raise the ladders on the other side of the town,
which is now undefended.

He commanded others to defend the town:
"For these," he said, "accept no ransom.
Let them not beg mercy!
King Richard shall never save them;
They shall die right away!"   4025
When King Richard heard him say so,
For scorn he began to laugh brightly,
And urged his men to be of good will,
"And endeavour to win this town
And rescue these folk who are within."   4030
The Saracens exercised their strength
To slay the Christians outright
Who had come over the wall.
Our folk all stuck together:
They shot arrows and bolts at the Saracens,   4035
And slew all those that they hit.
With fierce strength they gave them battle.
They were certain of good help
From King Richard who was outside.
Our Christian men ran about,   4040
And some hastened to the gates
While striking through all those they found,
And threw them from the tower,
Crying, "Sir King, help us!
You shall come in safely;   4045
In a little while, it shall be taken!"
Then they greeted King Richard
And let down the drawbridges,
And threw the gates wide open.
King Richard was the first who rode in,   4050
And after him, Robert de Turnham,
Robert of Leicester and Sir Bertram.
These rode in the vanguard;
None of them forbore to slay the hounds.
King Richard seized his axe in his hand   4055
And paid the Saracens their due!
He dealt such blows,
That everyone he hit immediately perished.
They slew every Saracen,
And took the Temple of Apollo.   4060
They knocked it down and burned Muhammad,[1]

---

1 The poet here imagines a wooden idol of Muhammad.

And he gave all the treasure of the town
To knight, squire, and page,
As much as they would have.
He left no Saracens alive, 4065
But King Richard raised up his flag
In a tower on a high pole,
And thus won the town in this way.
   Now be in peace, and listen closely!
I shall tell you of Sir Thomas, 4070
The noble baron of Multoun,
Who camped with many a mother's son
At Orglyous, a strong castle.
Listen now to what happened next!
The Saracens for treachery 4075
Soon sent out a spy
Who had been Christian in his youth.
He knew many an evil trick!
He came to Thomas and said thus,
And thought to have betrayed him: 4080
"Sir, I am a Christian man.
I escaped from prison and ran away.
Trust my speech well:
If you will do as I teach you,
You shall defeat them in a while. 4085
In all the town there is no treachery;
This I know; may the truth prosper!"
Thomas said, "Quickly tie him up!
Everything the scoundrel says is a lie;
He is of the Saracens' faith. 4090
He was sent to deceive us,
But he will regret coming here;
He shall quickly die.
So shall men teach him to lie!
Slit both of his ears, 4095
And tie a strong rope to his feet,
And hang him up until he dies!"
The scoundrel said, "I beg for mercy!
Don't put me to a vile death!
I shall truly tell you all that I can. 4100
If you find any falsehood in me,
In either word or in deed
That you can ever see or confirm,
Immediately strike off my head!

I was indeed sent to betray you: 4105
I shall tell you—listen how!
Before the gate there is a bridge—
Listen well and I shall say—
Under the bridge there is a trap
Covered carefully and fastened ingeniously, 4110
And underneath there is a hasp
Shut with a clasp and a bolt,
And in that hasp a pin is placed.
You must beware, if you will—
I would hate for you to fare badly— 4115
If you and your folk were in the middle
And the pin were struck out,
You should fall down there
Into a pit sixty fathoms deep.
Therefore, beware and take good care. 4120
In passing over the trap,
Many have fallen into evil circumstances.
It closes again by a counterweight,
Concealed where no one may see it."
"Now Saracen, tell me right away, 4125
What should we do in this danger?"
"You have horsemen and foot soldiers,
And good siege engines with you
That few Saracens know about.
Before you assail the town 4130
You should erect a catapult,
And so you shall badly frighten them.
Sling a great stone into the town,
And also, allow me to swiftly
Pass into the town again; 4135
And then you shall see
That they shall soon surrender the town.
But I beg a favour from you:
If I do win this town,
That you give me my reward." 4140
Said Thomas, "I grant you this."
With that covenant they parted ways.
The engine was drawn back and made all ready;
A great stone was cast into the town.
They slew men and knocked down houses 4145
Before any man was aware of them.
"We are dying! Help, Muhammad!" they cried.

On every side they hurried away
To hide themselves in woe and terror.
The traitor went into the town   4150
And said to the governor, Orgayl,[1]
"We're going to die, without fail!
He that threw the stone at you
Knew all about your treason:
How your bridge breaks apart,   4155
And all the trickery underneath,
And how it rejoins with a counterweight.
Beware, barons and burgesses!
It won't help you at all to shut your gates
To keep out him and his men.   4160
If you fight and defend yourselves
He will send more stones to you,
Destroy you and beat down the town.
He will let no house stand;
It is better to let him enter in peace   4165
Than that he kill you all herein;
Then we may be certain to live."
When he had given this advice,
They immediately did as he advised.
Each one of them cried, "Mercy, Thomas!   4170
Have here the keys of this city;
Do whatever you wish with it,
If you will only grant us our lives,
And those of our wives and children."
Thomas of Multoun seized the keys,   4175
And slung another stone
To Sir Muhammad's dwelling,
And knocked down a great turret.
The governor, Orgayl, came out,
With a hundred knights dressed like him: 4180
Barefoot, unarmed, and bareheaded.
"Mercy, Thomas! Don't spill our blood!
Take for yourself all the goods that we have.
If you will just save our lives,
Let us depart from here all naked."   4185
"Break the bridge," said Thomas, "that you have made,
And throw mortar and stone into the pit,
Or, by Jesus who sits in Heaven,

---

1 The governor's name relates to that of his city: see note to line 3974.

You shall all burn therein.
None of you all shall go,   4190
Nor run out, neither rich nor poor,
Unless you thoroughly fill the ditch
Up to the bank, in a hurry,
So that we may enter in quickly."
The Emir of the town was glad,   4195
And broke the bridge right away,
And cast stone and mortar into the pit.
Soon it was filled up and covered over
Up to the bank, and made all flat
And completely sound for the whole length and width,   4200
Truly, so that twenty men, and more besides,
Might ride in on armed steeds
And have entrance without fear.
Thus they came to that city.
The townsfolk came, all and some,   4205
And graciously welcomed them,
Crying mercy with loud voices.
For every one Christian man there were seven
Saracens in that city.
Right away they proffered gold   4210
And silver and brocades to Sir Thomas,
And with good will offered him
Lands, houses, and treasure,
To hold for him for ever more.
        The apostate came to Sir Thomas.   4215
"Mercy, Lord: I beg you to think
What you owe me for this town,
As you are a noble knight.
I ask no more than that you give me
Food and drink while I live.   4220
For with woolen clothes and bare feet
I shall walk in sleet and snow
To amend me of my sin,
In order to win the joy of Heaven!"
He cleanly confessed himself to a priest.   4225
Thomas granted with good will
This agreement between them,
And thus he left him unmolested,
Wherever he went in war or peace,
Always until the end of his life.   4230
Lords, listen to my lament!

You shall hear of a clever treason,
How the Saracens have pledged
To be avenged upon the Christian men.
This is how the Emir advised them: 4235
"When the Christians are in bed,
And while they're in their first sleep,
We should come armed, all together.
One shall remain within the courtyard
To open and unpin the gate, and   4240
Silently to undo the lock.
We shall come secretly in a troop
And slay Thomas of Multoun,
And with him every mother's son
That he has brought with him."   4245
Sir Thomas knew nothing of this.
They boiled flesh, roasted, and fried it,
And quickly went to supper.
There was abundant bread and wine,
Spiced wine, and clary, fine and good: 4250
And plenty of cranes, swans, and venison,
Partridges, plovers, and herons,
Larks and other small birds.
The Saracens, in order to dupe them,
Gave them the strongest wine to drink.   4255
They were weary, and greatly desired sleep;
They slept deeply, and began to snore.
The Saracens were all waiting outside,
And came armed to the gate.
The apostate stood ready there.   4260
They knocked at the door,
And he let it stay shut
And told Thomas what he heard,
And all that it meant.
Sir Thomas made no boast;   4265
He began to awake all of his folk.
"For God's love," he ordered them,
"Prepare yourselves quickly or you'll be dead!"
They jumped up and were afraid
Because of what he said to them.   4270
They armed themselves very readily,
And went out by a side door
Before the Saracens were aware.
So while they waited and gathered together,

And would have rushed in with strength, 4275
The Christians ran to the gates
And locked them securely with the key.
By that time the day began to break.
The Christians bent bows and crossbows,
And went throughout every street, 4280
Shooting arrows and bolts;
Many Saracens fell down dead.
They didn't leave, in any street or house,
Anyone alive in Orglyous,
Not burgess nor wife, nor young children. 4285
When they had made this reckoning,
Thomas truly gave his men
All the treasure and the cloth,
And every man had his share of
Silver and gold, every groat. 4290
There was no page so little
That he didn't have his wages
Of silver and gold and great treasure,
Enough to be rich forevermore.
Before he departed Thomas released 4295
Out of prison the Christian men,
Every palmer and pilgrim,[1]
And gave them incomes and houses there:
With them he brought order to the town again.
Whoever came there might well see 4300
King Richard's arms raised
On high in every prominent tower.
    Lords, now you have heard
How it fared in these towns;
How King Richard with his power 4305
Won the town of Sudan Turry;
Thomas Multoun won Orglyous
And slew every mother's son.
Of Ebedy we shall speak,
That has now securely locked its gate 4310
When Fulk D'Oilly besieged it,
So that he might not enter in.
The city was strong and bold:

---

1 Originally, a palmer was a pilgrim who had returned from the Holy
Land with a palm as proof of his or her pilgrimage; by the later
Middle Ages, "palmer" and "pilgrim" had become synonymous.

It was seven miles around.
It had thirty splendid towers by number, 4315
And a chief emir in every tower.
There were fifty thousand
Men of arms, by count,
Along with so many foot soldiers
Who came into the battle 4320
That no man could count
How many they would amount to.
Sir Fulk brought good siege engines,
Such that few Saracens knew of,
And had them raised on every side, 4325
To teach his enemies a new game.
He had a catapult pulled back,
And sent a stone to the great tower;
When that stone flew out,
The Saracens who saw it 4330
Cried "Alas!" and were in awe:
"It roars like thunder!"
The stone hit the tower so hard,
That it knocked it twenty feet away.
He threw a stone at another tower 4335
To make a new game for them:
He struck away all of one side,
And slew the dogs of false faith.
They beat down all the towers
In the town and on the wall. 4340
A splendid tower stood over the gate:
He bent back his engine and threw at it
A great stone that struck hard,
So that the tower broke all to bits,
The barrier, and the palisade: 4345
The gate burst, and the portcullis.
Thereto he gave another stroke
To break the oaken beams,
And slew the folk that stood therein.
The others fled, and were nearly insane, 4350
And said it was the devil's stroke.
"Alas, Muhammad! What does he mean,
This English dog called Fulk?
He is no man, he is a fiend
Who has stolen out of Hell! 4355
May he suffer an evil death

Because he besieges us severely.
If he casts more stones at us,
All this town will be beaten down.
He won't allow a house to stand!"   4360
Sir Fulk began to prepare himself
To assail the town with his folk.
Before he won the town with strength,
Many a man was slain there!
The town moats on every side   4365
Were very deep and wide,
And so full of mud that no man might swim them.
The wall stood right upon the brink:
No man might stand before it.
The archers of our land   4370
Shot in with slender arrows;
The townsfolk paid no attention.
The Saracens went up on the walls,
And shot with catapults and siege machines,
And stunned them with crossbow bolts.   4375
They slew many of our folk:
Their arrows were poisoned.
But when Fulk D'Oilly saw what was happening,
That his men would be slain,
He ordered them to withdraw: 4380
"And bring trees, and many a bough."
Many folk came to do his will.
The Christian men made themselves a shield
Of large doors and windows.
Some took boards and some took planks,   4385
And brought timber, and thatch,
And great beams, and wood,
And slung it into the mud,
And threw thatch on top of it,
So that Christian men might go up   4390
To the wall, and stand safely,
And give battle hand to hand:
A sorry beverage was brewed there![1]
Bolts and arrows flew thickly;
The English slew those that they captured.   4395
No man dared to look over the walls
Lest the Christians cast them down.

---

1 I.e., bitter suffering was inflicted.

And the Christians blew wildfire over the walls:
Right away many a house,
And many a land, and many a street   4400
Turned into a bright light.
Then the Saracens, because of the heat,
Pulled out their goods, and quickly fled:
"Alas!" and "Help!" they cried loudly.
The English men heard the cry: 4405
They were strong and fearless,
And well expected to win the town.
Those within defended themselves well:
Although one might fall down,
Another would leap upon the wall   4410
In the place where he stood,
And defended it well with a good heart.
There was no joy among the townsfolk:
They gathered together in council.
Then the Chief Emir said,   4415
"Lords, listen to me!
This siege is great, this fire is strong,
And we may not long endure.
They have great desire to slay us,
And they've set our town on fire!   4420
They won't grant us peace
Unless it's on the terms
That we forsake our god, Muhammad,
And accept Christianity,
And believe in Jesus and Mary.   4425
It would be disgraceful and wicked
For us to believe in a false religion!
So let every man arm himself who may—
Who is strong enough to bear weapons—
And let us strive to defend this town!   4430
In our army we have ten
For every one of the Christian men
He has brought here to fight with us.
Be bold and don't fear him at all!
It is better that we run out to battle   4435
Than to burn like wretches in our houses,
And fry in our own grease!
The English are faint and cowardly:
They lack food and drink.
We shall slay them all in battle,   4440

And fell them all in the field.
May he be hanged who will yield this town
To Christian men while he may live!"
But when he had given this counsel,
Every man threw on his arms   4445
And came to him all ready:
They were all very eager to fight.
They went very swiftly to their temple,
Every man armed in his livery,
And made their sacrifice there   4450
To Muhammad and to Jupiter,[1]
So that they would help them in their war:
"We never had such a need before now,
And here we vow to them
That if we win the victory this day,   4455
We will never cease
To fight with Christian rogues
Until they are all cut to pieces."
They divided their army in four parts,
And issued out at the four gates.   4460
         Sir Arcade led the first host,
Which spread out in all directions.
Sir Cudary led the other,
Together with his brother Sir Orphias.
Sir Materbe, valiant in armour,   4465
Led the third host with them;
Sir Gargoyle led the fourth.[2]
Wherever they rode, all the earth
Shook under their horses' hooves.
Sir Fulk perceived this and went to look.   4470
Their folk were arrayed in that plain,
Four score thousand, truly to tell,
Of footmen, knights, and squires,
And of lords with banners.

---

1 Again, the poet portrays the Saracens as polytheistic; Jupiter
   here joins Apollo (from line 3744) as another Roman god in their
   pantheon.
2 The names of these fictional Saracen knights are drawn from
   Greece (Arcadia), possibly from India (although the etymology
   of Cudary is uncertain), from the mythology of Ancient Greece
   (Orpheus), and from monstrosity (gargoyle). The origin of
   "Materbe" is unknown. See Larkin, n. 4467.

There were sixty emirs,   4475
To tell the truth, by certain count.
They rode armed, on well-caparisoned steeds,
Ready to await battle.
    Sir Fulk began to arrange his troops,
As they should conduct themselves.   4480
Foremost he set his crossbowmen,
And after that, his good archers,
And afterwards his staff slingers,
And others with shields and with spears.
He arrayed the fourth part   4485
With knife and dart, sword and axe.
The men of arms brought up the rear.
Fulk said, "Sirs, don't be afraid,
Although they have more troops than we!"
They blessed him and fell to their knees.   4490
"Father, and Son, and Holy Ghost,"
Said Fulk, "Guard the Christian host!
Mary mild, deliver our message!
May your Child help us at our need,
And preserve our honour, we pray you!   4495
We are ready to die for you,
And for His love who died on the Cross!"
The Saracens, with fierce hearts,
Seized their weapons.
They blew trumpets and began to pipe.   4500
The Christians were swift to the fight:
Every lord lifted up his banner
With his own family's coat of arms,
So that his men should know him,
And follow him at that time   4505
When they rode into battle.
The Saracens came with great will
Until the Christians might draw near them.
They prepared to shoot the crossbows,
And the archers aimed at them.   4510
Sir Fulk had a standard erected
With the arms of King Richard.[1]

---

1 Beginning in the reign of King Richard, the Royal Arms of
  England were three identical golden lions walking and facing
  outward (*passant guardant*), arranged in a column on a red field.
  See Ailes 52–63.

When the Saracens saw it,
They believed that King Richard was there.
All of those in the battle there   4515
Were greatly afraid of him.
Knights and proud emirs
Cried loudly, "Kill them outright!
Bring the city out of care!
May he be hanged who spares his foe!"   4520
Sir Arcade took a great lance,
And arrogantly came riding.
He bore it towards Fulk D'Oilly,
And Fulk met him with another:
Right on the field, in full charge,   4525
He hit him upon the shield.
It pierced right through his heart:
The misbelieving pagan died.
Sir Cudary came with pride
Against a brave Christian knight.   4530
He struck him with a falchion:[1]
Certainly, it would bite well.
He hit him then in the neck,
So that the head rolled off like a ball.
Orphias came on an Arabian steed;   4535
For pride he galloped at great speed.
He bore a great falchion in hand.
"Come fight with me now, whoever dares!"
Sir Fulk's nephew Sir John D'Oilly,
A young knight of great virtue,   4540
Took a long spear in hand—
The shaft was both stiff and strong—
And smote him so hard on his shield
That it split right in two,
And slew him there certainly,   4545
And said, "Dog, lie there
And rest until doomsday,
For now you've been paid your wages!"
When the hosts came together,
The archers might shoot no more.   4550

---

1 A sword with a broad, curved blade, often associated with
   Saracens, though also used by Christians in the poem. The
   pronouns are ambiguous in this passage, but it seems to be the
   Saracen knight who is killed.

Men of arms drew out their swords,
And soon heads rolled out of hoods.
They gave them many strokes
That shattered helmets and heads, so that
Brains fell to the shoulders;   4555
The Christian men slew them with might.
The foot soldiers and commoners
Took good staves in hand.
There was no Saracen in that troop
Who, if he had a knock   4560
With a well-placed staff
On helmet or head,
Didn't fall down, without fail,
Top over tail off his horse.
Soon, in just a little while,   4565
Most of them fell to the ground.
The lords saw how they fared,
And right away they fled hastily:
They meant to go to the town again.
Sir Fulk and his men were very eager   4570
To guard the road and hinder them:
On every side they blocked them,
So that none of them might escape.
The Christians quickly began to strike them.
When the foot soldiers were slain,   4575
They pulled down great lords
From steeds and armoured horses;
Immediately their heads were struck off.
It was truly seen that Jesus helped them.
The Saracens were slain altogether,   4580
And stripped naked to their shirts;[1]
But when they had unadorned them all,
Sir Fulk, that noble and wise man,
Let trumpets sound the victory call.
Then no man would bury the dogs;   4585
Christian men rested and made themselves merry.
Each man had a drink of good wine,
And when they had taken heart,
Refreshed themselves, and recovered,
Right away they broke the town gate.   4590

---

1 It was common practice for armies to take the armour and weapons
   of their slain enemies.

Sir Fulk rode in with his men,
And no Saracen awaited him.
They greeted every Saracen
That they met with such a toast
For the love of their Muhammad, 4595
That they struck the head from the shoulders.
The footmen came behind,
And killed everyone they might find
Either in house or in yard:
Man or woman, all went to the sword. 4600
The Christian men then quenched the fire.
There was more wealth of silver and gold
In that city than any man could imagine:
The Christian men had great plenty.
Sir Fulk said very courteously, 4605
"Every man keep his winnings,
To share and distribute among you!"
There was no need to fight for goods.
Sir Fulk made every Christian man,
In every lane and every street, 4610
To take heed and stay awake,
To guard by night and day,
In order to defend completely
From the Sultan Saladin.
On the town wall, on every corner, 4615
He had a banner set up
Displayed upon a broad shaft
With King Richard's arms portrayed,
As a sign to bear witness
That King Richard was their overlord. 4620
     When he had brought order to the town,
With his host he went armed
To Orglyous to Sir Thomas.
They went forth at great speed
To King Richard at Sudan Turry, 4625
And he took Sir Thomas and seated him nearby.
Each man told the others of his adventures.
The King of France came to them.
They turned toward Acre,
To dwell there after their labours, 4630
To reside and rest for a time,
And to heal those who had received wounds.
Afterwards, on a certain day,

King Philip ate with King Richard,
Dukes, earls, and barons,   4635
And the most renowned men of France:
With all of the noble knights
That they had brought from beyond the sea.
Thomas of Multoun, Fulk D'Oilly,
And earls and barons, truly,   4640
Of England, Gascony, and of Spain,
Of Lombardy, Aquitaine, and Germany.
Trumpets blew, drums rolled,
Food was prepared, and they went to wash.
They were set down at a table,   4645
And well served, without lie,
As they desired with fish and flesh:
The French men, Lombards, Gascoignes, and English.
There was plenty of rich wine,
Spiced wine and clary.   4650
After dinner the cloth was taken up,
And Richard was joyful about their arrival.
        After dinner they made merry;
They began to speak together.
King Richard said, "Every man tell   4655
How he has done, and what befell him,
Who has been in the most distress,
And who has done deeds of most prowess."
Richard said, "I myself won Sudan Turry,
And I had no mercy on the folk there.   4660
I and my host slew all that were there,
And won plenty of treasure therein.
Christian men remain there."
Thomas then spoke of his deeds:
"And I won Castle Orglyous.   4665
Maiden and youth, husband and wife,
My host slew, and spared no one.
I gave them all the treasure."
Then Fulk D'Oilly said,
"And I won the city of Ebedy.   4670
It gained them nothing to cry mercy:
What should dogs do but die?
The whole crowd hopped headless!
I made peace in this way:
Destroyed all the heathen blood.   4675
I gave all the goods that I found

Therein to Christian men,
And settled it in Christian hands."
Philip said: "And I did not do so.
I went to Taburet and Archane.   4680
The folk came out of both cities,
Fell on their knees and cried mercy.
I took ransom for every head;
They yielded every town to me,
And they set up my banner: 4685
We were accorded in this manner.
I never liked to slay men."
King Richard took it badly,
And began to look angrily at him.
"Cursed be he who allows that work!   4690
You well deserve to be reproached,
Since you would save Saracens!
In granting their lives in exchange for reward,
You do a great falsehood to God!
You have done a great shame to us: 4695
You deserve to have blame!
I refuse all such works,
And you, Sir King, if you did this,
You didn't do as I ordered you!
If you are ever again beset in battle,   4700
You shall find every one of them
To be your greatest foes!
If you had slain them all,
Then you might have been content,
And won all of the goods therein.   4705
Now you'll have to start all over again,
And you shall see that yourself."
Philip said, "I will go there again
To prove whether it's true.
If the folk deceive me,   4710
Or try to vex me,
I shall burn, slay, and destroy them!
They shall never have mercy!"
Richard said, "If I go with you,
You may have better fortune."   4715
In the morning they began to ride
With their host to Taburet.
The folk within shut the gates;
They called, "Philip, faint coward!

False wretch, you've broken your agreement! 4720
You gave us our lives in exchange for ransom.
From now until the world's end,
This town is no longer obliged to you!"
King Richard said, "Philip, now see
That I told you the truth—you may know it now!" 4725
Right away they knocked down Philip's banner,
And broke it up with great despite—
Broke it right into two pieces—
And threw it out into the ditch,
And set up one of their own, 4730
And told Philip, "Now do your best!"
Richard said, "Friends, don't delay!
Now we will quickly assail this town.
Every man exert his strength
To be avenged on these dogs!" 4735
When King Richard had thus spoken,
The Christian men made a great cry.
At once they won their way over the ditch.
The folk on the walls above
Defended themselves well 4740
In all ways that they might.
They threw down sticks and stones,
And hurt some of the Christians.
The archers backed away for dread.
Then they attacked the Saracens: 4745
They shot thickets of arrows and bolts,
And slew those that they reached.
No man dared to look over the walls.
The Christians mined under the walls.
Richard said, "I shall never again 4750
Sit on the ground, drink, nor eat,
Until I have won this town."
The wall tumbled down into the ditch;
The army entered in, and struck them down
With swords, axes, and sharp knives, 4755
And slew men, children, and women.
The army no longer wished to be there:
They began to travel toward Archane.
The folk of the town shut the gates
To keep King Philip out, 4760
And said, "Coward, go your way!
Here you have lost your prey.

You gave us our lives in exchange for ransom;
This town concerns you no more.
You took your payment all at once;   4765
You've lost your lordship here.
You are a false, cowardly wretch!
May whoever cares for you be hanged!
Do all that you can to us!"
Because they disparaged him so much,   4770
King Richard swore and was aggrieved:
"The misbelieving Saracens therein,
None of them shall save their lives!"
Arrows and bolts flew thickly;
The Christian men burnt the gates,   4775
They broke the walls, and in they went.
The Saracens fled, and quickly retreated;
The Christians followed, slew, and stabbed,
And gave all those folk their death;
Thus King Philip won Archane.   4780
        Richard said, "Philip, take for yourself
The goods of either city;
You might have done this before now.
Certainly, Philip, you are not wise.
You're forgiven the first transgression;   4785
You may learn from this, if you will.
Now let's both be friends,
But certainly, we shall be at odds
If you frequently engage in such foolishness
As to grant Saracens their lives.   4790
Beware, though you may covet gold,
Do not deceive us in these lands!
If you're found to engage in double-dealing again,
And thereby put us in peril,
Even if you were a child in our Lady's lap,   4795
You wouldn't get away without harm!
You shall have your fill of gold!"
Philip grieved inwardly, and held himself still;
He glowered, and began to sigh;
He greatly disliked King Richard   4800
For the words he had said to him.
King Richard did advise him:
"Be true, do as I teach you.
Let's go forth and invade this country,
To slay our foes and win the Cross!"   4805

King Philip without quarrel
Said, "In me there shall be no delay,
To aid this plan, however I can!"
King Richard and Philip with their armies
Went forth by the seacoast. 4810
Their navy came towards them,
With military ships, warships, many galleys,
Barges, and all manner of ships
That were loaded with all kinds of goods,
With armour, and with other provisions 4815
So that the host would lack nothing.
  Before Saint James's Day,[1]
When birds begin to chirp merrily,
King Richard turned his host to pass
Toward the city of Haifa, 4820
Henceforth by the seacoast
By the river of Chalyn.
Saladin heard tell of it,
And came quickly rushing after
With sixty thousand bold Saracens, 4825
And thought to do the Christians harm,
And overtook the rear guard,
And began a fierce battle.
They hastily drew their swords,
And slew many a Christian man. 4830
The rear guard was unarmed;
They fled in haste to King Richard.
When King Richard knew of this,
That the Sultan slew his men,
He mounted Favel of Cyprus, his reddish horse, 4835
Who was as swift as any swallow.
There was never found in all this world
A better steed to have in great need.
Right away his banner was unfurled;
The Saracens suddenly beheld it, 4840
And all those who might see the banner
Began to flee for fear.
King Richard rode after them,
And then they turned around,
And rushed together with such force 4845

---

1 25 July 1191; St. James was known as a defender of Christians
against the Islamic Moors in Spain.

As if all the world would fall down.
King Richard struck first
With his axe, so bitterly that
He hewed and carved them to pieces:
Many died under his hand.   4850
There was never a man on earth
Who fought better against them,
And many Christians, I tell you truly,
Took their death in that battle
On account of a cart that was Hubert Walter's,[1]   4855
That was stuck in the mire.
For Saladin's sons came there,
And seized the armour and weapons.
The carter lost his right hand;
Many a knight was slain there,   4860
For the armour and weapons would have protected forty,
But thirty were slain there with them.
King Richard came there with haste,
But he almost came too late!
He held his good axe in hand,   4865
And let many Saracens' blood!
There was no armour, truly,
So good that it might withstand his blows.
And also at that time William Longespée
Laid about on every side,   4870
So that everything went down that he smote
With his falchion, that bitterly bit.
The battle was uncertain,
And very perilous to his folk,
For the heat was so strong,   4875
And the dust rose among them,
And smothered the Christians' breath,
So that they fell dead upon the sand.[2]
More died of heat, in few words,
Than for the blows of spears or swords.   4880
King Richard was almost overcome,

---

1 The *Itinerarium* relates a similar episode, in which a cart called
   "the Standard," which holds a tower from which the king's flag
   flies, comes under an attack that, as in *RCL*, involves the loss of a
   defender's arm (Nicholson 237–38).
2 Ambroise recounts a similar episode of the crusaders being
   overcome with dust and heat; see Ambroise 118–19.

And nearly drowned in the dust.
He fell down to his knees
And called on Jesus to help,
For love of His Mother Mary;   4885
And as I find in the story,
He saw Saint George, the knight,[1]
Upon a good swift steed,
In armour white as a flower
With a Cross of red.   4890
All that he met in that place,
Horse and man, he felled to the ground,
And the wind began to grow calm;
They began to deliver stern strokes.
When King Richard saw that sight,   4895
He was glad and light in his heart,
And without fail, he eagerly
Began to assail the Saracens.
Bertram Braundys, the good Lombard,
Robert Tourneham, and King Richard   4900
Soon took the lives of
All those who charged against them.
The Saracens fled for refuge
To the mountain of Nazareth, without delay.
They were so rushed, at full speed,   4905
That many of their folk were lost.
King Richard went a great way
Toward the City of Haifa,
And thanked Jesus, King of Glory,
And Mary his Mother, for that victory.   4910
They all made great joy
For the winning of Haifa.
        In the morning, King Richard announced
Among his host that they should hasten
Henceforth along the seacoast   4915
To the City of Palestine.[2]
There they pitched their pavilions,

---

1   St. George was the patron saint of England; he was also associated
    with the Crusades, having appeared in a vision to Christians at
    Antioch during the First Crusade.
2   For the following episodes, including the battle of Arsuf and the
    capture of Jaffa, Ascalon, and Darum, see Gillingham, *Richard I*
    172–221.

And dwelled there all too long,
In order to await their provisions
That came by the sea, without fail.   4920
Truly, that was the worst dwelling
That Richard, our king, ever had!
Meanwhile the Sultan Saladin
Sent many a Saracen
To knock down many castles,   4925
Cities, towns, and turrets.
First they knocked down the castle
That was called Mirabel;
And afterwards the Castle Calaphyne
That was full of good siege engines.   4930
They felled the wall of Caesarea,
And all the tower of Arsuf.
They knocked down Jaffa Castle,
And the good Castle Toron.
They knocked down Pilgrims' Castle,   4935
And the good Castle of Figs;
The Castle of Saint Jorge Labane
They felled down and made all flat;
They felled the walls of Jerusalem,
And also the walls of Bethlehem.   4940
Maidens' Castle they let stand,
And the Castle of Aukes Land.
By that coast no more were spared:
They were all felled and beaten down,
And he did this without hesitation   4945
So that Richard should have no refuge.
When he had done this,
He sent unto King Richard,
And said that he would meet him
The next morning in the field, with vexation,   4950
And would ride to him with a lance
If he dared to await him.
Under the forest of Arsuf
He would test Richard's courage.
King Richard wasn't obstinate,   4955
But laughed greatly at that message.
He had it announced through his host
That they should, with determination,
In the name of the Holy Ghost
Rest that night before Arsuf,   4960

And get themselves all ready
To fight with the Sultan in the morning.
This battle would be on the eve of
The Feast of Saint Mary's Nativity.[1]
Many were the heathen men   4965
Who accompanied Saladin then:
From India, from Persia, from Babylon,
From Arabia and from Cesson,
From Africa and from Bogye,
From all the land of Alexandria,   4970
From great Greece and from Tyre,
And from many other empires:
From more lands than anyone can tell,
Except for He who made Heaven and Hell.[2]
That night King Richard was before Arsuf,   4975
Under the forest of Lysour.
With him there were many wise knights
Of England, strong of hand,
Many French folk and Templars,
Gascoignes and Hospitallers,   4980
A fair company from Provence,
From Apulia and Lombardy,
From Genoa, Sicily, and Tuscany;
There were many strong men
From Austria and Germany   4985
Who could fight well in the plain.
It was the fairest host of gracious
Christian knights to the world's end.
And you shall hear, as it is written,
How the battle was fought.   4990
    Saladin came by a mountain,
And his forces overspread hill and plain.
The spy said sixty thousand
Were in the first company,
With long spears and high steeds.   4995
Their battle gear was of gold and azure.
Sixty thousand came afterward,
Of Saracens stout and hard,

---

1 8 September.

2 The vast geographical range represented by Saladin's armies associates
the poem with many others, such as the *Song of Roland*, that portray
the East both as strangely united and as teeming with enemies.

With many a pennon of silk
And of green and brown sendal; 5000
There came almost fifty-five thousand
Along behind with Saladin;
They came unceasingly not far behind,
And their armour shone like fire.
Three thousand Turks came at last, 5005
With Turkish bows and crossbows.
They all at once struck
A thousand drums and more:
All the earth resounded under them.
There men might see a sight of wonder. 5010
Now we speak of Richard, our King:
How he came to battle with his troop.
He was armed in plates of steel,
And sat upon his horse, Favel.
Barons and knights well loved him, 5015
For he could well arrange a fight!
He gave the first battle to the Templars,
And to the Hospitallers,
And bade them go in God's name
To confound and shame the fiend. 5020
Jakes Deneys[1] and John de Nesle
Went in the front of that throng.
In this world there were
No better knights than they were.
Forth they rode, as I find, 5025
With fully twenty thousand knights,
And they met the Saracens,
And greeted them with deadly lances.
Many Saracens met their end,
And went to Muhammad and Apollo; 5030
And those of our side who received death
Went to Christ, our Saviour.
Jakes Deneys was a noble knight;
He did all he could to slay pagans.
He rode before his folk with his two sons 5035
To enrage the Saracens, and that was a pity.
Three thousand Turks came with arrogance

---

1 Jakes Deneys is probably James of Avesnes, one of the crusading
   army's leaders, who died at the Battle of Arsuf in 1191. See
   Appendix D4.

Between Jakes and his host,
So that no help might come to him
For anything that they could do. 5040
Nor might he withdraw himself,
Because of the folk of heathen religion.
It was a great pity, by Jesus Christ;
King Richard knew nothing about it,
For he was still behind 5045
To organize another twenty thousand
That the Duke of Burgundy would lead,
And the Earl of Bologne.
These came and did their duty
Against the heathen villains; 5050
And Jakes and his two sons
Were almost slain then.
He laid about on every side,
And conducted himself as a noble knight.
He slew twenty, and each son slew ten 5055
Of the vile heathen men.
And he killed nine after his horse was felled,
While covering himself with his shield.
He had no help from any Templar,
Nor from any Hospitaller. 5060
Nevertheless he fought bravely:
The Saracens didn't yet overcome him.
He laid about with his sword,
And ever he cried, "Jesus, Lord,
I shall die for your love: 5065
Receive my soul into Heaven above!"
The Saracens attacked him with a mace,
And right there they crushed him entirely,
Him and both of his sons.
Therefore King Richard was enraged. 5070
When King Richard knew of this,
That Jakes Deneys was dead,
"Alas, that is wrong!" he cried.
"I stayed behind for too long!"
He smote Favel with spurs of gold, 5075
Follow after him who would follow!
He held a lance in his hand;
He smote an emir in the shield.
The blow struck through the heathen's heart:
I understand that it smarted! 5080

King Richard withdrew his hand,
And with that lance he slew a king.
Just so he also killed an emir,
And five dukes, without fail.
With that same lance itself   5085
King Richard slew twelve kings.
The thirteenth he cleaved to the chin:
The lance burst; the Saracen died.
His axe hung on his front saddlebow;
Richard our King took it up again   5090
And he hit one on the shoulder bone
And right away cleaved him to the saddle!
And he so trimmed the crowns of some
That helmet and head both fell down!
No armour wrought with hands   5095
Might withstand King Richard's axe.
Don't be astonished at my tale:
The French poem (from which this English one is made),
Says that he slew a hundred
Before he rested himself at all.   5100
Many an English knight followed him,
Who eagerly helped him to fight
And laid about like they were mad
Until valleys ran with blood.
In their pavilions, the Saracens said   5105
That the Christians acted like wild lions,
And that Richard behaved with their folk
Like crafty greyhounds do with hares.
They leaped manfully upon their steeds,
And manfully gripped swords and spears.   5110
Many a man slew the other there;
Many a Saracen lost his brother,
And many of the heathen hounds
Gnawed the ground with their teeth.
Men could see where Richard was   5115
By the blood upon the grass!
He shed enough of blood and brains,
And many a horse dragged his guts.
There was many an empty saddle
That was mourned by the child in the cradle.   5120
He thought to rescue Jakes Deneys,
But before he came, he was slain.
For he and his sons

Were crushed, flesh and bone.
He took himself to his pavilion,[1]   5125
In despite of their god Muhammad.
There Richard dealt out blows on every side,
So that the Saracens no longer dared to stay.
At once he drove before him
Six thousand and seven score,   5130
Up against a high cliff.
They fled like deer that had been driven;
And for fear of King Richard,
They fell downward off the cliff,
And all burst asunder, horses and men,   5135
So that they never returned to life afterward.
The sultan, Saladin, saw that,
And was very certain he'd lose his life.
He left his pavilions and his tent,
And fled away, truly.   5140
When King Richard saw him fleeing,
He followed after, galloping fast.
He thought to slay the Sultan,
But, because he could not overtake him,
He took a bow from a footman   5145
And drew an arrow up to the barb,
And sent it directly to the Sultan
And struck him in the shoulder-bone.
Thus, the Sultan with hardship
Fled from the battle of Arsuf.   5150
Sixty thousand Saracens
Of heathen religion were slain there,
And only ten score of Christians:
Blessed be Jesus Christ therefore!
King Richard took the pavilions   5155
Of sendal and silk woven with gold.
They were shaped like castles,
With pennons of gold and silver.
Many noble tales were
Written thereon of wild beasts—   5160
Tigers, dragons, lions, leopards—
And all this King Richard won.
Bound coffers and great sacks

---

1 Larkin suggests that it may be Saladin's pavilion that Richard visits
   (n. 5125).

He had there, without number.
They had won so much treasure   5165
That they didn't know where to put it all.
King Richard went with honour
Into the city of Arsuf,
And rested himself there all night,
And thanked Jesus full of might.   5170
In the morning King Richard arose;
His deeds were praiseworthy, as was his fame.
He called Sir Gawter of Naples,
Who was his Master Hospitaller.[1]
He ordered him to take knights with him,   5175
Strong in arms and stout in battle,
And return again to the field
Where the battle had been fought,
And lead Jakes, the noble baron,
Into the town of Jerusalem,   5180
And bury his body there in the earth,
For he was a very worthy man.
All of King Richard's commands
Were carried out with no trouble.
Thus King Richard won Arsuf: 5185
God grant his soul great honour!
      In the morning he sent to the King of France,
And said to him without arrogance,
"Let's go to Nineveh,[2]
Which is a very strong city.   5190
For if we had won that town,
Then our game would be well begun!
If we had that and Macedonia,
Then we should go to Babylon.
Then we might ride safely   5195
For a hundred miles on either side!"
Richard and Philip dwelled in Arsuf.
Then a messenger came to say
That the Saracens would stand their ground
And ride in battle to them.   5200
In the plain of Odok, to say truly,
There they intend to live or die.

---

1   Probably Garnier de Nablus (d. 1192), the English Master of the
    Hospitallers.
2   The historical Richard did not attack Nineveh.

King Richard answered soon:
"I shall tell you, by Saint John!
If I knew what day it would be   5205
I would meet with them there!"
The messenger said, by his faith,
That it should be on the seventh day.
The time came, as he told:
The Saracens came into the field   5210
With sixty thousand and many more.
King Richard came against them then.
He divided his host into four,
As those said who were there:
Fulk D'Oilly on the one side,   5215
Thomas to remain on the other,
King Philip with the third part,
And King Richard with the fourth.
Thus they arrayed themselves, surrounding
The Saracens who were bold and strong.   5220
In every host, Christian men
Then raised Saracens' banners.
The Saracens then believed right away
That they were Saracens, every one.
As soon as Richard saw this,   5225
That the Saracens' host was surrounded,
He immediately raised his own banner.
Then the Saracens were greatly afraid,
And were terrified in an instant.
When the Christians recognized the banner,   5230
They battled on in that place,
And slew many a heathen hound.
King Richard rode upon Favel,
And slew outright on every side,
And all of his folk did, too.   5235
All four hosts did their utmost:
They destroyed many Saracens.
But alas, a Saracen host got away from them;
On the side of the King of France,
The host by chance passed by   5240
And went again into Nineveh:
Therefore King Richard grieved.
They put to death the Saracens
That they found there, the rich and poor,
The number that they put to death   5245

Was fifteen thousand, as I tell you.
King Richard went with his army
Toward the city of Nineveh.
King Philip went with him
With a great host, truly,   5250
Until they came to Nineveh
And set up their pavilions beside the city.
In the morning, when it was day, King Richard
Commanded all those who could to take arms
And hastily, without pity,   5255
To assail that city
With crossbows and other engines,
To see if they might win that city.
All the folk without complaint
Did King Richard's bidding.   5260
The engineers bent back catapults,
And sent stones into the city.
They threw in hard stones:
The Saracens knew it well!
They shot bolts from crossbows,   5265
And from slings on staffs that smite well;
They slung trebuchets also,
That caused great harm to them,
And blew wildfire from ingenious pipes,
To the great sorrow of those within.   5270
     Now the Saracens, every one, saw
That they should all go to death.
At once they sent a messenger;
He went forth to King Richard
And prayed, if he would consent,   5275
To have battle three against three:
Three of them, and three of his,
To see which of them would win the prize.
And whoever would have the higher hand
Would have the city and all their land,   5280
And have it forevermore.
King Richard granted them that,
And bade them come hastily.
The messenger went in on high
And said to the Emir   5285
That King Richard, without fail,
Well armed with spear and shield,
Would meet them in the field,

And with him two other barons,
Noble men of great renown,   5290
In order to fight with such three men
As you would send from this city.
Then three emirs, bold and valiant,
Were mounted on Arabian horses.
I shall tell you their names at once,   5295
What they were called, each one.[1]
Sir Archolyn rode in the front,
Cowderbras lingered and waited, and
Sir Galabre stayed where he was
To see who would ride to him.   5300
King Richard, the noble knight,
Prepared himself to face Sir Archolyn.
They smote grievous blows together:
He shall nevermore recover!
And he gave Richard a painful blow   5305
That struck off his helmet.
King Richard was greatly annoyed
By the stroke that he had there.
King Richard took his very strong axe
And vigorously struck the Saracen   5310
On the helmet above the crown:
He cleaved him to the saddlebow.
His life, truly, did not last long,
For King Richard was his priest.
Sir Cowderbras started to ride forth;   5315
Sir Thomas thought to await him.
They rode together, as we read,
So that they both fell to the earth.
They started up in that place,
And smote together with great blows.   5320
They fought very fiercely with sharp falchions;
There was strong battle between them.
Cowderbras treacherously
Smote Sir Thomas, without lie,
From his shield on to his shoulder-armour,   5325
So that it flew into the field.
Thomas was greatly annoyed,
And thought to trouble him more.
He took his mace of brass

---

1 The three emirs are fictional characters.

That never failed him in any cause, 5330
And gave him a painful blow
That split his helmet open
And completely shattered his skull.
He showed that he was a mighty man.
He quickly jumped out of his saddle, 5335
And went forth with the Arabian horse.
Sir Galabre stayed where he was
To see who would ride to him.
He didn't know whether it would be better
For him to fight or to turn around again. 5340
Sir Fulk D'Oilly saw this well.
He was loath to let him escape away.
He rode up to him upon a steed,
And that other rode against him.
They rode together with such fierce ire 5345
That both steeds fell to the ground,
And broke their necks in that place,
So that they lay dead upon the ground.
Their spears lay shattered on the field,
So they hit each other in the shield. 5350
Each gave the other dreadful strokes:
They sold their lives dearly.
Galabre was stout and valiant,
So that Fulk might not hit him soundly,
But at the last he gave him such a blow 5355
That he broke his shoulder bone,
And his arm as well:
Then his fighting was done.
He fell down on his knees and cried,
"I surrender, for Muhammad and Termagant!" 5360
But Sir Fulk would not have it so:
He smote the head from his body.
The lords of that city
Came before him and fell to their knees,
And brought the keys with them. 5365
They begged King Richard for mercy:
If he would save their lives,
They would be christened, men and women,
And go with him, without fail,
At the front of every battle, 5370
And hold that city in allegiance to him.
King Richard granted this with a generous heart.

He had a bishop come right away,
And had him christen every one:
Little, big, rich and poor   5375
Were christened at that time.
King Richard dwelled there peacefully for a while;
The commoners served him at his will.
No one of all that he had brought
Might better serve him than they did.   5380
    The chief Sultan of Heathenness[1]
had fled to Babylon,[2] certainly.
His sent for his council at that time,
And many bold pagans assembled.
Sixty thousand gilded spears in the field   5385
Were counted there,
Without even counting the foot soldiers
That had come there to do battle.
So said the spy
Who counted the folk on both sides: 5390
The Sultan had two hundred thousand
Heathen men to do battle.
Listen lords, young and old,
For the love of Him who Judas sold.[3]
He always sends strength and might   5395
To the men who love truth and righteousness:
This was clearly seen there.
Our Christian host, without doubt,
Was, as we find in books,
No more than eighty thousand.   5400
King Richard led thirty thousand,
For Philip and his men were worthless.
He had fifty thousand
By one side of that city,
That kept the bold Saracens within: 5405
None was so brazen as to pass out,
And King Richard lay on that other side,
Ready for battle every day

---

1 Saladin.
2 Another ahistorical battle. Only one of the *b* group manuscripts
   contains the conquest of Babylon, which appears in all of the *a*
   group manuscripts.
3 Judas Iscariot, one of Jesus' twelve apostles, who betrayed him for
   30 pieces of silver.

With catapults and siege engines,
With many arrows and bolts.   5410
No Saracen was so bold
As to look out over the walls.
The city was so very strong within
That no man might get to them.
Our strong engines, for the occasion,   5415
Broke their walls with hard stones,
Their gates and their barbican.
Be assured, the heathen men
Gave battle hard and strong,
So that many a man was slain therein.   5420
And if Philip had been honourable
At the siege of that city,
No one would have escaped then—
Not heathen king, nor Sultan—
Who wouldn't have been slain outright.   5425
For King Richard always, at night,
When the sun had gone to rest,
Would be ready with his host
To give hard and fierce battle
That no pagan might oppose,   5430
And slew down a great many of them,
And cast wildfire into the city.
The Saracens defended themselves well
With Turkish bows and bolts.
It was a fierce battle between them: 5435
So said those who saw it.
Arrows and bolts flew as quickly
As if they were thunder in the sky,
And wildfire to burn the folks.
The heathen men made a decision   5440
To fight with them in the field:
They would not yield the city.
They would not succeed with King Richard
To make a truce for any reward.
"For no price," said Richard then,   5445
"Until I have slain Saladin,
And burned those who are in the city!"
The translator then turned away
To the other side of the town,
And cried "Truce!" in a loud voice   5450
To the false King of France;

And he granted this, with wrongdoing,
For a portion of gold.
Otherwise the town would have been surrendered,
And all the Saracens slain;   5455
But the Sultan was very glad,
And all of their folk descended upon Richard,
For that other side was peaceful.
King Richard thought that Philip fought,
And yet he and his men did nothing at all   5460
But made merry all night long,
And were traitors in the fight.
Philip did not love to break heads,
But to do treason and take treasure.
Then King Philip sent word to Richard   5465
That he might no longer defend him:
For hunger, he and his men also
Must end the siege and go.
King Richard was woeful then,
And said, "Traitor, false man!   5470
He does himself great dishonour,
When for covetousness of treasure
He will give the Saracens respite.
It's a harm that such men live!"
He breaks the siege and begins to withdraw: 5475
Then the Saracens were wonderfully happy.
They made great joy among themselves,
Danced, and trumpeted, and sang merrily.
       The next day after that,
Messengers came from the Sultan,   5480
And greeted Richard in a courteous manner,
And said, "Sir, if it were your will,
My lord, the Sultan, sends a message to you
If you will grant it, at present.
You are strong in flesh and bones,   5485
And he is bold for the occasion;
You do him great harm, he says,
And destroy his country,
Slay his men and eat them, too.
All that you wage war on, you do so wrongfully.   5490
You crave sovereignty in this land,
And he wants you to understand well
That you have no right to it!
You say that your God is full of might:

Will you grant to prove by combat in the field,   5495
With spear and with shield,
With helmet, hauberk, and bright swords,
On strong steeds, good and swift,
Which has more power,
Jesus or Jupiter?   5500
And he sends to you to say this:
Will you accept a horse of his?[1]
In all the lands where you have gone,
You've never seen such a one!
Not Favel of Cyprus, nor worthy Lyard,   5505
Are anything in time of need compared to him.
And if you will, this same day
It shall be brought to you to try."
King Richard said, "You say well!
Such a horse, by St. Michael,   5510
I desire to have to ride upon,
For mine are weary and exhausted.
And I shall, for the love of my Lord
Who sits high in Heaven above,
Shed Saladin's blood with a spear,   5515
Even if his own horse is good.
If he will keep his promise
In the way that you've suggested,
I shall meet him in the field
As I must—God reward my soul!   5520
Bid him send that horse to me:
I shall learn what he's like.
If he's trusty, without fail
I shall take no other into battle!"
The messenger then went home   5525
And told the Sultan at once
How King Richard would meet him.
The rich and fierce Sultan
Then sent for a noble cleric,
A master necromancer,   5530
Who conjured, as I tell you,
Through the craft of the devil of Hell,
Two strong fiends of the air
In the likeness of two fair steeds,

---

1 Various chronicles record accounts of Saladin offering to give
   Richard a horse; see Appendix D4c for one example.

Both alike in hue and hair.   5535
As those who were there said,
No one had ever seen their equal.
The one was like a mare;
The other like a colt, a noble steed.
Wherever he was, in any situation,   5540
There was never king nor knight so bold
That he could hold him against his will
When his mother would neigh,
And keep him from running to her
To kneel down and suckle his mother.   5545
When that happened, the Sultan shamefully
Planned to quickly kill King Richard.
All this an angel did tell Richard,
Who came to him after midnight,
And said, "Awake, God's knight!   5550
My Lord wishes you to understand
That a horse shall come to you.
He is fair, and strong enough of body
To betray you if the Sultan has his way.
Have no fear of riding him: 5555
He shall help you in danger.
Obtain a tree, stiff and strong,
Even if it's forty feet long,
And fasten it crosswise over his mane:
All that he meets shall have destruction: 5560
With that tree he shall strike them down.
It is a fiend, I tell you!
Ride upon him in the name of God,
For he may cause you no shame.
Take a bridle," the angel said,   5565
"And fasten it well upon his head,
And you may turn him north and south
By the bit in his mouth.
He shall serve you at your will,
When the Sultan rides at you.   5570
Have here a spear head of steel:
He has no armour crafted so well
That it won't pierce it, if you're bold!"
But when the angel had told all this,
He went up to heaven again.   5575
In the morning his horse was sent to him.
Richard was overjoyed with the horse,

And quickly prepared a saddle.
Both his saddlebows were of iron,
So that they would be strong and lasting. 5580
They girded him tightly with a chain.
He cast a bridle upon his head,
As the angel had taught him.
He didn't forget to set two good hooks
Before him on the saddlebow. 5585
Then he stopped the horse's ears with wax,
And said, "By the twelve apostles,
Although you be the devil himself,
You shall help me in this danger!
He who bled on the Cross, 5590
And cruelly suffered five wounds,[1]
And afterwards rose from death to life,
And bought mankind out of Hell,
And then overthrew the devil's power,
And afterwards ascended into Heaven, 5595
Now in the Name of God,
For the Seven Names of God in Trinity,
I command you in His Name
That you serve me at my will!"[2]
The horse shook his head and stood quite still. 5600
     In the morning, as soon as it was light,
And King Richard was thus prepared,
Six sultans with a great company
Came out of the city,
And lined up along a river, 5605
With broad shields and shining helmets.
That day, without lying, there were counted
A hundred and even more
Of sultans and of heathen kings.
Even the least powerful brought with him 5610
Twenty thousand and ten.
Against one of our Christian men
There were a dozen, at the least:

---

1 Christ suffered five wounds on the Cross: in both of his hands and
   feet, and in his side. Christ's wounds were often a focus of religious
   devotion.
2 In this speech, Richard invokes some of the main elements of
   Christian belief as a means of controlling the diabolical horse. The
   Seven Names of God are an ancient Jewish tradition.

As men might see trees in a forest,
So fared the host of Saracens: 5615
They filled at least ten miles of coast!
They got into formation and awaited battle.
Messengers rode between
To King Philip and King Richard,
To see if they would keep the pledge   5620
That they had made the day before.
The Saracens were all ready:
There were three hundred thousand and more.
King Richard looked and saw—
Like snow lying on the mountains—   5625
Hills and plains covered
With bright hauberks and shining helmets.
It was a wonder to hear the noise
Of trumpets and of drums:
The sound seemed as though   5630
All the world above and under would fall.
Our Christian men made themselves ready.
King Richard feared nothing;
To his men he called, "To arms!"
And said, "Fellows, for love of the Cross,   5635
Be of good cheer!
And if we win the victory this day,
We will have conquered forevermore
All the nobility of the heathen world!
May He that made the sun and moon   5640
Be our help and our strength!
Behold how I myself shall fight
With spear, sword, and axe of steel:
Unless I use them well today,
Evermore, from hence forth,   5645
Hold me a faint coward!
May every Christian man and page
Have for his wages this night
The head of a Saracen,
Through God's help and mine, also!   5650
I shall do such work among them,
Those that I overtake,
That from now until doomsday
They'll speak of my vengeance!"
Our Christian men are armed well,   5655
Both in iron and in steel.

The King of France with his company
Is ready to assail the Saracens.
They ride above the Saracens
And set up formations and await battle, 5660
And block the land routes.
They could not flee into the open country,
Nor could any aid come to them,
Unless they were slain or captured!
The French boasted loudly and pretended 5665
To slay Saracens and crack crowns,
But as it's told in chronicles,
None of them was so bold
As to break the Saracens' battle formation
Until King Richard himself came. 5670
Now Richard went forth with his host
And surrounded them by another side,
Between them and the city
So that no Saracen might flee.
Then Richard had three companies: 5675
One assaulted the city,
And the other two he led with him.
He ordered that his horse be brought
That the Sultan had sent him.
He said, "With his own present 5680
I shall meet him, long before night."
Then he was ready to leap upon his horse,
But before he leaped into the saddle,
He attended to many things.
He wanted nothing but he had it: 5685
His men brought all that he ordered.
He commanded his men to fasten
A sturdy tree, forty feet long,
Securely upon his saddle,
So that it would fail for no reason. 5690
They did so, with hooks of iron
And good links that would endure.
There was no other fastening
Than iron chains, by all means,
And they were wrought very skillfully. 5695
The King's own heraldic device
Was placed both on the horse's girth
And on his breastplate.
His axe of steel lay before his breastplate,

And his mace on the other side.   5700
He himself was richly decked out
From the crest of his helmet to his toes.
He was armed wondrously well,
And all with plates of good steel,
And there above a mail coat,   5705
And a lance reliably wrought.
On his shoulder was a shield of steel
Fashioned well with three leopards;[1]
He had a lavishly ornamented helmet,
And his neck-mail was trusty and true.   5710
A white dove was on his crest,
Signifying the Holy Spirit;
The dove stood upon a Cross
Of gold wrought richly and well,
And so did Mary and John,[2] and God Himself,   5715
As He was nailed upon the Cross,
All as a sign of Him for whom he fought.
He didn't forget his spearhead:
He would have it upon his spear,
For God's Name was engraved thereon.   5720
        Now listen to the oath they swore
Before they went to battle.
If it should happen that Richard might
Slay the Sultan[3] in the field of battle,
He and all of his men should go,   5725
Every one of them, at their will,
Into the City of Babylon,
And he should have the Kingdom
Of Macedonia under his hand;
And if the Sultan of that land   5730
Might slay Richard in that field,
With sword or with spear under his shield,
Then the Christian men should go
Out of that land forevermore,
And the Saracens have their will far and wide.[4]   5735

---

1 See note to line 4512. Lions were also known as leopards.
2 The only one of Jesus' apostles to witness the Crucifixion.
3 Saladin.
4 In reality, Richard and Saladin never met in battle, though an
   apocryphal tradition grew up around the tantalizing idea that they
   might have. For examples, see Loomis.

King Richard said, "Thereto I promise;
Have my glove as my pledge, as a knight!"
They are armed and well equipped;
King Richard leaped into the saddle.
For whoever paid attention,   5740
That was a fair sight to see.
The steeds ran straight with great haste,
As hard as they might endure.
The fire sprang after their feet.
Drums beat and trumpets blew.   5745
There men might see in a moment
How King Richard, the noble man,
Encountered with the Sultan
Who was said to be Ruler of Damascus.
Saladin's trust was upon his mare.   5750
Therefore, as the book relates,
His crupper hung all full of bells,
And his breastplate and his saddlebow:
Men might hear the sound for three miles!
The mare began to neigh and ring her bells.   5755
For great pride, without lying,
The Sultan bore a broad falchion,
For he thought that he would have
Slain King Richard with treason there
When his horse kneeled down   5760
Like a colt that would suckle;
But Richard was wary of that fiend.
His ears were stopped fast with wax;
Therefore Richard was not afraid.
He spurred on the fiend that went under him,   5765
And gave the Sultan a marvelous blow.
On his shield, truly,
Was painted a serpent.[1]
With the spear that Richard held,
He struck him right through the shield.   5770
None of his armour might last:
Bridle and breastplate all burst asunder,
His girth and his stirrups also.
The mare fell down to the ground.
Despite all he could do, Richard made him fall   5775
Backward over his mare's hindquarters,

---

1 The heraldic symbol of the serpent connects Saladin with the devil.

His feet toward the earth;
The spear went out behind the Sultan.
Richard let him lie upon the green.
He smote the fiend with keen spurs;   5780
In the name of the Holy Ghost,
He drove into the heathen forces,
And as soon as he had come,
He broke their formation asunder,
For all that ever stood before him—   5785
Horse and man—went to earth,
For twenty feet around on every side.
Whomever he caught at that time,
There was no way to safeguard his life!
He made his horse ride throughout,   5790
And as bees swarm in the hives,
Christian men drove in after him,
Striking through those Richard had felled,
Through the middle and the back.
When the men of France knew   5795
That the Christians had the victory,
Then they were bold and took heart,
Spurred steeds and shook spears.
King Philip with a spear
Bore down a heathen king,   5800
And other earls and barons,
Strong men of great renown,
Slew the Saracens outright.
Many a noble knight of England
Did well there that day.   5805
Longespée of Salisbury
Felled to the ground with his sword
All that he found before him.
He was ever next to King Richard,
And the noble baron Sir Thomas,   5810
And Fulk D'Oilly, and Robert Leicester:
There were none better in Christendom!
Wherever any of them came,
They spared neither lord nor retainer,
Lest they not strike everyone down.   5815
The Saracens who were within the town
Wept with both their eyes
For the great sorrows that they saw,
And loudly began to cry "Mercy!"

They cast the gates open wide, 5820
And let them come in at their will.
The Christians have taken the city.
Right away then they hastily
Set banners upon the wall:
The arms of the King of England. 5825
When Saladin understood
That the city had surrendered,
He began to cry, "Alas, alas!
The glory of Heathenness is over!"
He began to flee right away, 5830
And all those who might follow were glad.
And King Richard, the noble knight,
When he saw the Sultan flee,
"Stay, coward!" he cried loudly,
"And I shall prove you false, 5835
And all of your cursed gods!"
King Richard rides quickly after;
The Sultan was sorely afraid.
He sees a great wood before him,
And quickly flees therein. 5840
King Richard drew close to the wood,
But hesitated because of the obstacles;
He might not enter because of his tree.
He soon turned his horse again
And met with a heathen king. 5845
He took his axe out of the ring,
And hit him high upon his helmet's crest,
And cleaved him down to the breast.
Another he stuck upon the shield
So that helmet and head flew into the field. 5850
To tell the truth in everything,
He slew six heathen kings.
As we find in the story,
More than sixty thousand
Riderless steeds roamed about, 5855
Up to their fetlocks in blood:
They wandered astray with great haughtiness;
Any man who wanted to might ride them.
The battle lasted until it was night,
But when they had slain outright 5860
All the Saracens they could overtake,
The Christians made great joy,

Kneeled and thanked God of Heaven,
And worshipped Him and His Seven Names.
Folk were slain on both sides.   5865
The Christian dead
Who lay there in the field
And yielded their souls to God
Numbered three hundred.
There was greater plenty of Saracens: 5870
Sixty thousand and even more.
Lo, such grace God sent there!
The Christians went into the city:
They found enough, without fail,
Gold and silver and precious stones,   5875
As well as meat and drink and other food.
In the morning when King Richard arose,
His deeds were noble, as was his fame.
Saracens came before him
And asked to become Christians.   5880
More than forty thousand
Were christened, as I find.
They made churches of the Christian religion,
And had their idols destroyed.
And those who would not become Christian,   5885
Richard had them slain, every one.
They divided the great treasure
Among the Christians with honour,
To earl, baron, knight, and knave,
As much as they wanted.   5890
They sojourned there for fourteen nights.
One day they prepared themselves,
And began to ride toward Jerusalem.
King Philip spoke prideful words:
"King Richard, listen to me!   5895
That rich City of Jerusalem
Even though you win it, it shall be mine!"
"By God," said Richard, "And St. Augustine,
And as God will reward my soul,
You shan't have half a foot   5900
Of the land that I win!
I want you to understand this well!
And if you want to have it," he said,
"Go and get it with your men!
This is my offer," said Richard, "See it here: 5905

I will come no nearer to the city!"[1]
He bent back a great crossbow,
And sent a gold florin flying to the city;
This was in order to signify
The honour due to Jesus Christ.   5910
The King of France became sick with ire;
The physician said without doubt
That he might not be well again
Unless he would return to France.
The King understood his advice,   5915
And said that it was true and good.
He ordered his ships prepared, big and small,
And went home on All Saints' Day.[2]
King Richard cried out against him
And said he did great villainy   5920
To travel home for sickness
Out of the land of Syria
Before finishing God's service,
For life or death by any means.
The King of France would not hear him,   5925
But left in this way:
And after that parting, truly,
Ever afterward they were at odds.
        King Richard, without boasting,
Went to Jaffa with his host.   5930
The King's pavilion, fair and fine,
He had erected in a garden.
Other lords all about spread
Their pavilions in a fair meadow.
King Richard with all his company   5935
Had the wall of the city built
So that there was never any in Saracen lands
So strongly built and of such great splendour.
That castle was strong and rich;
There was none like it in the world.   5940
Great plenty of all kinds of goods
Might come there by the sea.
He made there a guard of noble knights,

---

1 This seems to be the poet's attempt to explain why Richard never
   captured Jerusalem, a major objective of the Third Crusade.
2 1 November. Historically, Philip left the Crusade after the siege of
   Acre; see note to line 3756.

Stout in arms and strong in battle.
Sufficient men might go about   5945
For many miles without fear.
King Richard dwelled there with honour
Until Jaffa was made wholly secure.
    From there to Ascolan they went,
And found the walls all torn down.   5950
That city was large and fair:
King Richard felt pity for it.
He beseeched all the lords
Of the city to rebuild the wall;
And every one of the lords   5955
Granted him his request right away,
Except for the Duke of Austria:
He intended to deceive King Richard.
King Richard began to work
About the walls, without fail;   5960
So they each did, one and all.
Father and son, uncle and brother
Made mortar and laid stone
With their might, every one.
Every king and emperor   5965
Bore stones or mortar,
Except for the Duke, full of pride:
He would not help for anything.
One day King Richard met him,
And the King greeted him graciously   5970
And asked him, for his courtesy,
To do his share on the walls;
And he answered in this manner:
"My father was no mason or carpenter,
And though your walls should all tumble down,   5975
I shall never help to build them!"
King Richard felt great wrath,
And changed colour with rage.
He smote the Duke against the breast
With his foot, God knows,   5980
So that he fell down on a stone.
It was unluckily done, by St. Matthew!
"Fie on devils, vile coward!
May you be hanged hard in Hell!
Go quickly out of our company!   5985
May you be cursed by the Holy Ghost!

By the sides of Sweet Jesus,
If I find you, you traitor, among us
Three days from now,
I'll kill you myself!   5990
Traitor, we labour day and night,
In war, on night-watch, and in battle,
And you lie like a vile glutton
And rest in your pavilion,
And drink good strong wine,   5995
And sleep all night long!
I shall break your banner
And sling it into the river!"
The Duke went home so full of rage
That he hated his own life.   6000
He was so angry at that insult
That he quickly packed up his gear,
And swore by Jesus in the Trinity
That if he ever saw his chance,
He would be so avenged upon Richard   6005
That all the world would speak of it.
He kept his word all too well:
May he be hanged hard in Hell!
For through his treason and treachery,
And through his secret spying,   6010
He did a great shame to King Richard,
For which all England grieved.[1]
If he might have lived a little longer,
By the Holy Ghost,
He would have been lord and conqueror   6015
Over king, duke, and emperor.
All Christianity and pagan Heathendom
Should have been held under him.
The Duke of Austria hastily
Hurried away quickly with his men,   6020
And with him went the Duke of Burgundy,
The folk of France and the Earl of Bologne.

---

1   These lines probably refer to Leopold's capture of Richard
    following the Crusade, although the poem reorders events so that
    this occurs prior to the Crusade: see note to line 654. On Richard's
    humiliation of Leopold (which occurred at Acre and was motivated
    by Richard's and Philip's reluctance to share the spoils of war) see
    Gillingham, *Richard I* 224–26.

King Richard broke the Duke's banner
And cast it into the river,
And cried to him with a very loud voice, 6025
"Go home, wretch! Coward! And sleep!
Come no more in God's service,
Never again in any way!"
The Duke rode away then.
His heart began to burn with ire. 6030
King Richard left with his English,
Tuscans, Lombards, Gascoignes,
Scots, Irish, folk of Brittany,
Genoese, Basques, and folk of Spain,
And built the wall day and night 6035
Until it was made strong, in faith.
When King Richard with great difficulty
Had built the walls of Ascalon,
He took all his folk with him
And went forth at great speed. 6040
The first night in the Name of Mary
He lay at a town that was called Famiya.
In the morning he armed himself well
Both in iron and in steel;
By the sea-coast he went forth 6045
To Albary, a noble castle
That was a castle of the Saracens,
Full of stores and great riches:
Both fat flesh and lean,
Wheat and oats, peas and beans. 6050
King Richard won it, and sojourned there
Three months together,
And sent spies every way
To scout out the country.
　　　King Richard heard of Castle Darum, 6055
All about how it fared.
It was all full of Saracens
That were God's adversaries.
King Richard hurried there quickly,
In order to dismay the Saracens. 6060
He went there so quickly
He was there by St. James's Day.
He besieged Castle Darum
To take the castle and the town.
The castle was made of such stone 6065

That they didn't fear assault at all.
There was a ditch around the castle;
They had never seen one like it.
The Saracens cried in their language:
"Christian hounds of depraved madness,   6070
Unless you soon travel home,
You will receive your judgement here!"
When King Richard heard that cry,
He swore his oath by Saint Mary
That the Saracens should all be hanged   6075
Before such a fate should befall them.
The Christians attacked and they defended:
They sent out many arrows.
All that day and all that night,
They and the Christians continued the battle.   6080
The Christians saw that they couldn't succeed;
King Richard tried another plan.
King Richard had all the English
Cut rushes in the marshes
To fill the ditches of Darum,   6085
In order to take the castle and the town.
King Richard sent for two great engines
To cast stones for the occasion.
They were brought right away by water:
One was the Mate-Gryphon,   6090
Which was set up on a hill
To break down tower and castle.
The other was called Robynet,
Which was set on another hill.
King Richard placed a catapult   6095
That threw to another turret.
King Richard had the rushes
Bound fast, and cast into the ditch,
And made the ditches all flat.
The Saracens had no fear thereof,   6100
For they cast down wildfire:
The rushes caught fire quickly,
And burned right to the ground,
In just a little time.
Many hundreds were greatly   6105
Astonished at our Christians.
The catapults threw continuously,
And broke the walls by night and day.

All that the Robynet and
The Mate-Gryphon hit fell down,   6110
So that within a little time
The outermost wall was laid to the ground,
And filled the great ditch full,
And our men entered hastily.
Then our Christian men might well   6115
Enter into Castle Darum!
The Earl of Leicester, Sir Robert,
The truest knight in middle earth,
Was the first, without fail,
To assail Castle Darum.   6120
He lifted up his banner
And spurred on his war-horse.
The Saracens, with misfortune,
Fled up to the highest tower;
And many of them stood without   6125
And fought fiercely in great fear.
They gave many a hard blow
Against the earl, Sir Robert.
Many a helmet was stuck off there,
And many a helmet was cleaved.   6130
Shields fell, shorn in two;
Many steeds were stabbed also.
Robert Tourneham with his falchion
Cracked many a crown there.
The Longespée, the Earl of Richmond,   6135
Would spare no heathen hound.
King Richard came among them;
He didn't hold back from fighting well.
With his axe he felled to the ground
Many a one in a little time.   6140
He fought all on foot.
When the Saracens had sight
Of how plenteous was his payment,
None there dared to abide his strokes.
They went quickly—without exaggeration—   6145
And slew their steeds in their stable,
The fairest war-horses and steeds
That might bear a knight in any situation.
Wheat and flour, flesh and salted meat,
They set on fire all together.   6150
They had rather do so

Than help their foes with their provisions.
Richard saw this from the smoke,
And slew outright on every side
All that he might overtake: 6155
They might make no amends.
He began to assail the tall tower,
With bold men of great valour.
The Saracens in the tower on high
Saw that their dying day was near.   6160
They hastily cast wildfire
Among the Christian men.
The fire flew about so fiercely
That it hurt many Christian men.
They might not long suffer that pain;   6165
Immediately they withdrew themselves
A mile from Castle Darum.
They cast many barrels of wildfire across,
And soon within a little time,
Through the help of God's grace,   6170
The castle was all on fire,
From the tower to the outermost wall.
Their houses burned and their palisades;
Great smoke arose there, truly.
The Saracens in the high tower   6175
Were in very great agony.
They were almost burned in the heat,
And nearly suffocated in the smoke.
Ten of them cried there with one voice:
"Mercy, King Richard, honoured lord!   6180
Let us go from this tower,
And you shall have great treasure!
If you'll let us go with life and limb,
We'll give you a thousand pounds!"
"Nay!" said Richard. "By Jesus Christ,   6185
By His death and resurrection,
You shall never come down
Until your ransom is paid,
And yet afterward you'll be at my mercy,
Whether I will save or destroy you,   6190
Or else you will die right here."
"Lord," they said, "We shall serve you.
Do with us as you will,
As long as we may come to you.

We are yours to hang or draw, burn or slay;   6195
Our freedom, lord, is in your hands."
King Richard consented then,
And commanded every Christian man
To allow the Saracens to ransom themselves
Until the sun rose in the morning.   6200
It was done so, as I find.
King Richard had them bound fast
Upon a field beside the wall.
King Richard ordered them all brought out,
And he who paid a thousand pounds   6205
For his head might go unharmed.
And whoever would give so much,
He let them live until a certain time.
And he that paid no ransom,
Immediately his head was stricken off.   6210
And thus King Richard won Darum.[1]
God give us all His blessing!
        After the winning of Darum,
King Richard went to another town,
To Gatrys with a fair company   6215
To besiege that city.
Now listen how he won it,
And you shall hear of a bold man,
A stout and skillful warrior
Whose heart was never found to be faint.   6220
He that was the Lord of Gatrys
Had been a man of great worth,
And fierce to fight against his foes;
But by that time he was not so,
For he had fallen into old age,   6225
So that he might not wield arms.
But he managed a clever trick:
Listen now, in what way!
In the middle of the town upon a stage
He had a marble image made,   6230
And crowned it as a king,
And ordered his folk, old and young,
That they should never admit
To Christian folk, high nor low,
That they had any lord of rank   6235

---

1 On 22 May 1192.

In the city except for that image.
King Richard, the keen warrior,
Straight away began an assault there.
Right away his catapults were bent,
And he sent stones into the city.   6240
There Saracens cried "Mercy!"
They would cast the gates open wide
If it was Richard's will,
So that he wouldn't kill their people.
King Richard granted this, without lying,   6245
And they had entrance in peace.
King Richard asked at once
Where the lord of that city was,
And they answered to the King
That they had no other lord   6250
But that image of fine marble,
And Muhammad, their god, and Apollo.
King Richard stood, so says the book,
And looked at the image,
How massively he was made, and how stern,   6255
And said to them eagerly,
"O, Saracens," said Richard without fail,
"I marvel at your lord!
If I may, through my Lord so good
Who bought us all upon the Cross,   6260
Break his neck asunder with a shaft,
And if you see that great wonder,
Will you all believe upon my Lord?"
"Yes!" they said all together.
King Richard prepared a shaft for himself,   6265
With a trusty tree and natural skill:
And so that it would be strong and lasting,
He tightly bound to it
Four poles of iron and steel.
And King Richard, that great lord,   6270
Had a sharp spear-head set thereon.
When it was ready to be seen,
Favel of Cyprus was fetched forth,
And he set himself in the saddle.
He rode the course to the stage,   6275
And smote the image in the face
So that the head flew off of the body,
And slew five Saracens under it.

All the others then said
He was an angel and no man;   6280
And all became Christians there,
Old and young, less and more,
And hastily, without lying,
They brought forth their old lord
And told of his scheming.   6285
King Richard laughed with good intent,
And gave him the city to govern in joy,
Though he lived to be as old as Adam.
    King Richard retuned to Ascalon
By the sea, to say truly.   6290
There he stayed for two weeks
With many a bold and noble knight.
They pitched pavilions fair and well
To besiege a strong castle
That was a little beside them,   6295
Three miles from Castle Pilgrim,
With thick walls and ostentatious towers,
That was called Lefruyde.
The Saracens saw the King come,
And they very much expected to be captured.   6300
Their hearts were full of woe,
And by night they all fled away.
They opened up their gates very quickly,
And fled away by a hidden gate.
They dared not to await King Richard   6305
For all this wide middle earth.
King Richard truly won
This noble castle without a blow.
From there he went to Gybelyn,
Where the Hospitallers had dwelled,   6310
Together with the Templars,
And kept the city for many years.
When Baldwin was slain with sword,
Saladin took that town in hand.
In that city Saint Anne[1] was born,   6315
Who was chosen by Our Lady.
There they pitched their pavilion,
And with great force they won the town

---

1 The mother of the Virgin Mary, who according to these lines
  selected Anne as her mother.

And slew all the Saracens therein
Who would not believe in Christ's Name. 6320
    Then there came most wicked tidings
To Richard Coeur de Lion, our King:
How his brother John of England,
Who was the fiend's flesh and bone,
Through help of some of the barons 6325
Had seized the chancellor,
And intended, by force of arms,
To be crowned King in England
On the following Easter Day.[1]
Then King Richard answered, 6330
"What devil!" he said, "How goes this?
Does John think no more of me than this?
He thinks I will not live long;
Therefore, he will do me wrong,
And if he believed I were alive, 6335
He would not quarrel with me.
I will so avenge myself on him,
That all the world will speak of it!
If John crowns himself at Eastertime,
Where will he then dare to await me? 6340
There is no king in Christendom,
Truly, who will protect him.
I may not believe for anything
That my brother John will do this deed!"
"Yes, truly," said the messenger, 6345
"He will do so, by Saint Richard."[2]
King Richard believed in his heart
That all of this news was just a lie.
He then went forth from Gybelyn
To Bethany, a noble castle, 6350
And slew many a heathen man,
And won the noble city.
    Then other messengers came

---

1 On 15 April, Richard received word that John was overreaching
his authority in England, and on 29 May 1192 more messengers
arrived to say that John was conspiring with King Philip, though
no mention was made of his planning a coronation (Gillingham,
Richard the Lionheart 201–02, 209).

2 Larkin suggests that St. Richard (Richard of Chichester,
1197–1253) was "noted for brotherly love" and that therefore the
reference to him here "may well be ironic" (n. 6346).

And told King Richard, stout and fierce,
And swore that his brother John   6355
Would be crowned at Easter.
Richard was loath to withdraw his hand
Until he had won the Holy Land,
And slain the Sultan with a stroke of his sword,
And avenged Jesus, Our Lord.   6360
But afterward he thought to himself
That he would leave all his men there,
And with a private company
Would go thence into England,
And quickly put an end to the war   6365
Between him and his brother John,
And come again in haste
To fulfill what he had begun.
  And as he thought in his heart,
A stout Saracen burst in   6370
Who owed King Richard ransom
For the winning of Darum.
He spoke to the King openly
Among the people, poor and rich:
"Sire, you shall release me here,   6375
And all of our other hostages:
Through my ingenuity and my skill,
I shall win great treasure for you,
More than a hundred thousand pounds
Of florins (pure and of good quality)   6380
Of Saladin's chief treasure,
And great riches from their stores.
Thereto I offer my life as hostage,
And my children and my wife;
Unless I help you to win that plunder,   6385
May I die a horrible death!"[1]
Richard said, "You miscreant,
As you believe in Termagant,
Tell me now what folk it is:
I think it's all a deception."   6390
"Those who lead the treasure, without fail,
Sire, they are three thousand camels,

---

1 On 21 June 1192, Richard did indeed intercept a great caravan
  heading from Egypt to provide reinforcements and supplies to
  Saladin. See Gillingham, *Richard I* 206–08.

And there are also five hundred
Asses and mules, and even more,
That carry gold to Saladin,   6395
Refined silver, and fine treasure,
Wheat flour and spices,
Cloths of silk and gold as well."
King Richard said, "As God will judge you,
Are there many people to guard the treasure?"   6400
"Yes, Sire," he said, "there are sixty score
Of knights riding before,
And after, ten thousand
Of very strong heathen men.
I heard them say in whispers   6405
That they were afraid of you, Sir King."
King Richard said, "They shall find
That though they were sixty thousand,
And I were but myself alone,
I would fight them, every one.   6410
Tell, tell me right away,
Where may I find them tonight?"
The Saracen said, "I'll tell you
Where you should wait and linger.
Ten miles to the south of here   6415
You may find the heathen men.
There they will rest and abide
Until more folk come riding to join them."
The King equipped himself, and went directly,
Every one of his barons riding after.   6420
All that night with fair company
They rode forth by the way.
Then the spy said to the King,
"Sir, you should make your camp here.
They are lodged in this town: 6425
I will go and spy on their counsel.
I will go to them right away
And brew them a drink of woe,
And say to them that King Richard
Is at Jaffa to depart for England.   6430
They will believe me entirely,
And then they will go to rest.
Then you may go to them,
And slay them all, fast asleep."
"Fie, devil!" said the King.   6435

"May God now give you an evil ending!
I am no traitor, know you well,
To slay men while they sleep!
And I'll abide right here
Until I see the Saracens come riding.   6440
By clear day upon the fields
They shall see cloven shields and helmets.
Whether they're kings, dukes, or princes,
They shall make their endings here!"
The Saracen answered the King: 6445
"You have no peer in middle earth,
Nor is there any of such great renown.
You may well be named Coeur de Lion!
Therefore, I will not conceal
That there are twice as many Saracens   6450
As you have folk in this country,
I tell you for certain."
King Richard said, "God give you care!
My heart is not distressed by this,
For one of my Christian men   6455
Is worth nine or ten Saracens.
The more there are, the more I shall slay,
And avenge Jesus against His foes."
With that, the spy went forth
To spy on the heathen men.   6460
He spied all of their scheming and plotting,
And told it to Richard, our King.
He did cry, "To arms, make ready!
Coeur de Lion! Look how they go!"
Right away King Richard leaped   6465
Upon his good steed, Lyard;
And his English and his Templars
Leaped onto their war-horses,
And rushed into the heathen army
In the name of the Holy Ghost.   6470
        As the Saracens with their treasure
Were on their way to the Sultan,
King Richard smote among them.
No blissful song arose,
But they cried out to Pluto,[1]   6475

---

1 Pluto, another Roman deity, here joins Apollo and Jupiter in the
  poem's pantheon of pagan gods (see lines 3744 and 4451).

And to Termagant and Muhammad.
King Richard bore a king
Through the heart with a spear.
Afterward he drew his axe,
And slew many a heathen hound.   6480
Some he cleaved as far as the saddle;
Even the child in the cradle wept for it.
He cleaved a king to the saddlebow;
His god Muhammad didn't help him.
He sent many a heathen Saracen   6485
To the torments of Hell.
The Templars and the Hospitallers
Won many fair warhorses there.
They fought so long, so says the story,
That King Richard had the victory   6490
Through the help of his good knights,
Stout in arms and strong in battle:
And many escaped with deadly wounds,
Who did not live long thereafter.
They would never after meet   6495
King Richard again, by any way.
Now you may hear of the wealth
That Richard, our King, won there.
Without fail, five hundred and ten
Worthy horses and great camels,   6500
Six hundred horses—mighty steeds—
All loaded with rich treasures,
That were in coffers wonderfully bound
With fine silver and well-refined gold.
There were three hundred mules and more,   6505
That bore coins and spices;
Then afterward came fifteen hundred asses,
More or less, bearing wine and oil,
And as many with wheat bread.
It was a fortunate achievement for Richard!   6510
When he had won all of this treasure,
Then he went home to his men,
Into the noble City of Bethany,
With the wealth and the treasure.
He gave the rich and the poor   6515
Plenty of his winnings.
He gave them war-horses and steeds,
And divided his treasures among them.

Richard so distributed his gains
That he was beloved of all Christendom.　　　　6520
Thereafter, in a short while,
Messengers of great nobility came:
The Bishop of Chester was one,
And the other was the Abbot of St. Albans.
They brought him official letters,　　　　6525
Sealed with the barons' seals,
That told him his brother, John,
Intended to crown himself at once,
At Easter, by official judgement,
Unless he would come home first.　　　　6530
For the King of France with hostility
Has arrived in Normandy.
　　　King Richard said, "By God's pain,
The devil has too much power!
Some day they shall pay　　　　6535
For all of their boasts and their wrongdoing!"
And he dwelled there until All Saints' Day,[1]
And then he travelled to Jaffa.
He stuffed the castle with provisions
For seven years and still more.　　　　6540
I find in the book that he left
Fifteen thousand to look after that city,
To keep that land well
Out of Saladin's hand
Until he might come again　　　　6545
From England, as he intended.
And then that bold man, King Richard,
Went to the stronghold of Acre.[2]
Now we'll speak of Saladin,
His misery and his grief　　　　6550
When he learned of what happened,
For his treasure that was stolen,
And his men who were slain.
He reviled his god, and cursed his religion,
And swore he would be avenged,　　　　6555

1　1 November 1192. The poem's dating is inaccurate here; Richard
　　departed for England in October.
2　Richard arrived at Acre on 26 July 1192; the following day,
　　Saladin's army arrived at Jaffa.

If he might ever see his chance.'
At that time a spy came in,
And said this to Saladin:
"Lord," he said, "Be glad of heart,
For I bring you good tidings, 6560
A happy present for your heart.
King Richard has gone to Acre:
He will travel on to England,
For a message has come to him
That John, his brother—I swear to you— 6565
Will take his crown otherwise.
He has well supplied Jaffa,
With many a baron and noble knight,
Fifteen thousand, I know quite well,
Shall defend that castle 6570
Until he returns from his kingdom,
If he may succeed so well.
But see, Lord, without fail,
That you cut the tail from his body."[1]
Often was Saladin merry and woeful, 6575
But he was never so glad as he was then.
He gave the spy who brought him
That present a hundred bezants,
And also a fair warhorse,
And a richly furred robe. 6580
Then he would remain no longer:
He sent word on every side
That on pain of limb and life,
On their children and their wives,
They must come to him without delay 6585
To help him drive out of the land
King Richard with his great tail.
To him came many an emir,
Many a duke, and many a king,
And many a very noble lord 6590
Of Egypt and of Arabia,
Of Cappodocia and of Barbary,
Of Europe and of Ascalon,
Of India and of Babylon,
Of great Greece and Tyre also, 6595
And of many more empires and kingdoms:

---

1 See note to line 1776.

Of all heathen lands, I find,
From the Greek Sea to India.
    Neither Charlemagne nor Alexander,[1]
Whose fame is so great,   6600
Ever had such a host.
In the country where they lay,
The army stretched across five miles
And more, I believe, God help me.
It was twenty miles long;   6605
It was a host of great strength.
They came swiftly to the city of Jaffa;
The Christian men did shut the gates.
Within a little space,
On both sides many men were slain.   6610
That battle was so strong and fierce
That the brightness of the swords
Seemed without fail
To be the light of Heaven,
And always the Christians fought well,   6615
And slew Saracens, but it availed them nothing;
For it seemed there—let no man ask how—
As if they grew right out of the ground,
So that for no slaughter by keen swords
Could any effect be seen.   6620
The Christians fled into the castle,
And defended the gates very well.
The Saracens took the city
To be under their command and their judgement.
Then the Saracens began   6625
To make mines under the wall.
The Christian men, for the occasion,
Completely crushed them with stone.
The Saracens went about the wall
And threw and shot in everywhere;   6630
They shot many a burning,
Sharp arrow into Jaffa's Castle.

---

1   A French Christian king (742–814) and an ancient king of Macedon
    (356–323 BCE), respectively, both heroes of romance. It is curious
    that rather than being compared to Richard, as in the poem's open-
    ing lines, they are here compared to Saladin; the comparison flatters
    Richard's prowess, in that he can defeat an army that is bigger than
    even the largest armies of the greatest heroes.

They sought where they might best
Harass our Christian men the most.
At last they found a gate, 6635
Not soundly shut at that time.
There they found fierce battle
With very punishing swords and spears.
They yielded up a thousand men,
And of the Christians ten were slain. 6640
Although the Saracens were bold,
Men put them out of the gate.
The Saracens on no account
Might succeed that day.
At night by the clear moon, 6645
The Christians sent a messenger
To King Richard at the City of Acre
And prayed the King, for God's pity,
That he should come to them,
Or else they would all be captured. 6650
They told him the difficult circumstances
Of the Sultan's host, how it was,
And said that unless he came to them directly
They would be lost, every one.
King Richard answered at once: 6655
"Well I know the Sultan's might;
He will make a little trouble,
And then hastily he'll go his way.
I won't go to them on his account,
But I will soon send help." 6660
He called his nephew to him,
A baron of great virtue
Who was called Henry of Champagne,
And ordered him to go to the plain of Jaffa.[1]
"Take," he said, "Your host with you, 6665
And put an end to the Sultan's arrogance.
To arms!" he began to cry
Among his host: they should make haste
To go with Sir Henry,
To succor and defend Jaffa 6670
Against the Sultan Saladin,

---

1 In reality, Henry and Richard set off together, but Henry arrived first.
   The poem's account of Richard's rescue of Jaffa is an exaggerated
   version of the chronicle accounts (see Gillingham, *Richard I* 212–13).

And many a cursed Saracen.
In the morning there went with Sir Henry
Many a baron and hardy knight,
Gascoignes, Spaniard, and Lombards.   6675
By the command of King Richard
They went forth by the seacoast
Until they came to Palestine.
Then they saw all the country covered
With Saladin's host of heathen men;   6680
And when the Sultan heard of them,
He swiftly advanced toward them,
And when Duke Henry knew it,
He fled away, by Jesus Christ,
And didn't stop   6685
Until he came to Richard, our King,
And said he never saw nor heard
In all this wide middle earth
Half the number of men
That Saladin had on hill and dale.   6690
"No tongue," he said, "may count them:
I believe they've come out of Hell!"
Then King Richard answered,
"Fie on devils, vile coward!
I shall never, by God above,   6695
Trust in a Frenchman's love!
My men that are in Jaffa
May blame you for their deaths;
Because of your failure, I fear,
My good barons are hard pressed.   6700
Now, for the love of St. Mary,
Show me quickly to my ship!
Now to the ship, one and all,
Father and son, uncle and brother!
All that ever loved me,   6705
Now to the ship, for charity!"
All who might bear weapons
Went aboard the ship right away,
And went toward Jaffa
With the noble King Richard.   6710
        Now listen to my true tale,
Though I swear you no oath!
I want to read no romance
Of Partonope, nor of Ipomydon,

Of Alexander, nor of Charlemagne, 6715
Of Arthur, nor of Sir Gawain,
Nor of Sir Launcelot of the Lake,
Of Bevis, nor of Guy,
Nor of Urry, nor of Octavian,
Nor of Hector, that strong man, 6720
Nor of Jason, nor of Hercules,
Nor of Aeneas, nor of Achilles.[1]
I'll never believe, by my faith,
That in their day
Any of them did such bold deeds 6725
Of strong battle and great bravery
As did King Richard, without fail,
At Jaffa in that battle,
With his axe and his sword:
May Our Lord Jesus have his soul! 6730
It was before the middle of the night;
The moon and the stars shone very bright.
King Richard was come to Jaffa
With his galleys, all and some.
They looked up to the castle: 6735
They heard no pipe nor flute.
They drew near to the land
To see what they could learn,
And they could not detect,
By any sound of music, 6740
That living men were in the castle.
Then King Richard got very worried.
"Alas!" he said, "that I was born:
My good barons are all completely lost.
Robert of Leicester is slain, 6745
That was my own courteous official.
Each limb of his was worth a whole knight!
And Robert Tourneham who was so bold,
And Sir Bertram, and Sir Pypard,
Who were skillful and tough in battle; 6750
And also my other barons,
The best in all regions.
They may be slain and all torn apart;
How may I live longer, therefore?
If I had only come here sooner 6755

---

1 All heroes of romance and legend.

I might have saved them altogether!
Until I am avenged upon Saladin,
Certainly, I shall have no joy!"
Thus King Richard bewailed constantly
Until the dawn of the new day.   6760
A watchman then came to a battlement
And sounded a blast on a horn.
He only blew just one time,
But he made many a heart glad!
He looked down and saw the galley   6765
Of King Richard and his navy—
Ships and galleys that he knew well—
And then he blew a merrier note,
And piped, "Lords, up now! Arise!
Lord Richard has come to us!"   6770
When the Christians heard this,
They had great joy in their hearts, indeed!
Earl, baron, squire, and knight,
Rushed to the walls at once
And saw King Richard, their own lord.   6775
They cried to him with gracious words:
"Welcome, Lord, in the Name of God!
Now all our distress is turned to joy!"
King Richard had never, indeed,
Had half so much joy and bliss.   6780
"To arms!" he cried, "Prepare yourselves!"
And to those who had come with him,
"We have no life but one:
Sell it dearly, flesh and bone.
To claim our inheritance,   6785
We'll slay these hounds full of wrath!
Whoever is afraid of their threats,
May he never have sight of God's face!
I'll take my axe, that was made in
England, in my hand.   6790
I no more fear their armour
Than I do a ragged cloth!
Through the grace of God in Trinity,
This day men shall see the truth!"
He leaped to the land first of them all,   6795
And slew a dozen Saracens in a heap.
He began to cry in a voice loud and clear:
"Where are these heathen scoundrels

Who have taken the City of Jaffa?
I've come with my poleaxe 6800
To guarantee what I mean to do:
Wassail! I shall drink to you!"
He laid blows about on every side,
And slew the Saracens, in faith.
The Saracens fled and were checkmated; 6805
They ran out of the gate with sorrow.
In their hearts they were so eager
That they thought all of their gates too narrow.
They fled to the walls of the town,
And they fell down on every side. 6810
Some of them broke their necks,
Legs, and arms all together,
And every one cried in this manner,
As you shall hear afterward:
"Malcan staran nair arbru, 6815
Lor fermoir toir me moru!"[1]
That is to say, in English,
"The English devil is come:
If he meets us, we shall die!
Let's flee fast out of his way!" 6820
Out of the town every one of them fled;
They left not one there,
Except for four or five hundred
That Richard had killed.
He set porters at the gate, 6825
And stabled his warhorses.
He leaped upon his steed, Favel,
Well-armed in iron and steel.
The folk who had come out of the ships
Armed themselves all together, 6830
And many came out of the castle
Who were armed extremely well.
King Richard rode out of the gate:
He met two kings there,
With sixty thousand Saracens together, 6835
With shining arms and broad banners.
He hit one of them upon the hood
So that he slit him to the saddle.
The other he hit upon the hood

---

1 Mock-Arabic gibberish.

Till the stoke stopped at the waist,   6840
And his Templars and his barons
Behaved just like crazed lions:
They slew Saracens as quickly
As grass falls from the scythe.
The Saracens saw no better practice   6845
But to flee away, every one,
Unto Saladin's great army
That stretched fifteen miles across.
That same day the Sultan lost,
True to say, thirty-two thousand,   6850
For their armour was like wax
Against the axe of King Richard.
Many a Saracen and high lord
Yielded themselves to Richard, our king.
Richard took them as hostages, then: 6855
There were a thousand prisoners and more.
The chase lasted a long while,
Until the time of evensong.
Richard rode until after nightfall;
So many of them he put to death,   6860
That no number may tell
How many of them there were.
Richard left and went outside the town,
And there he pitched his pavilion.
And that night with a kind heart   6865
He encouraged his bold barons.
And you shall hear how on the following day
There was a day of sorrow:
For I understand there was the greatest battle
That ever was in any land.   6870
And you, who wish to learn of this battle,
Listen now, and you shall hear!
As King Richard sat at his supper,
And cheered his barons with a gracious manner,
And refreshed them with good wine,   6875
Two messengers came from Saladin,
And stood before King Richard,
With long beards and grey hair.
They were dismounted from two mules;
They were dressed in gold and silver.   6880
They held each other by the hand
And said, "King Richard, now understand

Our lord, Saladin, the high king,
Has sent you this petition:
That if you're so bold a knight,   6885
That you dare to face him in battle
After daybreak tomorrow,
You will be entirely deprived of bliss:
For your life and for your barons,
He wouldn't give two scallions!   6890
He will take you with great strength,
For he has folk of many lands:
Egyens, and folk of Turkey,
Moors, and folk of Arabia,
Basyles, and Embosyens—   6895
Very fierce knights of defense—
Egyptians, and folk of Syria,
Of India Major and of Cappadocia,
Medes, and folk of Asclamoyne,
Of Samaria, and of Babylon   6900
Two hundred knights without fail,
And five hundred emirs.
The ground is hardly able to bear
All the folk who have come to do you harm.
By our advice, you'll do well   6905
To turn again to Jaffa Castle.
There you may be safely guarded
Until you've sent after your army,
And if you see that you may not endure,
Turn back again to your own land."   6910
In anger Richard took up a loaf of bread,
And tore it to pieces in his hands,
And said to that Saracen,
"May God give you an evil ending,
And as for your lord Saladin,   6915
May the devil hang him with a cord!
May God send you a bad ending
For your message and your counsel!
Now go and say to Saladin
That in despite of his lord Apollo,   6920
I will await him in due course,
Even if he comes tomorrow before daybreak;
And even if I were all alone,
I would await every one of them!
And if the dog will come to me,   6925

204   RICHARD COEUR DE LION

My poleaxe shall be his doom!
And say that I defy him
And all his cursed company together.
Go now, and say to him thus:
May he have the curse of sweet Jesus!"　　　　　6930
The messengers went to Saladin,
And told the Sultan the beginning and end.
Saladin marvelled then,
And said Richard was no earthly man:
"He is a devil or a saint!　　　　　6935
I've never found his might to fail!"
Right away he made plans
To capture King Richard.
Richard paid no attention,
But lay all night and slept　　　　　6940
Until it was almost dawn;
Then he heard a melodious cry.
Through God's grace, an angel of Heaven
Then said to him, with gracious voice,
"Arise, and leap on your good steed, Favel,　　　　　6945
And turn again to Jaffa Castle.
You have slept long enough!
You shall find it difficult and hard
Before you come to that city:
You shall be surrounded, along with your army.　　　　　6950
After the battle do as I advise:
Make peace with the Sultan.[1]
Make a truce, and let your barons
Go to the river to do their pilgrimage
To Nazareth and to Bethlehem,　　　　　6955
To Calvary and to Jerusalem,
And then let them travel homeward,
And you follow after with your shipmen,
For you have enemies, I understand,
Both here and in your own land.　　　　　6960
Up!" said the angel, "and do well:
You've never had greater need!"
Richard arose as if he would go mad,
And leaped onto his good steed Favel,
And said, "Lords, arise now! Arise!　　　　　6965
Thus sweet Jesus has warned us!

1　In reality, peace talks were ongoing.

To arms!" he cried there,
To advance against the Saracens,
But Saladin, with his host,
Was between them and Jaffa.   6970
That was such a great sorrow to Richard
That he might not command his host,
But rose forth upon Favel,
And readied his lance to pierce very well.
Therewith without doubt he slew   6975
Three kings of the Sultan's troop.
His steed was strong, and he himself was good;
Neither horse nor man withstood him.
He hewed down the heathen bodies,
So that their horses fell to the ground.   6980
Whoever had seen his countenance
Would have always remembered him.
They began to fly to him as thickly
As bees out of the hive:
And with his axe he swept down   6985
The Saracens as a bear does sheep.
Englishmen and Frenchmen rode after;
They were eager to fight at that time.
They beat down upon the Saracens
With swords and with spears,   6990
And laid on with all their strength,
And slew the Saracens outright—
But that was of little concern to them.
There were so many all crowded together
That no slaughter in that battle   6995
Might be perceived, without fail.
There was a marsh outside of Jaffa
A mile broad, no less.
Richard the King, despite the Saracens,
Drove three thousand Saracens into that marsh.   7000
Then men might see the heathens
Lie and bathe there in that fen!
And those that wanted to come up for air
Had to drink of King Richard's cup.
Between the drowned and the slain,   7005
The Sultan lost of the heathen religion
Sixty thousand men in a little space,
As it is found in the French.
King Richard went again

To help his host with might and main: 7010
Now here, now there,
To command his host with his skill.
I've heard tell that no man ever saw
One man fell so many to the ground.
In the most perilous part of the battle 7015
King Richard saw, without fail,
His uncle, Sir Henry of Champagne,
Knocked off his horse down onto the field.
The Saracens had captured him,
And intended to slay him right away. 7020
It would have been his last day,
If King Richard hadn't come in haste.
King Richard cried in a loud voice,
"Help, God and the Holy Cross!
This same day shield my uncle 7025
From death at the hands of these wild dogs!
Lords," he said, "lay into them!
Let none of these hounds escape!
And I myself shall smite them,
If my poleaxe can strike any!" 7030
Men might see him with might and main
Shed the Saracens' blood and brains.
Upon that place that was green,
Many souls went to Satan.
By the blood-darkened field, 7035
Men might see where Richard fought.
The Templars came to help him;
There a fierce battle began.
They laid about as if they were mad,
Until valleys ran full of blood. 7040
Longespée was a noble knight;
He began to fight like a lion.
The Earl of Leicester, Sir Robert,
The Earl of Richmond, and King Richard
Slew many Saracens without fail. 7045
They so laid about in that battle
That wherever these same knights rode
They slew such a broad path
That four carts might pass;
So many Saracens lost their blood. 7050
On both sides many bodies
Were slain: strong, bold, and hardy.

And at the last, with great pain,
King Richard rescued the Earl of Champagne,
And set him upon a steed 7055
That was very good in any trouble,
And ordered him to stay by his side,
And not ride a foot away from him.
    Just then a messenger came quickly
To speak with King Richard, 7060
And said, "Sire, for charity,
Turn again to the City of Jaffa!
Both mountain and plain are covered.
Neither King Alexander nor Charlemagne
Ever faced such an army 7065
As is now about the city!
The gates have been set on fire
On the right side of Jaffa Castle;
Your men may come neither in nor out.
Lord, I'm very afraid— 7070
Because you may not ride to the city—
Of what may happen to you in the field!
And I warn you, without fail,
Your army is greatly diminished.
The bishop has been captured, 7075
And Jean de Nesle has been slain, truly.
William Arsuf, and Sir Gerard,
And the good Lombard Bertram Braundys,
All these have been slain, and many more!"
King Richard thought carefully then, 7080
And began to cry, "Turn to the rear,
Every man with his banner!"
And many thousands hastened before him
With swords and great lances,
With both falchions and maces. 7085
They made King Richard very angry;
They slew Favel under him,
And then King Richard was furious and fierce.
He drew his axe from his saddlebow,
And soon slew that same Saracen 7090
Who killed his steed under him;
Therefore the Saracen lost his life as reward.
Richard was on foot, and laid about:
Many died there under his hand.
He slew horse and man outright: 7095

All that his axe might reach,
Both before and behind.
While he was on foot, I find,
He slew a thousand and more:
Neither help nor aid ever came to them.   7100
Saladin's two sons came riding,
With ten thousand Saracens by their side,
And did cry to King Richard:
"Surrender, thief, traitor, coward,
Or I shall slay you in this place!"   7105
"Nay!" said Richard, "by God's grace!"
And with his axe he smote him so
That his waist flew in two:
Half the body fell down,
And the other half was left in the saddle.   7110
"From you," said King Richard, "I'm safe!"
His brother came to that battle
Upon a steed, with great violence.
He thought to bear King Richard down,
And gave him a wound through the arm   7115
That did our king a great injury:
There was poison upon the spearhead.
King Richard bravely smote him
So that man and horse fell dead to the ground.
"Lie there," he said, "you heathen hound!   7120
You shall never tell Saladin
That you made me lose my life!"
With that, five heathen dukes
Came with their host, undoubtedly,
And beset Richard, our king,   7125
And thought to give him his death.
King Richard in a little time
Had slain the five dukes,
And many hundreds of strong
Heathen men after them.   7130
And at the last, although it was late,
Richard went to the gate of Jaffa.
Then our Christian men were quite certain
That they should have victory in the battle.
The Earl of Leicester, Sir Robert,   7135
Brought our King his steed, Lyard.
King Richard leaped into the saddle,
And the Saracens fled as if they were sheep.

Our King rode after until it was night,
And slew all those that he might overtake.   7140
On hill and dale, there were slain
Ten hundred thousand heathen men
That night, without a lie.
King Richard won entry into Jaffa,
And thanked Jesus, King of Glory,   7145
And his Mother for that victory:
For since the world began,
A fairer battle was never won.
    In the morning he sent Robert de Sabloel,
And Sir William Wateville,   7150
Hubert and Robert Tourneham,
Hubert Walter, Gyffard, and John St. John,[1]
And bade them say to the Sultan
That he himself would fight
Against five and twenty men in the field,   7155
To determine God's right:
If he won, he would have the land
Forever in Christian men's hands;
And if the Saracens might slay him,
The land should forever be the Sultan's.   7160
And if he would not hear his proposals,
"Say that for three years, three months, and three days
I ask for a truce with the Sultan,
To go home and come again then."
The messengers went on their way   7165
And told the Sultan the beginning and end,
But he would not consent to that battle:
Five hundred against Richard, without fail!
In the morning, if he would come,
The truce should be established: 7170
Thus he told the messengers,
And they told it to Richard the fierce.
The next day he made an agreement
Of truce with King Richard,
Who could come away from Acre,   7175
Through all the land to the sea.
Then afterward, for all three years,
Christian men both far and near

---

1 Of these knights, only Hubert Walter has been identified as a real
    figure (see note to line 2831).

Could travel the way to Jerusalem,
To the Sepulchre and to Bethlehem, 7180
To the Mount of Olives and to Nazareth,
To Jaffa and to Maiden Castle,
And to all other pilgrimage sites,
Without harm or injury.[1]
    Thus King Richard, the bold man, 7185
Made peace with the Sultan,
And afterward, I understand, he
Went his way toward England,
And through treason was shot, alas,
When he was at Castle Gaillard.[2] 7190
The Duke of Austria in the Castle
With his host was arrayed very well.
Richard thought to abide there;
The weather was hot in the summertime,
And he thought he might have cooled himself off 7195
At Gaillard, under the Castle.
He took off his helmet there,
And made his face all bare.
A spy was there in the Castle,
Who spotted Richard for certain, 7200
And took an extremely strong crossbow
And a very long arrow,
And wrongfully struck King Richard
In the head, without doubt.
Richard let his helmet fall down, 7205
And ordered his men to ready themselves,
And swore by the sun and the sea
That until the Castle had been won,

---

1 Richard and Saladin agreed to the treaty of Jaffa on 2 September
  1192. It established a truce for three years and eight months.
  Richard surrendered Ascalon but retained Jaffa, and Muslims and
  Christians were to have free passage through one another's lands.
  For full details see Gillingham, *Richard I* 216–18.
2 After departing from the Holy Land, Richard was shipwrecked and
  captured by Leopold, Duke of Austria (see note to line 654). The
  poem, having relocated Richard's capture to before the Crusade,
  here skips ahead seven years to Richard's death on 6 April 1199.
  Richard died not at Castle Gaillard, but while laying siege to the
  castle at Chalus-Chabrol, south of Limoges, as part of his ongoing
  territorial dispute with Philip. He was shot in the shoulder and died
  when the wound became infected.

Never would any meat or drink
Ever sink into his body.   7210
He had Robynet, at that time,
Drawn up to the Castle's side,
And on the other side
He set up the Mate-Gryphon.
He threw stones to the Castle,   7215
And broke the walls, on that occasion,
And so within a little time,
They did ride into the Castle,
And slew before them and behind
All those who they ever might find against them.   7220
And always the arrow, by its point,
Was still stuck in Richard's head.
And when it was drawn out,
He died soon, without doubt,
And he commanded that in any event   7225
Men should bring him to his father.
They didn't stop for anything, soft or hard,
Until they were at Fontevraud.
At Fontevraud, certainly,
His bones lie by his father's.[1]   7230
He was called King Harry, truly:
He held all England by right.
King Richard was a conqueror.
God give his soul much honour!
No more is said of him in English,   7235
But may Jesus who dearly bought us
Grant his soul peace and rest,
And ours, too, when it comes there,
And that it may be so,
All say amen, for charity.   7240

---

1   This is more or less true, although according to Richard's wishes
    his brain and entrails were buried at the Abbey of Charroux, and
    his heart at Rouen. The rest of his body was interred at Fontevraud,
    as the poem claims.

Appendix A: The Middle English Richard Coer de Lyon

[The Middle English *Richard Coer de Lyon*, on which this translation is based, was written in the early fourteenth century, perhaps near London. Its basic verse form is octosyllabic rhyming couplets; as this was a popular form for Anglo-Norman romance, it may well have been adapted from the poem's posited Anglo-Norman source. Lines generally have four stresses:

/   x / x / x /   x
The spousyng was idon that nyght

although occasionally—perhaps due to scribal errors in the text's transmission—they have only three:

/   x / x / x
Twoo knaves and a mayde

The syllable count per line is less strict than the number of stresses, and here, too, there is variation. Lines typically have seven to nine syllables, generally alternating between stressed and unstressed.

Students new to Middle English will encounter two unfamiliar letters: þ, or thorn, which makes the "th" sound, and ȝ, or yogh, which is used where in Modern English you would normally expect a "y" or "g" at the beginning of words, or a "gh" in the middle or at the end. It may also help to know that "-yd" and "-es" endings are frequently pronounced as separate syllables; the final -e on nouns may or may not be pronounced, depending on whether it is needed for the metre (but never before a vowel or an initial h-). For example:

/   x / x / x /x
Be fforn the elevacyon,

/   x / x /   x   / x
The qwene fel in swowne adon.

More than anything else, the rhyme ties the lines together (see Putter, "Metres").

Four brief passages of the Middle English *Richard Coer de Lyon* are included below. These examples demonstrate the poem's original language and prosody and will allow for some close reading of select passages. They include three of the poem's fabulous episodes: Henry II's marriage to the mysterious Cassodorien and its abrupt ending; Richard's reaction to his first, unintentional act of cannibalism; and Richard's message to Saladin following his second cannibal feast. I have also included one of the poem's many battle scenes, which focuses on Richard's martial prowess.

I've transcribed these selections directly from the Cambridge, Gonville and Caius College manuscript, although I've silently expanded abbreviations, added punctuation, and modernized *u/v* in accordance with modern conventions. Attentive readers may notice select lines that differ from my translation or from other modern editions, where modern editors have preferred an alternative manuscript witness. The first and final selections also give a glimpse of the composite nature of any modern edition: in selection 1 starting at line 228, and in selection 4 starting at line 6850, there are leaves missing from the Cambridge, Gonville and Caius College manuscript, so the missing lines are supplied by Wynkyn de Worde's 1509 printed edition. Note, for example, that de Worde uses "th" rather than "þ."]

1. Cassodorien's Marriage (ll. 185–234)

þe spousyng was idon þat ny3t;
þeratte daunsyd many a kny3t.
Mekyl joye was hem among.
A preest on morwe þe messe song;
Be fforn þe elevacyoun,
þe qwene fel in swowne adon.
þe folk wondryd and were adrad.
In to a chambyr sche was lad,
Sche seyde, "For I am þus ishent,
I dar nevere see no sacrement."
Here fadyr on morwe took hys leve;
No lengere wolde he þere beleve.
þe kyng dwellyd wiþ hys qwene;
Chyldren þey hadden hem bytwene,
Twoo knaves and a mayde,
Forsoþe, as þe book us sayde.

Rychard hyghte þe fyrste, iwis,
Off whom þis romaunce imakyd is.
Jhon þat oþer forsoþe was.
þe þrydde hys sustyr Topyas.
þus þey dwellyd in fere
To þe ffyfftenþe ȝere.
On a day before þe rode,
þe kyng at hys masse stode.
þere com an erl of gret pouste
"Sere," he sayde, "hou may þis be
þat my lady, ȝoure wyf, þe qwene,
þe sacrement ne dar nought sene?
Geve us leve to don here dwelle,
Fro þat begynnes þe gospeller
Tyl þe messe be sungge and sayd,
And ȝou schalt se a queynte brayd."
þe kyng grauntyd wiþ good wylle,
To holden here wiþ strengþe stylle.
"Neyþer for wele neyþer for woo
Let here nought out fro kyrke goo."
And whene þe belle began to ryng,
þe preest scholde make þe sakeryng
Out off þe kyrke sche wolde away.
þe erl, for gode, sayde, "Nay,
Lady, þou schalt here abyde
For ony þyng þat may betyde."
Sche took here doughtyr in here hond,
And Johan her sone she wolde not wonde,
Out of the rofe she gan her dyght,
Openly before all theyr syght.
Johan fell frome her in þat stonde,
And brake his þygh on þe grounde;
And with her doughter she fled her waye,
That never after she was isey.

2. First Episode of Cannibalism (ll. 3194–3226)

When Kyng Richard hadde restyd a whyle,
A knyght hys armes gan unlace.
Hym to counfforte and solace,
Hym was brouȝt a sop in wyn:
"þe hed off þat ylke swyn
þat I off eet," þe cook he bad,

"Ffor feble I am, feynt and mad.
Off myn evyl now I am ffere;
Serve me þerwiþ at my sopere!"
Quod þe cook, "þat hed I ne have."
þenne sayde þe kyng, "So God me save,
But I see þe hed of þat swyn,
For soþe, þou schalt lese þyn!"
þe cook seygh non oþir may bee,
He ffette þe hed and leet hym see.
He ffel on knees and made a cry,
"Loo, here þe hed, my lord, mercy!"
Hys swarte vys whenne þe kyng seeþ,
Hys blake berd and hys whyte teeþ,
Hou hys lyppys grennyd wyde,
"What devyl is þis?" þe kyng cryde,
And gan to lawȝe as he were wood.
"What? Is Sarezynys flesch þus good,
And nevere erst I nought wyste?
By Goddys deþ and hys upryste,
Schole we nevere dye for defawte
Whyl we may in any assawte
Slee Sarezynys, þe flesch mowe taken,
Seþen and roste hem and doo hem baken,
Gnawen here fflesche to þe bones.
Now I have it prouvyd ones,
For hungyr, ar I be woo,
I and my ffolk schole eete moo!"

3. Richard's Message to Saladin (ll. 3521–62)

Whene þey hadde eeten þe cloþ was folde.
Kyng Richard gan hem to beholde;
On knees þey askyd leve to gon,
But off hem alle was þer nouȝt on
þat in message was þedyr come,
þat hym hadde levere have ben at home,
Wiþ wyf, frendes, and here kynde,
þenne al þe good þat was in Ynde!
Kyng Rychard spak to an old man:
"Wendes hom to ȝoure Sawdan,
Hys malycoly þat ȝe abate,
And says þat ȝe come to late.
To slowȝly was ȝoure terme igesseyd,

Or ȝe come þe fflesch was dressyd
þat men scholden serve wiþ me
þus at noon and my meyne.
Say hym it schal hym nouȝt avayle
þough he forbarre oure vytayle,
Brede and wyne, ffysch, fflessche, samoun and cungir,
Of us non schal dye ffor hungyr,
Whyle we may wenden to ffyȝt,
And slee þe Sarezynes dounryȝt,
Wassche þe fflesche and roste þe hede.
Wiþ oo Sarwzyn I may wel fede
Wel a nyne or a ten,
Of my goode Crystene men."
Kyng Richard: "I schal waraunt,
þer is no flesch so norysschaunt,
Unto an Ynglyssche man,
Partryk, plover, heroun, ne swan,
Cow, ne oxe, scheep, ne swyn,
  As þe hed off a Saryzyn!
þere he is fat and þerto tendre,
And my men are lene and sclendre.
Whyl any Sarezyn quyk bee
Lyvande now in þis cuntrée,
For mete wole we noþyng care:
Aboute ffaste we schole ffare,
And every day we schole eete
Also manye as we may gete.
To Yngelond wole we nought gon,
Tyl þey be eeten, everylkon."

4. King Richard at Jaffa (ll. 6833–62)

Kyng Richard rod out at þe ȝate;
Twoo kynges he fond þerate,
Wiþ syxty þousand Sarezynes fers,
Wiþ armes bryȝte and brode baners.
þat on upon þe hood he hytte
þat to þe sadyl he hym slytte.
þat oþir he hytte upon þe hood,
þat at þe gyrdylstede it stood;
And hys Templers and hys barouns,
And Hospytalers egre as lyouns
þey slowen Sarezynes also swyþe

As gres ffalliþ fro þe syþe.
þe Sarezynes sey3en no betere won
But flowen agayn everylkon,
Unto Saladynes grete hoost
þat fyfftene myle lay a coost.
Twoo and þrytty þousand, forsoþe to say,
The Sowdan loste that same daye,
For theyr armure fared as waxe
Ayenst Kynge Rychardes axe.
Many a Sarasyne and hygh lordynge
Yelded them to Rycharde, our kynge.
Rycharde put them in hostage tho:
There were a thousande prysoners and mo.
The chase lasted swyþe longe,
Tyll þe tyme of evensonge.
Richard rode after tyll it was nyght,
So many of them to deth he dyght,
That no nombre it may accounte
How many of them it wolde amounte.

Appendix B: Calls to Crusade

1. **"Pope Urban II's Call for a Crusade," in Dana C. Munro, "Urban and the Crusaders,"** *Translations and Reprints from the Original Sources of European History,* **vol. 1, no. 2 (Department of History of the University of Pennsylvania / P.S. King, 1895), pp. 5–8**

[At the Council of Clermont on 10 November 1095, Pope Urban II announced an ambitious plan to reorder the world. Pilgrimage to Christian holy sites in Jerusalem had become more dangerous, as the arrival of Seljuk Turks from Central Asia had unsettled internal politics in the Islamic world; the popular preacher Peter the Hermit had been publicly urging the necessity of military aid to the Christians in Jerusalem; and the Byzantine Empire— including Constantinople, the seat of the Greek Orthodox church—was under threat from the Turks and had requested Urban's help. In addition, Europe was beset by internal turmoil. Responding to these manifold pressures, Urban proposed a massive military undertaking that would unite the Christian world against the "infidels" who threatened it. No direct transcription of his speech survives, although several writers report the gist of his speech after the fact. The version below is recorded by Robert the Monk, who may have been present at Clermont but who was writing 25 years after the fact.]

Oh, race of Franks, race from across the mountains, race chosen and beloved by God as shines forth in very many of your works set apart from all nations by the situation of your country, as well as by your catholic faith and the honor of the holy church! To you our discourse is addressed and for you our exhortation is intended. We wish you to know what a grievous cause has led us to your country, what peril threatening you and all the faithful has brought us.

From the confines of Jerusalem and the city of Constantinople a horrible tale has gone forth and very frequently has been brought to our ears, namely, that a race from the kingdom of the Persians, an accursed race, a race utterly alienated from God, a generation forsooth which has not directed its heart and has not entrusted its spirit to God, has invaded the lands of those Christians and has depopulated them by the sword, pillage and fire; it has led away a part of the captives into its own country, and a part it has destroyed by cruel tortures; it has either entirely destroyed the churches of God or appropriated them for the rites of its own religion. They destroy the altars, after having defiled them with their uncleanness. They circumcise the Christians, and the blood of the circumcision they either spread upon the altars or pour into the vases of the baptismal font. When they wish to torture people by a base death, they perforate their navels, and dragging forth the extremity of the intestines, bind it to a stake; then with flogging they lead the victim around until the viscera having gushed forth the victim falls prostrate upon the ground. Others they bind to a post and pierce with arrows. Others they compel to extend their necks and then, attacking them with naked swords, attempt to cut through the neck with a single blow. What shall I say of the abominable rape of the women? To speak of it is worse than to be silent. The kingdom of the Greeks is now dismembered by them and deprived of territory so vast in extent that it cannot be traversed in a march of two months. On whom therefore is the labour of avenging these wrongs and of recovering this territory incumbent, if not upon you? You, upon whom above other nations God has conferred remarkable glory in arms, great courage, bodily activity, and strength to humble the hairy scalp of those who resist you.

Let the deeds of your ancestors move you and incite your minds to manly achievements; the glory and greatness of king Charles the Great, and of his son Louis, and of your other kings, who have destroyed the kingdoms of the pagans, and have extended in these lands the territory of the holy church. Let the holy sepulchre of the Lord our Saviour, which is possessed by unclean nations, especially incite you, and the holy places which are now treated with ignominy and irreverently polluted with their filthiness. Oh, most valiant soldiers and descendants of invincible ancestors, be not degenerate, but recall the valor of your progenitors.

But if you are hindered by love of children, parents and wives, remember what the Lord says in the Gospel, "He that loveth father or mother more than me, is not worthy of me." "Every one that hath forsaken houses, or brethren, or sisters, or father, or mother, or wife, or children, or lands for my name's sake shall receive an hundredfold and shall inherit everlasting life." Let none of your possessions detain you, no solicitude for your family affairs, since this land which you inhabit, shut in on all sides by the seas and surrounded by the mountain peaks, is too narrow for your large population; nor does it abound in wealth; and it furnishes scarcely food enough for its cultivators. Hence it is that you murder one another, that you wage war, and that frequently you perish by mutual wounds. Let therefore hatred depart from among you, let your quarrels end, let wars cease, and let all dissensions and controversies slumber. Enter upon the road to the Holy Sepulchre; wrest that land from the wicked race, and subject it to yourselves. That land which as the Scripture says "floweth with milk and honey," was given by God into the possession of the children of Israel. Jerusalem is the navel of the world; the land is fruitful above others, like another paradise of delights. This the Redeemer of the human race has made illustrious by His advent, has beautified by residence, has consecrated by suffering, has redeemed by death, has glorified by burial. This royal city, therefore, situated at the centre of the world, is now held captive by His enemies, and is in subjection to those who do not know God, to the worship of the heathens. She seeks therefore and desires to be liberated, and does not cease to implore you to come to her aid. From you especially she asks succor, because, as we have already said, God has conferred upon you above all nations great glory in arms. Accordingly undertake this journey for the remission of your sins, with the assurance of the imperishable glory of the Kingdom of Heaven.

When Pope Urban had said these and very many similar things in his urbane discourse, he so influenced to one purpose the desires of all who were present, that they cried out, "It is the will of God! It is the will of God!" When the venerable Roman pontiff heard that, with eyes uplifted to heaven he gave thanks to God and, with his hand commanding silence, said:

Most beloved brethren, today is manifest in you what the Lord says in the Gospel, "Where two or three are gathered together in my name there am I in the midst of them." Unless the Lord God had been present in your spirits, all of you would not have uttered the same cry. For, although the cry issued from numerous mouths, yet the origin of the cry was one. Therefore I say to you that God, who implanted this in your breasts, has drawn it forth from you. Let this then be your war-cry in combats, because this word is given to you by God. When an armed attack is made upon the enemy, let this one cry be raised by all the soldiers of God: It is the will of God! It is the will of God!

And we do not command or advise that the old or feeble, or those unfit for bearing arms, undertake this journey; nor ought women to set out at all, without their husbands or brothers or legal guardians. For such are more of a hindrance than aid, more of a burden than advantage. Let the rich aid the needy; and according to their wealth, let them take with them experienced soldiers. The priests and clerks of any order are not to go without the consent of their bishop; for this journey would profit them nothing if they went without permission of these. Also, it is not fitting that laymen should enter upon the pilgrimage without the blessing of their priests.

Whoever, therefore, shall determine upon this holy pilgrimage and shall make his vow to God to that effect and shall offer himself to Him as a living sacrifice, holy, acceptable unto God, shall wear the sign of the cross of the Lord on his forehead or on his breast. When, truly, having fulfilled his vow he wishes to return, let him place the cross on his back between his shoulders. Such, indeed, by the twofold action will fulfill the precept of the Lord, as He commands in the Gospel, "He that taketh not his cross and followeth after me, is not worthy of me."

2. "Pope Gregory VIII, *Audita tremendi*, October 29, 1187," in *Crusade and Christendom: Annotated Documents in Translation from Innocent III to the Fall of Acre, 1187–1291*, edited by Jessalynn Bird, Edward Peters, and James M. Powell (U of Pennsylvania P, 2013), pp. 5–9

[While the First Crusade captured Jerusalem and established four crusader states (the Principality of Antioch, the Counties of Edessa and Tripoli, and the Kingdom of Jerusalem) along the Mediterranean, by 1187 Saladin—Sultan of Egypt and Syria— had recaptured all but a tiny fraction of this territory. When news of a catastrophic Christian loss at Hattin and the subsequent fall of Jerusalem reached Pope Urban III, he supposedly died of grief. His successor, Gregory VIII, almost immediately called for a new crusade in this encyclical, *Audita tremendi*, issued on 29 October 1187. According to its most recent editors, from whose edition this selection is taken, this was "not only the most impassioned plea for a crusade ever issued by a pope until then, but the fullest detailed account of crusaders' spiritual and temporal rewards and privileges to date" (4). Richard Coeur de Lion, then Count of Poitou, was the first to take the Cross (without the permission of his father, Henry II). He inherited the English throne in July 1189, and a year later he set out for the Holy Land.]

GREGORY, Bishop, servant of the servants of God, to all Christ's faithful who receive this letter, greeting and apostolic benediction.

When we heard of the severity of the awesome judgment that the hand of God visited on the land of Jerusalem, we and our brothers were disturbed by such a great horror, afflicted by such sorrows, that we scarcely knew what to do or what we should do, save that the psalmist laments and says, "O God, the gentiles have invaded your inheritance, they have sullied your holy temple, they have laid waste Jerusalem; they have left the dead bodies of your saints as meat for the beasts of the earth and food the birds of the air ..." [Ps 78:1–2].[1] In fact, because of the conflict which the malice of [Christian] men has recently brought on the land by the inspiration of the devil, Saladin approached those parts with a host of armed troops. They were confronted by the king and the bishops, the Templars and the Hospitallers, the barons and the knights, with the people of the land, and with the Lord's cross (through which from memory and faith of the suffering of Christ, who hung there and redeemed the human race, was believed to be a sure safeguard and a desired defense against the attacks of the pagans), and after the battle was joined, our side was defeated and the Lord's cross was captured. The bishops were slaughtered, the king captured, and almost all our men were either put to the sword or taken prisoner. Very few are believed to have escaped. Also, the Templars and Hospitallers were beheaded in his [Saladin's] presence. With the army defeated, we do not think our letter can explain how they next invaded and seized every place so that only a few remained outside their power. Still, though we use the words of the prophet: "Who will give me water for my head and a font of tears for my eyes, and I will weep night and day for the death of my people" [Jer 9:1], we ought not despair now and decide to mistrust and believe that God is so angry with his people that in his anger with their commission of a multitude of sins he will not quickly pardon when he is pleased by their penance and, after tears and groans, will lead them to exaltation.

Indeed, whoever does not mourn at least in his heart in so great a cause for sorrow not only is ignorant of the Christian faith, which teaches us to join in all suffering, but of our very humanity. For from the magnitude of the dangers and their barbarous

---

1 The editorial material in brackets is from the original source edition.

ferocity thirsting for the blood of Christians, and adding all their power in this cause to profane the holy and erase the name of God from that land, whoever thinks we should be silent should decide. Of course, when the prophets worked previously with total desire, later the apostles and their followers worked so that divine worship should be in that land and should spread from it to every part of the world by every means great and wonderful. God, through whom all things were made, who wished to take on flesh through his divine wisdom and his incomprehensible mercy and desired to achieve our salvation through the weakness of our flesh, hunger, thirst, the Cross, death and resurrection, according to the words "And he has worked salvation in the midst of the land" [Ps 73:12] has himself decided to work for this end. Neither can tongue speak nor the senses understand what that land has now suffered, how much it has suffered for us and for all Christians, that we read it endured under its ancient population. Moreover, we ought not believe that these things happened because of the unjust act of the judge but rather by the iniquity of an unworthy people, since we read that at the time when the people were being converted to the Lord, "one thousand were persecuted and two were fleeing from ten thousand" [Dt 32:30]. On the contrary, however, the army of Sennacharib was overcome by an angelic force. But "that land also devoured its inhabitants" [Nm 13:33] and was not at peace for very long, nor could it restrain those who broke the law. Nor did it give teaching to those who would seek the heavenly Jerusalem, which they could not attain save through the exercise of good works and after many temptations. But they could long ago fear those things, when Arroasia [Edessa] and other land fell into the hands of the pagans [1144], and it was clearly foreseen if the people who remained had again done penance they would have pleased God whom they offended by their sins. For his anger is not quick, but he puts off the punishment, and gives time for repentance. But, finally, he does not lose his judgment in mercy, but exercises his protection for the punishment of sinners and for the surety of those to be saved.

We, therefore, should heed and be concerned about the sins not only of the inhabitants of that land but also of our own and those of the whole Christian people so that what is left of that land may not be lost and their power rage in other regions. For we hear from every direction of scandals and conflicts between kings and princes, among cities, so that we lament with the prophet and are able to say: "There is no truth, no knowledge of God in the land: lying, murder and adultery abound, and blood pursues blood" [Hos 4:1–2]. For this reason, everyone must understand and act accordingly, so that by atoning for our sins, we may be converted to the Lord by penance and works of piety and we may first alter in our lives the evil that we do. Then we can deal with the savagery and malice of our enemies. And, what they do not fear to try against God, we will not hesitate to do for God. Therefore, sons, consider how you came into this world and how all pass on, and thus you will pass on. Use the time for penitence and doing well insofar as it regards you, with thanks. Give yourselves, give after yourselves, because you, who cannot make even a gnat upon the land, have nothing of your own. We do not say, dismiss, but send us forth in the heavenly harvest which you have and deposit with him "upon whom the rust does not destroy, nor the worms, nor the thieves dig up and steal" [Mt 6:20]. Work for the recovery of that land in which for our salvation Truth has arisen from the land and did not disdain to carry the forked wood of the cross for us. Pay attention not to earthly profit and glory, but to the will of God who himself taught us to lay down our souls for our brothers. Give your riches to him, which whether willingly or unwillingly, you do not know to which greedy heirs they will be left. It is certainly not new, nor unusual, that that land is persecuted by a divine judgment that, after being beaten and corrected, it may obtain mercy. Of course, the Lord could preserve it by his will alone, but it is not for us to know why he would do this. Perhaps he wished to experience and bring to the notice of others if someone is understanding and seeking God, who having offered himself embraces the time of penance joyfully. He sacrifices himself for his brothers; though he may die young, still he accomplishes much. Heed how the Maccabees, afire with the divine zeal of the law experienced extreme dangers for the freedom of their brothers. They taught that not only riches but their persons should be sacrificed for their brothers, exhorting and saying to each other: "Gird yourselves and be powerful sons because it is better for us to die in battle than to witness the desecration of our nation and our saints" [1 Mc 3:58–59]. Indeed, they were subject to one law; you by the incarnation of our Lord Jesus Christ have been led to the light of truth and instructed by the many examples of the saints. You should act without trepidation and do not fear to give away earthly possessions, which will last for such a short time, for those goods we are promised that "neither eye has seen nor ear has heard nor have they entered into the heart of man" [1 Cor 2:9], as the Apostle says: "That the sufferings of this time are not worthy to be compared to the future glory which will be revealed in us" [Rom 8:18].

We promise full remission of their sins and eternal life to those who take up the labor of this journey with a contrite heart and a humble spirit and depart in penitence of their sins and with true faith. Whether they survive or die, they should know that they, after they have made a true confession, will have the relaxation of the penance imposed, by the mercy of almighty God, by the authority of the apostles Peter and Paul, and ours. Their goods, from their reception of the cross, with their families, remain under the protection of the holy Roman Church, as well as the archbishops and bishops and other prelates. They should not face any legal challenge regarding the things they possess legally when they received the cross until their return or their death is known for certain, but they should also keep legally all their goods. Also, they may not be forced to pay interest if they have a loan. They should not travel in precious clothing, and with dogs or birds, or with others that display ostentation and luxury, but in modest garb and demeanor, they should do penance rather than affect vainglory. Dated at Ferrara on the fourth Calends of November [29 October 1187], the sixth indiction.

Appendix C: Cannibalism

1. Crusader Cannibalism

[Numerous scholars have connected the cannibalism scenes in *RCL* to episodes of actual, rumoured, or feigned cannibalism during the First Crusade. Over time, accounts of the crusaders' cannibalism changed. The initial reactions of horror and disgust by eyewitnesses and near-contemporaries gradually turned to appreciation of cannibalism's ability to inspire terror in the enemy, particularly as the cannibalism was displaced either by making it a clever ruse or by blaming it on a group of lower-class men known as the Tafurs: an abject other within the ranks of the crusaders, characterized by their poverty, ferocity, and aptitude for manual labour. When the Tafurs' cannibalism is first represented in a literary text, the late-twelfth-/ early-thirteenth-century Old French *Chanson d'Antioch*, it is openly celebrated. The following selections a, g, and i refer to events at Antioch; a, b, c, d, e, f, and h refer to events at Ma'arra.]

a. From "Daibert, Archbishop of Pisa, Duke Godfrey, Advocate of the Holy Sepulchre, Raymond, Count of St. Gilles, and the entire army of God, to the Pope and all the Christian faithful (September, 1099)," in Malcolm Barber and Keith Bate, translators, *Letters from the East: Crusaders, Pilgrims and Settlers in the 12th–13th Centuries*, Crusade Texts in Translation (Ashgate, 2010), pp. 33–34

[This letter was sent from the leaders of the First Crusade to Pope Urban II.]

However, because these successes bred arrogance among some of us, God placed Antioch in our path, a city impossible to storm by human strength alone. There he detained us for nine months, and during the siege so humbled us that eventually all our pride and arrogance turned to humility. When, indeed, we were humbled to the point that the whole army could muster scarcely a hundred good horses, God opened up for us His abundant mercy and guided us into the city, placing the Turks and all their possessions in our hands. As we thought we had acquired these by our own efforts and failed to magnify God in a worthy manner for bringing us this success, we were besieged by such a huge number of Saracens that none of us dared set foot outside the city. Moreover, famine was so rife in the city that some people were ready to eat human flesh. It would take too long to recount all the misery we suffered there [...] Our army defeated the enemy, but was continuing to suffer from hunger and fatigue, as well as from quarrels among our leaders, so it set out for Syria where it captured the Saracen cities of Barra and Marra as well as the fortresses in that region. While we were resting there our Christian soldiers were so hungry that they ate the decomposing corpses of the Saracens.

b. From the *Gesta Francorum* (c. 1100), in Rosalind Hill, editor and translator, *The Deeds of the Franks and the Other Pilgrims to Jerusalem* (Thomas Nelson and Sons, 1962), p. 80

The Franks stayed in that city for one month and four days, during which time the bishop of Orange died. While we were there some of our men could not satisfy their needs, either because of the long stay or because they were so hungry, for there was no plunder to be had outside the walls. So they ripped up the bodies of the dead, because they used to find bezants[1] hidden in their entrails, and others cut the dead flesh into slices and cooked it to eat.

c. From Raymond d'Aguilers, *Historia Francorum qui Ceperunt Jherusalem* (c. 1102), edited and translated by John Hugh Hill and Laurita L. Hill (American Philosophical Society, 1968), p. 81

Now the food shortage became so acute that the Christians ate with gusto many rotten Saracen bodies which they had pitched into the swamps two or three weeks before. This spectacle disgusted as many crusaders as it did strangers, and as a result of it many gave up without hope of Frankish reinforcements and turned back. The Saracens and Turks reacted thus: "This stubborn and merciless race, unmoved by hunger, sword, or other perils for one year at Antioch, now feasts on human flesh; therefore we ask, 'Who can resist them?'" The infidels spread stories of these and other inhuman acts of the crusaders, but we were unaware that God had made us an object of terror.

---

1 Gold coins produced in the Middle East.

d. From Fulcher of Chartres, *A History of the Expedition to Jerusalem 1095–1127* (c. 1106), translated by Frances Rita Ryan (U of Tennessee P, 1969), pp. 112–13

Here our men suffered from excessive hunger. I shudder to say that many of our men, terribly tormented by the madness of starvation, cut pieces of flesh from the buttocks of Saracens lying there dead. These pieces they cooked and ate, savagely devouring the flesh while it was insufficiently roasted. In this way the besiegers were harmed more than the besieged.

e. From Guibert of Nogent, *The Deeds of God through the Franks: A Translation of Guibert of Nogent's Gesta Dei per Francos* (c. 1109), edited and translated by Robert Levine (Boydell, 1997), p. 146

There was another kind of man in this army, who was barefooted, carried no arms, and was not permitted to have any money. Dirty, naked, and poor, he marched in front of everyone, feeding on the roots of herbs, and on the most wretched things that grow. A Norman, well-born, said to have been formerly a knight, but now a foot-soldier, he saw them wandering without a leader, and laid aside his arms and the clothing he wore, wishing to declare himself their king. He had himself called Tafur, a term taken from the barbarian language. Among the pagans they are called Tafur whom we call, to speak less literally, Trudennes, that is, men who kill time, that is, who pass their time wandering aimlessly here and there. It was the Tafur's custom, whenever the people he was leading arrived at a bridge to be crossed, or at a narrow pass to be traversed, to rush forward to observe very carefully, and if he saw that anyone of his men possessed two deniers,[1] he would quickly separate him from the general group, order him to purchase arms, and assign him to the section of the army that bore weapons. However, those in whom he saw a love of the simple life, who had no impulse or desire to save money, he made members of his inner circle. Perhaps some might think that these men were not useful for the general good, and that he could have fed others what he was uselessly giving to them. But no one can describe how useful they were in carrying food, in collecting tribute, in hurling stones during the sieges of cities. They were better at carrying heavy burdens than the asses and mules,

---

1 French coins of low value, sometimes called silver pennies in English sources.

and they were as good at hurling projectiles as the machines and launchers. Moreover, when pieces of flesh were found among the pagan bodies at Marra, and elsewhere, during a terrible famine, a hideous rumor (based on something that had been done furtively and very rarely) circulated widely among the pagans, that there were some men in the Frankish army who eagerly fed upon the corpses of Saracens. To circulate this rumor among them even more vividly, the men carried the battered corpse of a Turk out in full view of the other Turks, set it afire, and roasted it as if the flesh was going to be eaten. When they learned what had happened, thinking that the charade was real, they grew even more afraid of the fearlessness of the Tafurs than of our other leaders.

f. From Ralph of Caen, *The Gesta Tancredi of Ralph of Caen: A History of the Normans on the First Crusade* (c. 1118), edited by Bernard S. Bachrach and David S. Bachrach (Ashgate, 2005), p. 116

This flood brought with it terrible hunger as all of the grain brought into camp rotted. No more was brought in from anywhere and victory was delayed. The bread floated away and hunger increased. It is shameful to report what I heard and what I learned from the authors of this shame. For I heard that they said that they were forced by the lack of food to begin to eat human flesh. Adults from among the gentiles were put into the cooking pot and their youth were fixed on spits and roasted. In devouring them, the Christians looked like wild beasts, like dogs roasting men. They threatened at the end that they would eat the limbs of their own if foreign ones were lacking unless the capture of the city or the bringing in of foreign grain lessened their starvation.

g. From William of Malmesbury, *Chronicle of the Kings of England* (c. 1127), translated and edited by J.A. Giles (Henry G. Bohn, 1847), p. 380

And now, everything which could be procured for food being destroyed around the city, a sudden famine, which usually makes even fortresses give way, began to oppress the army; so much so, that the harvest not having yet attained to maturity, some persons seized the pods of beans before they were ripe, as the greatest delicacy; others fed on carrion, or hides soaked in water; others passed parboiled thistles through their bleeding jaws into their stomachs. Others sold mice, or such dainties, to those who required them; content to suffer hunger themselves, so that they could procure money. Some, too, there were, who even fed their corpse-like bodies with other corpses, eating human flesh; but at a distance, and on the mountains, lest others should be offended at the smell of their cookery.

h. From Orderic Vitalis, *The Ecclesiastical History* (c. 1142), edited and translated by Marjorie Chibnall (Oxford UP, 1975), p. 141

The bishop of Orange fell sick there and, departing from earth, passed to heaven. During this time the army suffered terribly from hunger and was forced to devour without scruple things that were filthy, strange, disagreeable, and even forbidden. Some even ate the flesh of Turks and, though the more highly-born and stricter men were ashamed and horrified to hear about it, they forbore to punish the offence because of the terrible famine. It was not even regarded as the most heinous of crimes, because they were willingly suffering starvation for God and were attacking his enemies with their teeth as well as their hands. It is true that they acted unlawfully, but overriding necessity forced them to violate the law. Because of the famine in the camp they snatched at everything and rejected nothing. Some men ripped open the bodies of Turks, because they found in their bowels bezants and gold that they had swallowed, and carried it off. Many died of starvation there.

i. From William of Tyre, *A History of Deeds Done beyond the Sea* (c. 1184), translated by Emily Atwater Babcock and A.C. Krey, 2 vols. (Columbia UP, 1943), vol. 1, pp. 222–23

When it seemed impossible to discover any way of preventing these machinations,[1] Bohemond, a man of unusually keen and clear-sighted mind, is said to have addressed the chiefs as follows: "My lords and brethren, leave all responsibility in this matter to me; for with the help of God, I will find a fitting remedy for this malady." Then the conference of leaders broke up and each returned to his own camp.

As the shades of evening began to come on apace and throughout the camp the usual preparations for dinner were in progress,

---

1 The passage refers to damage done by an influx of enemy spies; "Bohemond" is Bohemond I of Antioch (c. 1054–1111), one of the leaders of the First Crusade.

Bohemond, mindful of his promise, caused certain Turkish prisoners to be brought forth. He handed them over to the headsman with orders that they be strangled. He then had a huge fire built as if preparing dinner and directed that the bodies, after being prepared with care, should be roasted. His people were instructed that if any question arose about the meaning of such a meal, they were to answer that thenceforward, by decision of the chiefs, the bodies of all enemies or spies seized should furnish meat for the tables of the leaders and the people in the same fashion.

The news that these measures were being taken in Bohemond's camp spread through the army. All the members of the expeditions ran thither in wonder at the novelty of the idea. The spies who were at that time in the camp were terrified. They believed that what was rumored to have been decreed was actually so, and without pretense, and drew their own conclusions from it. Apprehending that a similar fate might overtake them also, they left the camp at once and returned to their own land. To the chiefs who had sent them they reported that this people surpassed every other nation and even beasts in cruelty. To seize the cities and castles of their enemy, together with all property of every description, to cast into prison, to torture cruelly in enemy fashion, or even to kill did not satisfy them. These Christians must also fill their stomachs with the flesh of their enemies and feast on the fat of their foes.

Such were the rumors which penetrated to the farthest parts of the Orient and terrified, not merely neighboring nations, but even those far remote. The entire city of Antioch trembled also, frightened at the novelty and cruelty of the measure. Thus the zealous efforts of Bohemond brought about the elimination of this pest of spies, and our plans were less often divulged to the enemy.

j. From the *Chanson d'Antioch* (c. 1200), in Carol Sweetenham and Susan Edgington, *The Chanson D'Antioche: An Old-French Account of the First Crusade*, Crusade Texts in Translation (Ashgate, 2011), pp. 200–02

Meanwhile back in the Christian army scarcity was the order of the day. There was little if any food and morale was low. Lord Peter the Hermit was in his tent when the King of the Tafurs came to see him, accompanied by more than a thousand of his followers. All of them had stomachs swollen by hunger. "My lord," they said, "for holy charity's sake tell us what to do. In truth, we are dying of hunger and deprivation." Lord Peter replied: "That is because you cannot bring yourselves to do what needs to be done. Go and fetch those [dead] Turks lying over there on the battlefield. They would taste perfectly all right if you cooked and seasoned them properly." The King of the Tafurs said, "You're right, you know." He left Peter's tent and had his beggar army summoned: when all assembled there were more than ten thousand. They flayed the Turks, cutting off the skin, then boiled and roasted the flesh; they ate their fill, although there was no bread to go with it. The pagans were absolutely terrified. Alerted by the smell of meat cooking, they all hung over the walls. The beggars had an audience of twenty thousand pagans, every last Turk sobbing and heartbroken as they watched their own people being eaten. "Alas Lord Mohammed! This is appallingly cruel behaviour! Make sure you take vengeance on those who have put you to such shame and insulted you beyond belief by eating your own people. These are not Frenchmen—they are living devils! May Mohammed curse them and their Christian religion! If that is the sort of thing they are capable of, we shall be humiliated and defeated."

Now the King of the Tafurs along with his numerous companions set to work with a will. They used their sharp keen knives to skin the Turks down on the battlefields; they carved them into joints in full view of the pagans and boiled or barbecued them till they were done to a turn. Then they gobbled them eagerly without bread or any seasoning, saying to each other: "This is absolutely delicious—much better than pork or roast gammon. More fool anyone who dies among this kind of plenty." The King and his barons ate to their hearts' content. The smell of roast Turk was so strong that the cry went up all over Antioch: the Franks were eating the Turks they had killed. The infidels crowded up onto the ramparts, while the walls were completely full even of Saracen women. Garsion went up to the highest windows with his son Sansadoine and his nephew Ysoré; there must have been a good thousand infidels, both young and bearded with age. Garsion addressed them: "In the name of Mohammed, look! See how these devils are eating our own people." The King of the Tafurs looked up at the assembled infidels, including large numbers of women and girls. He called all his followers together and marched them off to the communal graves. They exhumed the bodies and carried them all up onto a hill; they flung the decomposing ones into the Orontes and skinned the others, hanging the meat to dry in the wind. Count Robert came up to them with Bohemond and Tancred, the highly esteemed duke of Bouillon, Count Hugh of Vermandois and the noble and sagacious bishop of Le Puy; all the commanders without exception accompanied them, but every last one in armour and carrying weapons. They all came to a halt in front of the King of the Tafurs and asked him jocularly: "How's it going?" "In faith," replied the King, "I must say I feel very well fed. There is plenty to eat though I wouldn't say no to a drink to wash it down." "Certainly," said the duke of Bouillon, "have a drink." He had a bottle of good wine from his own private supply presented. The King of the Tafurs had a swig and passed it round. Meanwhile Garsion was leaning over the palace balconies. He called to Bohemond and Count Hugh by name to get their attention. "My lord," said Garsion, "you have been very poorly advised in having our dead flayed and exhumed. By Mohammed, you know this is terrible behaviour." "My lord," replied Bohemond, "none of this can be laid at our door. We did not order it and it wasn't on our initiative. The responsibility lies with the King of the Tafurs, their leader. They are a ferocious people who detest you: as far as they're concerned Turkish flesh tastes better than spiced peacock. The King of the Tafurs fears nobody."

2. Religious Cannibalism

[As is still the case today, in the Middle Ages the Eucharist was central to the religious belief system of the Catholic Church. At a crucial moment in every Mass (the consecration), the words of a priest transformed a thin wafer of bread and a cup of wine into the literal body and blood of Christ. The Eucharist would then be consumed, in a sacrament known as Communion, either by the priest and the members of the congregation, or—more often, except on Easter—by the priest on behalf of the congregation. Though this transformation was ordinarily an invisible one, the doctrine of transubstantiation and ritual of Communion brought Christian believers into direct contact with their God, and bound them together with one another. In *RCL*, for example, Heather Blurton has noted that in the case of Cassodorien, "Willingness to participate in eating a body—in this case the body of Christ—is the litmus test for belonging to the community" (124). Stories of miracles involving the Eucharist, often designed to prove Christ's real presence in the ceremony, proliferated from the late twelfth century and often literalized the sacrifice of Christ and the cannibalism implicit in Communion (see Rubin).]

a. From Robert Mannyng, *Handlyng Synne* (early fourteenth century), edited by Frederick J. Furnivall, EETS o.s. 119 and 123 (Kegan Paul et al., 1901), lines 9999–10074; translated by Katherine Terrell

There was a man of religion, famous for giving alms. But because the devil wanted to destroy him, he didn't believe in the sacrament[1] and said that it was not Jesus, who was conceived through virtue, and the bread that was raised at the consecration was not Jesus. And although he performed the service, he didn't believe it.

He told this tale to two abbots, who wrote the tale down: it ought to be told to everyone who is against Christendom, until it is proven by the clergy whether it be faith or heresy.

These abbots showed him the right way with all of the examples they could tell, and he said that it was a lie, unless he saw it with his own eyes. "Make it so that I can see it, and then I will believe that it may be so." These abbots prayed for seven whole nights that God would show him, though His power, the flesh and blood on the altar, to confirm his pure belief; and he himself especially prayed that God would show him in the body. "Lord," he said, "You shouldn't be angry with me for any misbelief, but show the very truth that You are the sacrament of the Mass, so that I may make others certain when I have seen You with my eyes!" The abbots lay in prayer until all seven nights had passed; on the seventh day, they came to the church, and took the other man with them. A seat was prepared for the three of them to behold the sacred mystery of the Holy Sacrament, which was shown in their presence. Between them sat this same man of whom the story first told.

When the Eucharist was laid on the altar, and the priest had said the words, all three thought that truly, before the priest, there lay a living child in actual form of flesh and blood; this the three saw where they stood. When the priest should divide the sacrament, an angel was sent down from heaven, and sacrificed the child right there; as the priest divided it, the angel cut it apart. The blood of that child, both God and man, ran into the chalice.[2]

This man hurried as quickly as possible to partake of the Eucharist, so as to be full. He thought the priest brought morsels of the newly-slain child on the paten,[3] and offered him a morsel

---

1 The Eucharist.
2 The wine cup used during the Eucharist.
3 The plate used to hold the bread during the Eucharist.

of the flesh with all of the fresh blood on it. Then he began to cry, with a loud voice, "Mercy! God's Son of Heaven! The bread that I saw lie on the altar, it is Your Body: I see it with my eyes! Through the sacrament the bread is all turned into flesh and blood: this I believe, and ever I shall, for truly we see it all."

When he and they were all certain, the form of the bread changed again: he partook of the sacrament like the others, and was a good man forevermore. And all others will be better who hear this tale, or read these words.

b. From "On the Feast of Corpus Christi" (late fourteenth century), in *The Minor Poems of the Vernon Manuscript*, edited by Carl Horstmann, EETS o.s. 117 (Kegan Paul et al., 1901), pp. 174–77; lines 129–207; translated by Katherine Terrell

["On the Feast of Corpus Christi" is a late fourteenth-century poem based on earlier versions, found in the Vernon Manuscript (Bodleian Library, MS. Eng. Poet. a. 1).]

One time a Jew and a Christian man traveled together. And along the way, as was proper, the Christian man heard the bells ring for Mass. The Christian man said, "Wait for me here, while I go to my prayers!" The Christian man went into the church, and the Jew began to grumble, because he thought his companion was spending too long at Mass. The Jew rose up and went forth into the church, to observe. Then he saw at the altar the priest hold a beautiful child over his head, badly wounded in hands and feet. Moreover, he saw that there was no woman or man in all the church who didn't kneel and hold up their hands; and from that child he saw another just like it fly to each person, and come to rest between their hands. The Jew stayed until the priest consumed the Eucharist: then he saw him eat the child that he held between his hands, and the Jew thought that everyone in the church with him did, also. The Jew was frightened and concealed himself where his companion had told him to wait, and said to himself, "Christian men have a grisly life!"

After the Mass, the Christian man came to the room where the Jew was. The Jew asked, "How are you?" The Christian man said, "Better than you; because I have seen my God, the way seems easier to me." The Jew said, "By my skull, you ought to have a full belly! Had I eaten so much, I wouldn't want any food for three days." "Truly," said the Christian man, "Today I've not had so much as a sight of any earthly kind of food that my mouth might eat." "Let be! I saw with my two eyes how you and the others each held a bloody child, and afterwards you ate it, I won't lie: wherefore I say that your religion is not good." The Christian man began to get angry at his words: "You lie, Jew! You are hateful to me. Your religion is false, and so are you. You won't believe anything but what you see. Therefore I'll go on alone; I won't keep company with you anymore." The Jew said, "Fellow, don't get upset because I tell you what I saw and thought, but tell me some other proof, whereby I might believe." "This is the reason," said the Christian man, "that God will not allow you to see with your eyes the sacrament that is so secret: how His flesh is hidden from us Christians within the bread. Because your kin made Him die, therefore you see Him all bloody." "Fellow," said the Jew then, "Help me to become a Christian man, for I had rather be christened than to ever see such a sight again." Then the Jew was christened—and others, too—because of the miracle that happened there. What better proof would men ask of this bread that is God's flesh, of which each part is entirely God?

3. Literary Cannibalism

a. From Geoffrey of Monmouth, *The History of the Kings of Britain* (c. 1138), edited and translated by Michael Faletra (Broadview, 2008), pp. 207–08

[Geoffrey of Monmouth's Latin *History* was one of the most popular texts of the Middle Ages. Largely fictional, it purported to tell the history of Britain from its origins to the seventh century CE. This selection concerns the British king Cadwallo, who— like Richard—inadvertently accepts a cannibalistic meal and is thereby healed of an illness. Unlike in *RCL*, however, the flesh that heals Cadwallo (in a clear echo of the Eucharist) is lovingly sacrificed.[1]]

Cadwallo then decided to go to King Solomon of the Armorican Britons to ask for counsel and support in returning to his own kingdom. But when he turned his sails toward Armorica, such mighty storms blew up unexpectedly that his men's ships were all scattered in a short space of time, no two remaining together. The helmsman of the king's ship was then seized with such a great fear that he let the rudder go and let Fortune take the ship

---

1 For analysis of this episode, see Heng, *Empire* 52–61.

where it would. In constant peril of death all night long, the ship was tossed back and forth by the oncoming waves. At dawn on the next day, they landed on the island known as Guernsey, and, with great effort, made it ashore. Grief and anger over the loss of his companions constantly afflicted Cadwallo's thoughts, such that for three days and nights he refused to eat and lay ill in bed. Then, at sunrise on the fourth day, a great desire to eat meat came upon him, and he called Brian to him and explained what he desired. So Brian took up his quiver and bow and set off across the island, hoping to catch some kind of wild beast. However, although he traversed the entire island, he was unable to find what he was looking for, and was deeply concerned at not being able to fulfill his lord's desire. Indeed, he feared that the king's illness might lead to death if he were unable to satisfy his appetite. Then he had a new idea: he sliced a piece of flesh from his own thigh, set up a spit, and roasted it, presenting it to the king as venison. Cadwallo, thinking it to be the flesh of a beast, ate it and began to feel better, marveling that he had never before tasted meat of such a sweet flavor. Once his appetite was sated, he became much more merry and cheerful, and within three days his health was completely restored.

b. From *The Alliterative Morte Arthure* (late fourteenth century), edited by Edmund Brock, EETS 8 (Trübner, 1865), lines 941–1103; translated by Katherine Terrell

[*The Alliterative Morte Arthure*, a tale of King Arthur's exploits and ultimate downfall, is widely considered one of the masterpieces of fourteenth-century poetry. Written in alliterative metre (which is based on patterns of stress and alliteration rather than rhyme), it is ultimately based upon the *History* of Geoffrey of Monmouth, who originated much of the Arthurian tradition—including this tale of Arthur's battle with a cannibalistic giant on Mont Saint Michel. While the giant's cannibalism is more typical than Richard's in its overt monstrousness, he blends civilized dining habits with monstrous aberration in a way that is reminiscent of *RCL*.]

The king climbs the crag   with chasms quite high,
To the crest of the cliff   he climbs aloft,
Casts up his visor   and keenly he looks,
Caught of the cold wind   to comfort himself.
Two fires he finds,   flaming full high: 945
The fourth of a furlong   between them he walks;
The way by the waterfalls   he wanders alone,
To learn of the warlock,   where that he dwells.
He fares to the first fire,   and even there he finds
A weary woeful widow   wringing her hands,   950
And groaning on a grave   with grisly tears,
Newly made in a mound,   since midday it seemed,
He saluted that sorrowful one   with suitable words
And asked about the fiend   fairly thereafter.
Then this woeful wife   woefully him greets,   955
Clambered up on her knees   and clasped her hands,
Said, "sorrowful sir,   you speak too loud!
Were the warlock aware,   he would war on us all!
Cursed may be the carl   that carried off thy wit,
That would have thee wander   in these wild lakes!   960
I warn thee, for worship,   you wish for sorrow!
Whither bound thee, bloke?   Unblessed you seem.
Scheme you to strike him   with thy sword rich?
Were you wittier than Wade   or Wawain either,
You win no worship,   I warn thee before.   965
You signed yourself unsecurely   to seek these mountains,
Six such as you would be too simple   to assemble with him alone,
For, if you see him with sight,   thy heart will not serve
To sign you securely,   he seems so huge.
You are fine and fair,   and in thy first flower,   970
But you are fated to fall, by my faith,   and that afflicts me.
Were fifty such as you on a field   or on a fair earth,
The fellow would with his fist   fell you at once!
Look! Here lies the duchess dear   (today was she taken),
Dead deep underground,   down in the earth.   975
He has murdered this mild one;   I know not what it meant.
Without mercy on earth;   I know not what it meant.
He has forced and defiled her,   and left her fated to die;
He slew her savagely   and slit her to the navel.
And here I have embalmed her   and buried her thereafter.   980
For dole of the defenseless   I may never feel delight.
Of all the friends she had,   none followed after
But I, her foster-mother   of fifteen winters.

To travel from this hilltop　try will I never,
But here be found in field　till I am fated to die." 　985
Then answers Sir Arthur　to that old wife,
"I am come from the conqueror,　courteous and noble,
As one of the noblest　of Arthur's knights,
Messenger to this manure,　for amendment of the people,
To meet with this master man　that this mountain holds, 　990
To treat with this tyrant　for treasure of lands
And take truce for a time,　till better may tide."
"But these words are but waste,"　quoth the wife then,
"For both land and territory　he cares little or less;
Of rents of red gold　reckons he never, 　995
For he will live outside the law,　as himself thinks,
Without license of leader,　as a lord on his own.
But he has a kirtle on,　kept for himself,
That was spun in Spain　by special ladies,
And after sewn in Greece　very skillfully together. 　1000
It is hidden all with hair,　wholly all over,
And bordered with the beards　of burly kings,
Curled and combed　so that men may conceive
Each king by his color,　in the country where he dwells.
Here the revenues he robs　of fifteen realms, 　1005
For every Easter eve,　however it happens,
They send it to him certainly,　for peace among the people,
Securely at that season,　with certain knights.
And he has asked Arthur　all these seven winters:
Therefore inhabits he here,　to horrify his people 　1010
Till the Britons' king　has burnished his lips
And sent his beard to that bold one　with his best barons.
Unless you have brought that beard,　betake thee no further.
For it is a bootless burden　you bring, otherwise.
For he has more treasure　to take when he likes 　1015
Than ever Arthur owned　or any of his elders.
If you have brought the beard　he will be more blithe
Than if you gave him Burgundy　or Great Britain.
But look now, for charity,　that you chasten your lips,
That no words escape thee,　whatever happens. 　1020
Look that thy present be prepared　and press him but little,
For he sits at his supper;　he will be soon displeased.
And then agree to my advice　and remove thy armor,
And kneel in thy kirtle　and call him thy lord.
He sups all this season　with seven boy children, 　1025
Chopped in a charger　of chalk-white silver,

With sauce and seasoning   of precious spices,
And piment quite plenteous   of Portuguese wine.
Three mournful maidens   revolve his spits,
And abide his bedtime,   his bidding to work;   1030
Four such would be fated to die   within four hours
Before he was filled with the filth   for which his flesh yearns."
"Yes, I have brought the beard,"   said he, "I like it the better.
I will betake me there,   and bear it myself;
And, dear, if you will demonstrate   where that devil dwells, 1035
I shall allow thee and I our lives,   our Lord so help me!"
"Fare fast to the fire,"   she quoth, "that flames so high,
There that fiend fills him,   find him when thee likes.
But you must seek more south,   sideways a little,
For he will have sent   himself six long miles."   1040
The source of the smoke   he sought straightaway,
Signed himself securely   with certain words,
Till sideways he reached   the sight of the man.
How unseemly the sot sat,   supping all alone!
He lay leaning at length,   lodging foully,   1045
The thigh of a man's leg   lifted up by the haunch,
His back and his buttocks   and his broad loins
He warms at the bonfire,   and breechless he seemed.
There were roasts very rude,   and pitiful roasts,
Human beings and beasts   both skewered together,   1050
A cauldron crammed full   of christened children,
Some spitted as meats,   and maidens turned them.
And then this comely king,   because of his people,
His heart bleeds for grief   on the ground where he stands!
Then he fastens on his shield,   shrinks no longer,   1055
Brandishes his broad sword   by the bright hilt,
Rushes toward that ruffian   right with a resolute will
And hastily hails that hulk   with haughty words:
"Now, all-wielding God   that we all worship,
Give thee sorrow and sadness,   sot, where you lie,   1060
For the foulest fiend   that ever was formed!
Foully you feed yourself!   The Fiend have thy soul!
Here is a curry unclean,   carl, by my truth!
Chaff of all creatures,   you cursed wretch!
Because you have killed   these christened children,   1065
Have made martyrs,   and brought out of life
Those that here are brochetted   and broken with your hands,
I shall render thy reward   as thou have richly deserved,
Through the might of St. Michael   who maintains this mount!

And for this fair lady   that you have left fated to die   1070
And thus forced on field   for filth of thyself,
Prepare thee now, dog-son,   the devil have thy soul!
For you shall die this day,   through dominance of my hands!"
Then grieved the glutton,   and glared horribly,
He grinned as a greyhound   with grisly rusks,   1075
He gaped, he groaned   with grudging looks,
For grief of the good king   who greets him with anger.
His hair and his tresses   were all tangled together
And slobber slid from his face   a half foot long.
His face and his forehead,   all over his front,   1080
Was like the skin of a frog,   and freckled it seemed.
He was hook-nosed like a hawk,   with a grey-hued beard,
And haired to the eye-holes   with hanging brows.
Harsh as a hound-fish,   to whoever looks hard,
Was the hide of that hulk,   wholly all over!   1085
Ears had he, full huge,   and ugly to show,
With eyes quite baleful,   and burning, in truth.
Flat-mouthed as a flounder,   with sneering lips,
And the flesh in his foreteeth   foul as a bear's.
His beard was fierce and black,   that reached to his breast,   1090
Corpulent as a dolphin,   with carcass quite huge,
And quivered all the flesh   in his foul lips:
Each twisted like an outlaw,   it flared out at once.
Bullnecked was that bloke,   and broad in the shoulders,
Badger-breasted like a boar,   with very large bristles,   1095
Rude arms like an oak   with rugged sides,
Limbs and loins very loathsome,   believe you for truth,
Shovel-footed was that scoundrel,   and stumbling he seemed,
With unshapely shanks   shoving together,
Thighs thick as a monster,   and thicker in the haunch,   1100
Grown fat as a boar,   very grisly he looks!
Whoever truly measures   the length of that lad
From the face to the foot   would find five fathoms long!

Appendix D: Richard I and the Third Crusade

1. Richard's Character

a. From *The Itinerarium Peregrinorum et Gesta Regis Ricardi* (c. 1220), in Helen J. Nicholson, editor and translator, *The Chronicle of the Third Crusade: The Itinerarium Peregrinorum et Gesta Regis Ricardi*, Crusade Texts in Translation (Ashgate, 1997), p. 146

The Governor of the Ages had conferred on him a generous character and endowed him with virtues which seemed rather to belong to an earlier age. In this present age, when the world is growing old, these virtues hardly appear in anyone as if everyone were like empty husks; and so they are wonderful and memorable in the few people where they do appear. King Richard had the valour of Hector, the heroism of Achilles; he was not inferior to Alexander, nor less valiant than Roland. No, he easily surpassed in many respects the most praiseworthy figures of our times. Like another Titus, "his right hand scattered help." Also, which is very unusual for one so renowned as a knight, Nestor's tongue and Ulysses' wisdom enabled him to excel others in every undertaking, both in speaking and acting. His skill and experience in action equaled his desire for it; his desire did not betray a lack of skill or experience.[1]

If anyone perhaps may think that he could be accused of rash actions, you should know that he had an unconquerable spirit, could not bear insult or injury, and his innate noble spirit compelled him to seek his due rights. So he may not unreasonably be excused. Success had made him better able to do everything, since "Fortune favors the brave" [Virgil, *Aeneid*, Bk. 10 v. 284].

---

1 The Greek Achilles and Trojan Hector were famed heroes of the Trojan War; the Macedonian king Alexander the Great became a romance hero, as did Roland, a military leader under Charlemagne. The Roman emperor Titus was best known for ending a Jewish rebellion by capturing Jerusalem in 70 CE. The Greek Nestor was praised for his wisdom, while his fellow Greek Ulysses (Odysseus) was famed for his cleverness, in the Trojan War and its aftermath.

So, although Fortune works her will as she pleases, King Richard "could not be overwhelmed by the hostile waves of life" [Horace, *Epistolae*, Bk. 1 no. 2 v. 22].

He was tall, of elegant build; the colour of his hair was between red and gold; his limbs were supple and straight. He had quite long arms, which were particularly convenient for drawing a sword and wielding it most effectively. His long legs matched the arrangement of his whole body. With the not insignificant addition of his suitable character and habits, his was a figure worthy to govern.

He gained the greatest praise not so much for his noble birth as for the virtues which adorned him. But why should I labour to extol such a great man with immense praises? "He does not need another to commend him, although he has deserved it fully; fame accompanies the deed." He far excelled others both in his good character and in physical strength. He was memorable for his military power; his magnificent deeds overshadowed all others, no matter how glorious. He would have been thought really fortunate—speaking in human terms—if he had not had rivals who were jealous of his glorious deeds. The sole reason for their hatred was his greatness; because you will never torture the envious more than by serving virtue.

2. Richard in Sicily

[This section comprises two excerpts from the *Chronicle* of Roger of Howden, who was a parson and royal clerk who served both Henry II and Richard I and who accompanied Richard on crusade between August 1190 and August 1191; his account is therefore of particular value as a source for that year. The first selection below concerns the siege of Messina and attests to the uneasy relationship between Richard and King Philip of France. The second highlights Richard's religious devotion, something that *RCL* shows in a distinctly different way.]

a. Roger of Howden, "The Siege of Messina" (c. 1200), in *The Annals of Roger de Hoveden*, translated by Henry T. Riley, 2 vols. (H.G. Bohn, 1853), vol. 2, pp. 158–59

When the citizens of Messina saw that the king of England had placed knights and men-at-arms with his sister in the castle of Le Baniare, and had taken possession of the monastery of the Griffons, they had suspicion of him, believing that he would seize the whole of the island, if he could: consequently they were disposed to be easily excited against him. Accordingly, on the third day of October, a disagreement arose between the army of the king of England and the citizens of Messina, and to such a pitch did the exasperation on both sides increase, that the citizens shut the gates of the city, and, putting on their arms, mounted the walls. On the king's troops perceiving this, they made a vigorous attack on the city gates: but our lord the king rode to and fro through the army on a steed of the greatest swiftness, beating back with a staff such of his men as he could reach, trying to restrain them from making the attack. However, he was unable so to do: and at last returned to his lodging, where, putting on his armour, he went out again to put an end to the affray if he possibly could. He then embarked in a boat and repaired to the palace of king Tancred, to consult with the king of France on the affair that had taken place. In the meantime, however, through the mediation of the elders of the city, the discord was allayed: and arms being laid down on both sides, each party returned home.

On the ninth day of October there came to the king of England [many dignitaries from the King of Sicily, as well as King Philip of France], for the purpose of making peace between them and the king of England.

Now when the terms of peace had been for some time under consideration, and they had nearly come to a conclusion thereon, the citizens of Messina, collecting in great multitudes, proceeded to the mountains, and waited in readiness, treacherously to fall upon the king of England; while others made an attack on the lodging of Hugh Le Brun. On this, their shouts, which were far from subdued, came to the ears of the king of England, who immediately leaving the conference with the king of France and the other persons above-named, ordered all his men to put on their armour, and he, with a few followers, climbed a steep hill, which no one could have supposed he could possibly have done, and having, with great difficulty, reached the top of the hill, there took to flight with all possible speed and re-entered the city, the king pursuing them with the edge of the sword.

On this, the knights and men-at-arms of the king of England bravely attacked the citizens at the gates and walls of the city, and, suffering many hard blows from stones, at one moment effected an entrance into the city gates, while at another they were driven out. Here there were slain five knights of the king of England's people, and twenty men-at-arms, while the King of France was looking on, and giving them no assistance, although they were of one brotherhood with him in the pilgrimage. As for the king of France, he and his people entered the city, and made their way through them in perfect safety.

However, the men of the king of England at last exercised their strength with such effect, that by main force they burst open the city gates and mounted the walls in all directions, and so having entered the city, they took possession thereof, and immediately hoisted the banners of the king of England on the fortifications around the walls. At this the king of France was greatly indignant, and demanded that the banners of the king of England should be lowered, and his own set up; this, however, the king of England would not permit, but still, that the wishes of the king of France might be satisfied, he lowered his own banners and gave the city into the charge of the knights Hospitallers, and the Templars, until everything should have been complied with that he demanded of Tancred king of Sicily.

b. Roger of Howden, "Richard Does Penance" (c. 1200), in *The Annals of Roger de Hoveden*, translated by Henry T. Riley, 2 vols. (H.G. Bohn, 1853), vol. 2, pp. 176–77

In the same year [1190] Richard, King of England, the Divine grace inspiring him thereto, being sensible of the filthiness of his life, after due contrition of heart, having called together all the archbishops who were with him at Messina, in the chapel of Reginald de Moyae, fell naked at their feet, and did not hesitate to confess to God, in their presence, the filthiness of his life. For the thorns of lustfulness had departed from his head, and it was not the hand of man who rooted them out, but God, the Father of Mercies, who wisheth not for the death of a sinner, but rather that he may turn from his wickedness and live, looked upon him with the eyes of mercy and gave him a heart to repent, and called him to repentance, for he received the penance imposed by the bishops before named, and from that hour forward became a man who feared God, and left what was evil and did what was good. O happy the man who so falls as to rise with greater strength still! O happy the man who after repentance does not relapse into faultiness and a course of ruin!

3. Richard at Acre

a. Letter from Richard I to William Longchamp, Bishop of Ely (1191), edited and translated by Peter Edbury, in *The Conquest of*

Jerusalem and the Third Crusade: Sources in Translation, Crusade Texts in Translation (Ashgate, 1998), pp. 178–79

[In this letter, Richard details his campaign in Cyprus and his capture of Acre, as well as his disappointment with the subsequent departure of King Philip of France. After the capture of Acre, in the summer of 1191, Philip had had enough of crusading and left for France. Curiously, given the *RCL* poet's predilection for denigrating Philip, in the *a* version of the poem he does not desert the Crusade until considerably later: line 5918.]

Richard, King of England etc., to his justiciar in England, greetings.

You know that we have suffered much from illness since we undertook our journey, but by the mercy of God we are restored to full health. Enough has been told you of how divine mercy added to our honor at Messina. Then, as we were continuing our pilgrimage journey, we were diverted to Cyprus where we hoped to find the refuge of those of our number who had been shipwrecked. But the tyrant, who, revering neither God nor man, has usurped the name of Emperor, hurriedly brought a strongly armed force to bar us from the port. He robbed and despoiled as many as possible of our men who had suffered wreck and imprisoned those dying of hunger. Not unnaturally we were spurred to revenge. We did battle with our enemy and, thanks to divine assistance, obtained a speedy victory. Defeated and fettered, we hold him together with his only daughter. We have subjected to ourselves the whole island of Cyprus with all its strong points. Then, happy and rejoicing, we entered the port of Acre, and not long after the arrival of the king of France and ourselves we recovered the city of Acre with the Holy Cross and took 1700 captives. But within 15 days the king of France left us to return to his own land. We, however, place the love of God and his honor above our own and above the acquisition of many regions. We shall restore the land of Syria to its original condition as quickly as possible, and only then shall we return to our lands. But you may know for certain that we shall set sail next Lent. We order you to attend faithfully to furthering our affairs.

Witnessed by myself at Acre, on the sixth day of August (1191).

b. From Richard of Devizes, *The Chronicle of Richard of Devizes of the Time of King Richard the First* (c. 1192), edited by John T. Appleby (Nelson and Sons, 1963), pp. 42–45

[The account of the late-twelfth-century English chronicler Richard of Devizes shares with the author of *RCL* esteem for Richard and disdain for the French.]

The king of the English, who would brook no delay, on the third day of his coming to the siege had his wooden castle that had been built in Sicily and was called "The Griffon-Killer" built and set up. Before dawn on the fourth day the machine stood against the walls of Acre, and because of its great height it overlooked the city beneath it. As soon as the sun rose, the bowmen upon it kept up an unceasing rain of arrows on the Turks and Thracians. The stone-throwers, skillfully placed, broke down the walls by repeated shots. Even more effective than these were the miners, who opened a way for themselves underground and dug under the foundations of the walls. Ladders also were placed against the walls, and the troops on the ramparts kept watch for an entry. The king himself ran about through the ranks, ordering, exhorting, and inspiring, and he was thus everywhere beside each man, so that to him alone might be ascribed what each man did.

Even the king of the French himself did not act slothfully, but he also made as much of an assault as he could on a tower of the city called the Accursed Tower.

At that time the most illustrious men Karakush and Meshtub, the most powerful princes of the infidels after Saladin, ruled over the besieged city. After a struggle of several days, they promised, through interpreters, to surrender the city and pay ransom. The king of the English wanted to conquer these despairing men by force, and he wanted the vanquished to pay with their heads for the freeing of their bodies. Through the agency of the king of the French, however, they were granted their lives and the safety of their bodies, on condition that after the surrender of the city and of everything they had, the Lord's Cross would be given back.

All the most excellent and well-born fighting men of the infidels were then in Acre and they were nine thousand in number. Many of them, by swallowing many gold pieces, made purses of their bellies, for they knew in advance that whatever anyone might have of any value would be counted as an offense and would lead him, if he resisted, to the gallows and be booty for the victors. All of them therefore came out before the kings completely defenseless and with no money outside their skins and were put into safekeeping. The kings entered the city with triumphant banners and divided it with its furnishing in half between themselves and their armies, except only the bishop's seat, which its bishop received by common consent. The captives also were divided. Meshtub fell by lot to the king of the English, and Karakush, like a drop of cold water, fell into the burning mouth of the thirsty Philip, King of the French.

c. Two Accounts of the Killing of Hostages at Acre

[These two accounts, from eyewitnesses on each side of the conflict, record the failure of negotiations between Richard and Saladin in August of 1191 and the slaughter of a large number of Muslim hostages. These events are covered in *RCL*—with a vastly inflated number of hostages—in lines 3699–3756.]

i. From Bahā' al-Dīn Ibn Shaddād, *The Rare and Excellent History of Saladin, or al-Nawādir al-Sultāniyya wa'l-Mahāsin al-Yūsufiyya* (c. 1198–1215), translated by D.S. Richards, Crusade Texts in Translation (Ashgate, 2002), pp. 164–65

There was a steady stream of envoys concerning the drawing up and implementation of the agreement until the enemy received what they sought, the prisoners and the money specified for that term. In all it was the Holy Cross, 100,000 dinars, and 1,600 prisoners. They sent their trusted men who testified to everything, apart from the prisoners to be specified on their side, for they had not finished selecting and naming them so that they could be fetched. They kept procrastinating and wasting time until the first term elapsed, which it did on 18 Rajab [11 August]. At that time they sent demanding the prisoners. The sultan said to them, "Either you send our men to us and you receive what has been specified for this term, while we give you hostages for the rest which you will get in the remaining terms or you give us hostages for what we hand over to you until you send our men out to us." They replied, "We shall do none of that, but do you deliver to us what this term demands and be satisfied with our word, until we hand over your men to you." The sultan refused this, as he knew that, if they received the money, the Cross and the prisoners, while they still had our men, he could not be sure that they would not act treacherously and then the loss for Islam would be so great that it could hardly be repaired [...]

When the king of England saw that the sultan hesitated to hand over the money, the prisoners and the Cross, he dealt treacherously toward the Muslim prisoners. He had made terms with them and had received the surrender of the city on condition that they would be guaranteed their lives come what may and that, if the sultan delivered what was agreed, he would free them together with their possessions, children, and women folk, but that, if the sultan refused to do so, he would reduce them to slavery and captivity. The accursed man deceived them and revealed what he had hidden in his heart. He carried out what, according to the subsequent reports of his co-religionists, he had intended to do after taking the money and the prisoners. He and all the Frankish forces, horse and foot, marched out at the time of the afternoon prayer on Tuesday 27 Rajab [20 August] and came to the wells beneath the Tell al-'Ayyadiyya. They brought their tents forward as far as that and then moved on into the middle of the plain between Tell Kaysan and al-'Ayyadiyya. Our advance guard had withdrawn to Tell Kaysan when the Franks moved their tents forward to Tell al-'Ayyadiyya. The enemy then brought out the Muslim prisoners for whom God had decreed martyrdom, about 3,000 bound in ropes. Then as one man they charged them and with stabbings and blows with the sword they slew them in cold blood, while the Muslims' advance guard watched, not knowing what to do because they were at some distance from them. The Muslims had already sent to the sultan and informed him of the enemy's move and their new position and he had sent reinforcements. When the enemy had finished, the Muslims attacked them and a great battle ensued, in which men were killed and wounded on both sides. It continued until nightfall.

In the morning the Muslims investigated what had happened, found the martyrs where they had fallen and were able to recognize some of them. Great sorrow and distress overwhelmed them for the enemy had spared only men of standing and position or someone strong and able-bodied to labor on their building works. Various reasons were given for this massacre. It was said they had killed them in revenge for their men who had been killed or that the king of England had decided to march to Ascalon to take control of it and did not think it wise to leave that number in his rear. God knows best.

ii. From Ambroise, *The History of the Holy War: Ambroise's Estoire De La Guerre Sainte* (c. 1194–99), translated by Marianne Ailes (Boydell, 2003), pp. 107–08

The hostages who had been held at Tyre arrived. The time set for the fulfillment of the terms passed; two more weeks passed, indeed more than that, from the time when they said they would keep their word to the Christians. In this way the sultan defaulted and in so doing he acted in a false and treacherous manner when he did not redeem or deliver those who were condemned to death. Because of this he lost his renown, which was great, for his name was celebrated in every court of the world. But God, having tolerated him for a time, brings down His enemy and upholds and supports His friend, glorifying and controlling His work. But He would not support and exalt Saladin any more, for whatever he did, resisting and working against the Christians, he accomplished only because it was God's will to work through these means to bring back His people who had gone astray and whom He wished to bring back to His way.

When King Richard knew for sure and realized without doubt that in truth Saladin was only putting him off, he was then very annoyed and displeased that he had not already moved the army on. And when he knew that Saladin would do nothing more for him and that he had no care for those who had defended Acre for him, then was the matter examined at a council where the great men gathered and decided that they would kill most of the Saracens and keep the others, those of high birth, in order to redeem some of their own hostages. Richard, King of England who killed so many Turks in that land, did not wish to worry his head about it any more, but [in order to] bring down the pride of the Turks, disgrace their religion and avenge Christianity, he brought out of the town, in bonds, two thousand and seven hundred people who were all slaughtered. Thus was vengeance taken for the blows and the crossbow bolts. Thanks be to God the Creator.

4. Richard at Jaffa

a. Letter of Richard I, King of England, to N. (1 October 1191), in Malcolm Barber and Keith Bate, translators, *Letters from the East: Crusaders, Pilgrims and Settlers in the 12th–13th Centuries*, Crusade Texts in Translation (Ashgate, 2010), p. 91

[Richard's letter from Jaffa to "N."—as Barber and Bate note, "a standard anonymous initial, which would enable recipients in the royal administration to insert appropriate names"—suggests that "Richard wanted the letter to achieve wide circulation, rather in the manner of ecclesiastical encyclicals" (91). The letter attests to Richard's feelings about Philip's early departure from the Crusade, as well as his esteem for James of Avesnes, who died at Arsuf (and who is probably the Jakes Deneys of lines 5021–5182).]

Richard, by the grace of God King of England, Duke of Normandy and Aquitaine, Count of Angers, to his beloved and faithful N., greetings.

You should know that after the capture of Acre and the departure of the king of France who thus so cravenly abandoned his pilgrimage vow and promises against God's will—to his eternal shame and that of his kingdom—we set out for Jaffa, but on approaching Arsuf we were met and savagely attacked by Saladin and his Saracens. But God had pity on us and we lost nobody that day except James of Avesnes, a great man whose merits had recommended him to the whole Army. He had served God like a pillar in the Christian Army for several years, always ready and devout, a truly religious Christian. Afterwards with God's blessing we reached Jaffa which we fortified with ditches and a wall with the intention of furthering Christian affairs as best we could. On that very day, the vigil of the Nativity of the Blessed Mary, Saladin lost a huge number of his nobles and in his flight, as though bereft of any help or plans, he destroyed the whole of the land of Sulia. Three days before Saladin's route a lance caused us a wound in the left side, but thanks to God's grace it has already healed. Know, however, that with God's grace we hope to regain the holy city of Jerusalem and the Sepulchre of the Lord in less than twenty days after Christmas and then we will return home.

Witnessed by ourselves at Jaffa on 1 October.

b. From Richard of Devizes, *The Chronicle of Richard of Devizes of the Time of King Richard the First* (c. 1192), edited by John T. Appleby (Nelson and Sons, 1963), pp. 73–79

[In the summer of 1192, Richard became seriously ill. This excerpt from the *Chronicle* of Richard of Devizes records Richard's illness, along with the excessive eating habits of the crusaders in the Holy Land and the hunger that results. It then places an extraordinary speech in praise of Richard in the mouth of Safadin, Saladin's brother.]

The king's army grew weaker day by day in the Promised Land, and, in addition to those wounded in battle, many thousands of them died every month from the very great extremes of cold by night and heat by day, coming so close together. As it appeared that everyone was going to die there in any case, each one chose whether he would die in bed or in battle. On the other hand, the pagans' strength increased greatly, for their boldness grew at the Christians' plight and their army had recently been increased by fresh troops from various places. They were accustomed to the climate, the place was their native land, the work was healthful, and the scarcity of food was curative. Amongst our men, on the contrary, what brought an advantage to their foes was a disadvantage to them. If, indeed, our men were on short rations for even one day of the week, they were weakened for seven weeks to come. The common people among the French and English feasted together everyday in a splendid fashion, no matter how great the cost, as long as their money held out, and with all due respect for the French, they ate till they were sick. The traditional custom of the English was always observed, and with proper ceremony they drained their cups to the sound of clarions and the clangour of trumpets. The merchants of the province who brought provisions to the camp, were astonished at these extraordinary ways and could scarcely believe what they saw to be true, that one host of people, and that a small one, should consume three times as much bread and a hundred times as much wine as would sustain several or even countless hosts of pagans. And rightly did the Lord's hand fall upon those who had deserved it. Such hunger followed such gluttony that their teeth scarcely spared their fingers when their hands offered their gullets less than they were accustomed to eating. To these calamities and others, grave and numerous in themselves, was added the much greater misfortune of the king. The king took to his bed, very ill indeed. His fever was continuous, and the physicians whispered of an acute semi-tertian fever. They were the first to give way to despair, and from the king's dwelling dire despair was diffused throughout the camp. Rare was the man amongst those many thousands who did not think of flight, and the supreme confusion of dispersal or surrender would have followed, if Hubert Walter, Bishop of Salisbury, had not quickly called a council.

By earnest pleading he attained this result: an agreement was made that the army would not disperse till a truce had been asked for from Saladin; all the armed men stood in their ranks more stoutly than ever; and, hiding the cowardice of their hearts behind fierce faces, they lyingly declared that they were ready for battle; no one spoke of the king's illness, lest so sorrowful a secret should be spread amongst the enemy. Everyone knew for certain that Saladin feared the onslaught of the whole army less than that of the king alone. If he had known that the king was ill in bed, he would already have pelted the French with ox-dung and have made those choicest drinkers, the

English, drunk with fear. Meanwhile, as was his habit, there came to see the king a certain Safadin, a pagan, Saladin's brother, a man of long military experience, very polished and wise, whom the king's magnanimity and munificence had won over to his friendship and to favoring his side. When the king's servants greeted him with less than their usual warmth and would not let him in to talk with the king, he said through an interpreter: "I realize that you are in great grief, and I know the cause. My friend, your king, is ill, and therefore you close his doors to me." With his cheeks all wet with tears, "O God of the Christians," he said, "if You are God, do not allow such a man, so necessary to Your people, to die so suddenly." He was received into the assembly and spoke thus: "I prophesy truly that if this man should die, things being as they are now, all you Christians will perish, and all this region will be ours on the next day without a struggle. Did we fear that brave king of France who was conquered even before he came to battle? Whatever strength he had brought together in 3 years was destroyed in the brief space of three months. He will never come back here for anything, for we have always held this sign to be true. I do not say this in heat, but calmly—that those whom we find to be cowards at the beginning we find to be ever worse thereafter. But this king, amongst all the princes of the Christian name that the round circle of all the world embraces, alone is worthy of the honour of a leader and the name of the king, for he began his work well, he continued it even better, and if he remains with you a while longer, he will finish it perfectly. It is no new thing for us to fear the English, for this man's father had such fame amongst us that even if he had come into our country unarmed we would all have fled, even though we were armed, for it would be deemed no disgrace to flee from him. That terror to us, the outstanding man of his time, has died, but like a phoenix has risen up again a thousand times better in his son. We knew, even whilst his father was alive, who this Richard was, for all during his father's life we had our observers in those parts who reported to us both the king's deeds and the rise and fall of his sons. His father loved this one above all his brothers because of his uprightness, and chose him rather than his older brothers to rule over his people. Nor was it unknown to us that when he was made duke of Aquitaine he overcame the tyrants of the province, whom none of his ancestors could conquer, with such speedy strength that he became an object of fear to the king of France himself and to all the rulers of the lands around his borders. No one [dared take] to himself anything that was Richard's, but he, on the other hand, was forever extending his boundaries at the expense of his neighbors. We also knew that he did not cease waging war against two of his brothers, one of whom was already crowned king and the other was already count of Brittany, because they have risen up against their blessed father, until he wore them both out and gave them to eternal rest. We even know by name all the cities of your part of the world (I tell you this so that you may marvel all the more), and we also know that the king his father was defeated by their treachery at Le Mans, died at Chinon, and was buried at Fontevrault. I keep silent, but not through ignorance, concerning the one who made himself the author of a death so very welcome to us.

"If this Richard, whom I love as much as I fear, were removed from our midst, how little would we fear and what scant attention would we pay to that youngest son, who sleeps at home in clover! We know that Richard, who, greater even than his father, succeeded to the throne, set forth against us in the very year of his crowning. Even before he set out, the number of his ships and soldiers was not unknown to us.

"We knew, at the very time it was taking place, how speedily he captured Messina, the most strongly fortified city of Sicily, and, although none of us would believe it, nevertheless our fears increased, 'and fame added false fears to true.'

"'His courage, unable to stand still in one place,' proceeded through a boundless region, and everywhere he left signs of his strength [...] I swear to you by the great God that if, after he had become master of Acre, he had immediately led his army to Jerusalem, he would not have found a single one of our people in all the bounds of the Christians' lands. Rather would we have given him inestimable treasure to induce him not to go on and not to persecute us any further. But, thank God, he was burdened with the king of the French and held back by him, like a cat with a hammer tied to its tail. Nevertheless, although we are his rivals, we found nothing in Richard to which we could take exception save his bravery, nothing to hate save his skill at arms. But what glory is there in fighting a sick man? And although this morning I would have wished that he and all of you might receive a death sentence, now you are to be pitied because of your king's misfortune. I shall arrange with my brother either for a perpetual peace for you or, at the least, for a firm and lasting truce. However, until I come back to you, let none of you speak of it to the king lest his illness become worse, for he is of such great and noble heart that even if he were now due to die he would not consent to the transaction unless he saw that his was the better part of the bargain."

He wanted to say more, but his tongue, faltering and stopping through grief, would not carry on to the end. He covered his face with his clenched fists and wept bitterly. The bishop of Salisbury and the closest members of the king's household who were present conferred upon these matters secretly and agreed to what they termed a most hateful and unwanted truce, although they had earlier proposed to buy it at any price. Having shaken hands with them, Safadin, his face expressionless and his grief concealed, went back to Saladin at Jerusalem.

c. "Gift of a Horse" (mid-thirteenth century), in Peter Edbury, editor and translator, *The Conquest of Jerusalem and the Third Crusade: Sources in Translation*, Crusade Texts in Translation (Ashgate, 1998), pp. 117–18

[While the demonic horse of *RCL* is clearly fictional, chronicle accounts do contain several examples of horses that Richard received as gifts from Saladin. Below is one version of the story.[1]]

Some of the Saracens returned to their camp. Saladin demanded to know why they had returned without capturing the castle. They told him that the king of England had come and had relieved it. Saif al-Din, Saladin's brother, asked where the king was. They pointed him out on a small hill with his men. Saif al-Din was concerned with good and honour, and he sent one of his mamluks[2] with a restive horse for him which was in great pain in the mouth. He charged him to say to the king that it was totally unacceptable that a king should be fighting against the Saracens on foot. The king, who was well aware of Saracen malice, realized that the horse was in pain and told the messenger to ride the horse at a gallop. Once he had done so he could see that it was restive. He said to him, "Thank your lord. Take him his horse and say that it is not out of any love between us that he has sent me a restive horse so as to take me." The mamluk returned and took it to his lord and told him that Richard had realized that the horse was restive. Saif al-Din was shamed and ordered the same mamluk to take him another one, more amenable than the first. The king ordered the smith to pull out the horse's canines and incisors. This was done immediately and when the man had extracted them he had a bridle put on it and had someone ride it. The horse was now easy to handle. The king mounted and did many feats of arms.

---

1 See Broughton, *Legends* 100–02, for further analogues.
2 I.e., slaves.

Appendix E: National and Family Legends

[Numerous legends circulated about Richard's family both during and after his lifetime. His mother Eleanor of Aquitaine (who is replaced in *RCL* by the fictitious Cassodorien) was a particular focus of controversy, although as Gerald of Wales attests in the first selection, Richard's inheritance from his father could be seen as equally problematic.]

1. From Gerald of Wales (Giraldus Cambrensis), *On the Instruction of Princes* (c. 1216–23), in *The Church Historians of England*, translated by Joseph Stevenson (Seeleys, 1858), 5.1.224–25

Also, there was a certain Countess of Anjou, of remarkable beauty, but of an unknown nation, whom the count married solely for beauty, who was in the habit of coming very seldom to church, and there manifested very little or no devotion in it; she never remained in the church until the celebration of the secret canon on the Mass, but always went out immediately after the gospel. At length, however, this was remarked with astonishment both by the count and also by others; and when she had come to the church, and was preparing to depart at her usual hour, she saw that she was kept back by four soldiers at the command of the count; and immediately throwing off the robe by which she was held, and leaving there with the rest her two little sons, whom she had with her under the right sleeve of her robe, she took up under her arm the two others, who were standing on the left, and in the sight of all flew out through a lofty window of the church. And so this woman, more fair in face than in faith, having carried off her two children with her, was never afterwards seen there.

Moreover, King Richard was often accustomed to refer to this event; saying that it was no matter of wonder, if coming from such a race, sons should not cease to harass their parents, and brothers to quarrel amongst each other; for he knew that they all had come of the devil, and to the devil they would go. When, therefore, the root was in every way so corrupt, how was it possible that the branches from such a stock could be prosperous or virtuous? [...]

Wherefore it is sufficiently known how the Norman tyrants reigned in the island of which they took possession, not by natural descent or legitimately, but, as it were, by a reversed order of things; for which reason few or none of them departed this life by a praiseworthy end.

2. Legends of Eleanor of Aquitaine

[Richard's mother, Eleanor (1122–1204), was a powerful and controversial figure. Soon after she became Duchess of Aquitaine at age 15, she married King Louis VII of France. She accompanied him on the unsuccessful Second Crusade, and the marriage produced two daughters. However, it was not a happy marriage, and the couple repeatedly sought an annulment, which was granted in 1152 on the grounds of consanguinity (although the lack of a male heir was probably the more important factor). In the same year, Eleanor married Henry, Duke of Normandy and Count of Anjou, who became King of England in 1154. They had eight children, two of whom (Richard and John) became kings of England.

The excerpts below show the development of negative legends about Eleanor, starting within her lifetime with rumours about her activities on crusade and the breakup of her first marriage, and expanding after her death into accusations of adultery and murder.]

a. From John of Salisbury, *Memoirs of the Papal Court* (c. 1164), translated by Marjorie Chibnall (Nelson and Sons, 1956), pp. 52–53

In the Year of Grace 1149 the most Christian King of the Franks reached Antioch, after the destruction of his armies in the east, and was nobly entertained there by Prince Raymond, brother of the late William, Count of Poitiers. He was as it happened the Queen's uncle, and owed the king loyalty, affection, and respect for many reasons. But whilst they remained there to console, heal, and revive the survivors from the wreck of the army, the attentions paid by the prince to the queen, and his constant, indeed almost continuous, conversation with her, aroused the king's suspicions. These were greatly strengthened when the queen wished to remain behind, although the king was preparing to leave, and the prince made every effort to keep her, if the king would give his consent. And when the king made haste to tear her away, she mentioned their kinship, saying it was not lawful for them to remain together as man and wife, since they were related in the fourth and fifth degrees. Even before their departure a rumour to that effect had been heard in France, where the late Bartholomew Bishop of Laon had calculated the degrees of kinship; but it was not certain whether the reckoning was true or false. At this the king was deeply moved; and although he loved the queen almost beyond reason he consented to divorce her if his counsellors and the French nobility would allow it. There was one knight amongst the king's secretaries, called Terricus Gualerancius, a eunuch whom the queen had always hated and mocked, but who was faithful and had the king's ear like his father's before him. He boldly persuaded the king not to suffer her to dally longer at Antioch both because "guilt under kinship's guise could lie concealed," and because it would be a lasting shame to the kingdom of the Franks if in addition to all the other disasters it was reported that the king had been deserted by his wife, or robbed of her. So he argued, either because he hated the queen or because he really believed it, moved perchance by widespread rumour. In consequence, she was torn away and forced to leave for Jerusalem with the king; and, their mutual anger growing greater, the wounds remained, hide it as best they might.

b. From Walter Map, *De Nugis Curialium/Courtiers' Trifles* (1181–92), edited and translated by M.R. James (Clarendon, 1983), pp. 475–77

To him[1] Henry, son of Matilda, succeeded, and upon him Eleanor, Queen of the French, cast her unchaste eyes, and contrived an unrighteous annulment, and married him, though she was secretly reputed to have shared the couch of Louis with his father Geoffrey. That is why, it is presumed, their offspring, tainted at the source, came to nought.

c. From William of Tyre, *A History of Deeds Done beyond the Sea* (c. 1184), translated by Emily Atwater Babcock and A.C. Krey, 2 vols. (Columbia UP, 1943), vol. 2, pp. 179–81, 196

[William records the visit of King Louis VII of France and Eleanor to her uncle, Raymond, Prince of Antioch, during the Second Crusade. At first Raymond eagerly welcomes Louis and

---

1 King Stephen of England.

seeks his aid in furthering his plans to conquer several neigh-
bouring cities. This passage records the breakdown of their
friendship.]

Raymond had already more than once approached the king pri-
vately in regard to the plans which he had in mind. Now he came
before the members of the king's suite and his own nobles and
explained with due formality how his request could be accom-
plished without difficulty and at the same time be of advantage
and renown to themselves. The king, however, ardently desired
to go to Jerusalem to fulfill his vows, and his determination was
irrevocable. When Raymond found that he could not induce the
king to join him, his attitude changed. Frustrated in his ambi-
tious designs, he began to hate the king's ways; he openly plotted
against him and took means to do him injury. He resolved also
to deprive him of his wife, either by force or by secret intrigue.
The queen readily assented to this design, for she was a foolish
woman. Her conduct before and after this time showed her to
be, as we have said, far from circumspect. Contrary to her royal
dignity, she disregarded her marriage vows and was unfaithful
to her husband.

As soon as the king discovered these plots, he took means to
provide for his life and safety by anticipating the designs of the
prince. By the advice of his chief nobles, he hastened his depar-
ture and secretly left Antioch with his people. Thus the splendid
aspect of his affairs was completely changed, and the end was
quite unlike the beginning. His coming had been attended with
pomp and glory; but fortune is fickle, and his departure was
ignominious.

Some people attribute this outcome to the king's own base
conduct. They maintain that he received his just deserts because
he did not accede to the request of a great prince from whom he
and his followers had received kind treatment. This is of especial
interest, because these persons constantly affirmed that if the
king would have devoted himself to that work, one or more of the
above-named cities might easily have been taken [...]

The King of the Franks passed a year among us. Then, at the
time of the spring crossing, after celebrating Easter at Jerusalem,
he returned to his own land with his wife and nobles. On his
arrival there, remembering the wrongs which he had suffered
from his wife on the journey and, in fact, during the entire pil-
grimage, he decided to put her away. An annulment was solemnly
granted in the presence of the bishops of his realm on the grounds

of blood relationship. Immediately, without lapse of time, and even before she returned to Aquitaine, her paternal inheritance, she was taken to wife by Henry, Duke of Normandy and Count of Anjou. Shortly after the marriage, Henry succeeded Stephen, King of the Angles, who died without male children.

The King of the Franks, happier in his second choice, then espoused Maria, daughter of the Emperor of Spain, a maiden pleasing to God and highly esteemed for her saintly life and character.

d. From Richard of Devizes, *The Chronicle of Richard of Devizes of the Time of King Richard the First* (c. 1192), edited by John T. Appleby (Nelson and Sons, 1963), pp. 25–26

Queen Eleanor, an incomparable woman, beautiful yet virtuous, powerful yet gentle, humble yet keen-witted, qualities which are most rarely found in a woman, who had lived long enough to have had two kings as husbands and two kings as sons, still tireless in all labours, at whose ability her age might marvel [...] Many know what I would that none of us knew. This same queen, during the time of her first husband, was at Jerusalem. Let no one say any more about it; I too know it well. Keep silent!

e. From Gerald of Wales (Giraldus Cambrensis), *On the Instruction of Princes* (c. 1216–23), in *The Church Historians of England*, translated by Joseph Stevenson (Seeleys, 1858), 5.1.223–24

But it is a matter of sufficient notoriety how Queen Eleanor had conducted herself at first in the parts of Palestine beyond the sea; and how when she returned she had behaved herself towards her first as well as her second husband [...] Also Geoffrey, Earl of Anjou, when Seneschal of France, had carnally known Queen Eleanor; of which, as it is said, he frequently forewarned his son Henry, cautioning and forbidding him in any wise to touch her, both because she was the wife of his lord, and because she had been known by his own father.

As it were to crown all these enormities, which were already too enormous, King Henry, as common report declared, dared by an adulterous intercourse to defile this so-called Queen of France, and so took her away from her own husband, and actually married her himself. How, then, I ask, from such a union could a fortunate race be born?

f. From *A Thirteenth-Century Minstrel's Chronicle* (c. 1260), *Récits d'un ménstrel de Reims: A Translation and Introduction*, translated by Robert Levine (Edwin Mellon P, 1990), pp. 12–13

The barons agreed that the king[1] should marry, and they gave him the Duchess Eleanor, who was a very evil woman. She held Maine, Anjou, Poitou, Limoge, and Touraine, and easily three times the land held by the king. Now it happened that he wanted to go beyond the seas, to deliver the Holy Land from the hands of the Saracens. He took the Cross, and gathered many men, and they prepared for their expedition. Embarking upon the sea at St. John's Day, they sailed for a month at the mercy of the winds, arriving at Tyre, for that was the only land held by Christians in Syria. He remained there for the entire next winter, and did nothing but spend his resources.

When Saladin perceived that he was weak and hesitant, he offered battle several times, but the king would not engage in a fight. When Queen Eleanor saw the king's weakness, and she heard men speak of the goodness and strength and understanding and generosity of Saladin, she conceived a great passion for him in her heart, and she sent him greetings through one of her interpreters. He understood that, if he could arrange her escape, she would take him as her lord, and would give up her faith.

When Saladin understood the letter she had sent him through her interpreter, he was very pleased, for he knew that she was the most aristocratic and wealthiest lady in Christendom. Therefore he had a galley prepared, and brought from Ascalon, where he was, to Tyre, together with the interpreter. They arrived at Tyre a bit before midnight.

By means of a hidden door, the interpreter climbed up to the queen's bedroom, where she was waiting for him. When she saw him, she said: "What news?" "Lady," he said, "look at the galley that stands ready and waiting for you. Hurry, before we are seen." "My word," said the queen, "this has been done well." She quickly took with her two women, and two boxes full of gold and silver, intending to have them brought to the galley. When one of her ladies saw what was happening, she left her bedroom as quietly as possible, going to the bed of the king, who was asleep, waking him, and saying to him, "Sir, unfortunately the queen intends to go to Ascalon with Saladin, and his boat is waiting for her in the harbor. For God's sake, sir, hurry."

---

1 King Louis VII of France.

When the king heard this, he jumped up, got dressed, went out and ordered his entourage to arm themselves, and he went off to the harbor. There he found the queen, with one foot in the galley, and he took her by the hand, and brought her back to her room. The king's entourage captured the galley and its crew, for they were too surprised to defend themselves.

The king asked the queen why she wanted to do this, and she replied, "In the name of God, because you are not worth much. I heard so much about Saladin that I love him better than I love you. Be sure that you understand that you will never hold me." The king quickly departed, leaving her heavily guarded, and decided to return to France, for his money was running out, and in the East he had acquired only dishonour.

He set out again on the sea, together with the queen, and returned to France, where he consulted with all his barons about what to do with the queen. After he told them what she had done, the barons said, "My God, the best advice we can give you is to let her go, since she is a devil, and we fear that, if you keep her any longer, she will have you killed. In addition, she has given you no[1] child." The king foolishly agreed, and carried out this plan; he should have cloistered her, so that his land would have remained great all his life, and the disasters of which you are about to hear would not have taken place.

The king returned Queen Eleanor to her land, and she immediately sent for King Henry of England, who had ordered Saint Thomas of Canterbury killed. He came willingly, married her, and did homage to the king for the very sizeable land that he took over. Henry took Eleanor back to England, and kept her until he had three sons with her, of whom the eldest was named Henry Courtmantel, a fine and competent knight, who, however, did not live long. The second was named Richard, a fine, competent, generous, chivalrous man, and the third was named John, an evil, treacherous man, who did not believe in God.

g. From the *French Chronicle of London* (early fourteenth century), in *Chronicles of the Mayors and Sheriffs of London and the French Chronicle of London*, translated by Henry Thomas Riley (Trübner, 1863), p. 232

1162: In this year the queen was shamefully hooted and reviled at London Bridge, as she was desiring to go from the Tower to Westminster; and this, because she had caused a gentle damsel to be put to death, the most beauteous that was known, and imputed to her that she was the King's concubine. For which reason, the queen had her taken and stripped all naked, and made her sit between two great fires in a chamber quite closed, so that this very beauteous damsel was greatly terrified, for she thought for certain that she should be burnt, and began to be in great sorrow by reason thereof.

And in the meantime the queen had caused a bath to be prepared, and then made the beauteous damsel enter therein; and forthwith, she made a wicked old hag beat this beauteous damsel upon both her arms with a staff; and then, so soon as ever the blood gushed forth, there came another execrable sorceress, and brought two frightful toads upon a trowel, and put them upon the breasts of the gentle damsel; whereupon they immediately seized her breasts and began to suck. Two other old hags also held her arms stretched out, so that the beauteous damsel might not be able to sink down into the water until all the blood that was in her body had run out. And all the time that the filthy toads were sucking on the breasts of this most beauteous damsel, the queen, laughing the while, mocked her, and had great joy in her heart, in being thus revenged upon Rosamonde. And when she was dead, the queen had the body taken and buried in a filthy ditch, and with the body the toads.

3. Englishmen with Tails

[The rumour that Englishmen had tails may have started with a story of the mistreatment that St. Augustine suffered at the hands of the English during the Anglo-Saxon period (see the selection from the poet Layamon, below). It was certainly in wide circulation by the twelfth century and, as the chronicler Richard of Devizes attests, was a popular slur against the English even in Richard's day. Richard of Devizes records the insult being used in Sicily, as does *RCL*: but *RCL*'s poet has the French deploy it more often than the Greeks and later has the Muslims take it up as well.]

a. From Richard of Devizes, *The Chronicle of Richard of Devizes of the Time of King Richard the First* (c. 1192), edited by John T. Appleby (Nelson and Sons, 1963), pp. 19–20

Before the arrival of King Richard in Sicily, the Griffons were stronger than all the other rulers of that region [...] They made peace with all who recognised the King of France as lord, and then they sought full revenge for their injuries from the King of the English and his tail-bearing men. (The paltry Greeks and Sicilians called all those who followed that king "Englishmen" and "tailed"). The English, therefore, were denied all trade with the country by edict, and they were slain both by day and by night by forties and fifties, wherever they were found unarmed. The slaughter increased every day, and it was planned to continue with this madness till every one of them was either killed or put to flight. The King of England, that fearful lion, was aroused by these tumults and roared horribly, burning with a rage worthy of such a breast. His raving fury terrified his dearest friends.

b. From Layamon's *Brut* (c. 1205), edited by Frederic Madden, 3 vols. (Society of Antiquaries of London, 1847), vol. 3, lines 29535–600; translated by Katherine Terrell

[Layamon was a Middle English poet who adapted Wace's Anglo-Norman *Roman de Brut*. While the origin of the legend is in doubt, it may have been first recorded by William of Malmesbury, in his 1125 *Gesta Pontificum*.[1]]

Then St. Augustine went forth, east and west and south and north, and afterwards throughout England, and turned it to God's hand. He taught clerics, he erected churches, he healed the sick through God's might. And so he went southward, so that he came to Dorchester: there he found the worst men that dwelled in that land. He told them of God's teaching, and they heaped scorn upon him; he taught them of Christianity, and they sneered at him. There stood St. Augustine and his clerics with him, and spoke of Christ, God's son, as had been their custom, and they went to him with evil intent, and took the tails of fish and hung them on his cope on each side. And they ran beside him and pelted him with bones, and attacked him with grievous stones, and drove him out of that place. They were hateful to St. Augustine, and he became exceedingly angry. He went five miles from Dorchester and came to a hill that was tall and fair, and there he knelt on bended knee and called upon God to avenge him upon those cursed folk who had vanquished him with their evil deeds. Our Lord heard him in Heaven and sent his vengeance against the wretched folk who had hung the fish tails on the clerics. Then tails came upon them; therefore they may be

---

1 See Broughton, *Legends* 93–97, for further examples.

tailed. That tribe was shamed, for they had muggles,[1] and in each company men call them mugglings, and always every free man speaks foul of them, and English freemen in foreign lands for that same deed have a red face, and many a good man's son in foreign lands who never came near there is called wicked.

---

1 A rare word that seems to mean "fishtails" in this context.

Works Cited and Recommended Reading

Manuscripts and Early Printed Editions

a version

MS Cambridge, Gonville and Caius College 175/96
MS London, BL Additional 31042 (formerly London Thornton)

b version

MS London, College of Arms HDN 58 (formerly Arundel)
MS Oxford, Bodleian 21802 (formerly Douce 228)
MS London, BL Egerton 2862
MS London, BL Harley 4690
MS Edinburgh, National Library of Scotland Advocates' 19.2.1
(Auchinleck)

Early Printed Editions

Wynkyn de Worde, 1509
Wynkyn de Worde, 1528

Editions of *Richard Coer de Lyon*

Brunner, Karl, editor. *Der Mittelenglische Versroman über Richard Löwenherz*. Wilhelm Braumüller, 1913.
Larkin, Peter, editor. *Richard Coer de Lyon*. TEAMS Middle English Texts Series. Medieval Institute Publications, 2015.

Other Primary Sources

Ambroise. *The History of the Holy War: Ambroise's Estoire De La Guerre Sainte*. Translated by Marianne Ailes. Boydell, 2003.
Bahā' al-Dīn Ibn Shaddād. *The Rare and Excellent History of Saladin, or al-Nawādir al-Sultāniyya wa'l-Mahāsin al-Yūsufiyya*. Translated by D.S. Richards. Crusade Texts in Translation. Ashgate, 2002.

Barber, Malcolm, and Keith Bate, translators. *Letters from the East: Crusaders, Pilgrims and Settlers in the 12th–13th Centuries.* Crusade Texts in Translation. Ashgate, 2010.

Bird, Jessalynn, Edward Peters, and James M. Powell, editors. *Crusade and Christendom: Annotated Documents in Translation from Innocent III to the Fall of Acre, 1187–1291.* U of Pennsylvania P, 2013.

Chronicles of the Mayors and Sheriffs of London and the French Chronicle of London. Translated by Henry Thomas Riley. Trübner, 1863.

Edbury, Peter, editor and translator. *The Conquest of Jerusalem and the Third Crusade: Sources in Translation.* Crusade Texts in Translation. Ashgate, 1998.

Fulcher of Chartres. *A History of the Expedition to Jerusalem 1095–1127.* Translated by Frances Rita Ryan. U of Tennessee P, 1969.

Gerald of Wales (Giraldus Cambrensis). *On the Instruction of Princes. The Church Historians of England.* Translated by Joseph Stevenson. Seeleys, 1858, 5.1.132–241.

Guibert of Nogent. *The Deeds of God Through the Franks: A Translation of Guibert of Nogent's Gesta Dei per Francos.* Edited and translated by Robert Levine. Boydell, 1997.

Hill, Rosalind, editor and translator. *The Deeds of the Franks and the Other Pilgrims to Jerusalem.* Thomas Nelson and Sons, 1962.

John of Salisbury. *Memoirs of the Papal Court.* Translated by Marjorie Chibnall. Nelson and Sons, 1956.

Layamon. *Layamon's Brut.* Edited by Frederic Madden. 3 vols. Society of Antiquaries of London, 1847.

Levine, Robert, translator. *A Thirteenth-Century Minstrel's Chronicle (Récits d'un ménstrel de Reims): A Translation and Introduction. Studies in French Civilization 4.* Edwin Mellen, 1990.

Map, Walter. *De Nugis Curialium / Courtiers' Trifles.* Edited and translated by M.R. James. Clarendon, 1983.

Morte Arthure. Edited by Edmund Brock. EETS 8. Trübner, 1865.

Munro, Dana C. "Urban and the Crusaders." *Translations and Reprints from the Original Sources of European History,* vol. 1, no. 2. Department of History of the U of Pennsylvania / P.S. King, 1895.

Nicholson, Helen J., editor and translator. *The Chronicle of the Third Crusade: The Itinerarium Peregrinorum et Gesta Regis Ricardi.* Crusade Texts in Translation. Ashgate, 1997.

"On the Feast of Corpus Christi." *The Minor Poems of the Vernon Manuscript.* Edited by Carl Horstmann. EETS o.s. 117. Kegan Paul et al., 1901.

Orderic Vitalis. *The Ecclesiastical History.* Edited and translated by Marjorie Chibnall. 6 vols. Oxford UP, 1975.

Ralph of Caen. *The Gesta Tancredi of Ralph of Caen: A History of the Normans on the First Crusade.* Edited by Bernard S. Bachrach and David S. Bachrach. Ashgate, 2005.

Raymond d'Aguilers. *Historia Francorum qui Ceperunt Jherusalem.* Edited and translated by John Hugh Hill and Laurita L. Hill. American Philosophical Society, 1968.

Richard of Devizes. *The Chronicle of Richard of Devizes of the Time of King Richard the First.* Edited by John T. Appleby. Nelson and Sons, 1963.

Robert of Brunne. *Handlyng Synne.* Edited by Frederick J. Furnivall. EETS o.s. 119 and 123. Kegan Paul et al., 1901.

Roger of Howden. *The Annals of Roger de Hoveden.* Translated by Henry T. Riley. 2 vols. H.G. Bohn, 1853.

Sweetenham, Carol, and Susan Edgington, editors and translators. *The Chanson D'Antioche: An Old-French Account of the First Crusade.* Crusade Texts in Translation. Ashgate, 2011.

William of Malmesbury. *Chronicle of the Kings of England.* Edited and translated by J.A. Giles. Henry G. Bohn, 1847.

William of Tyre. *A History of Deeds Done beyond the Sea.* Translated by Emily Atwater Babcock and A.C. Krey. 2 vols. Columbia UP, 1943.

Critical Works

Akbari, Suzanne. "The Hunger for National Identity in *Richard Coer de Lion.*" *Reading Medieval Culture: Essays in Honor of Robert W. Hanning,* edited by Robert M. Stein and Sandra Pierson Prior, U of Notre Dame P, 2005, pp. 198–227.

Ambrisco, Alan S. "Cannibalism and Cultural Encounters in *Richard Coeur de Lion.*" *Journal of Medieval and Early Modern Studies,* vol. 29, 1999, pp. 499–528.

Anderson, Carolyn. "Constructing Royal Character: King Richard in *Richard Coer de Lyon.*" *Publications of the Medieval Association of the Midwest,* vol. 6, 1999, pp. 85–108.

Blurton, Heather. *Cannibalism in High Medieval English Literature.* Palgrave Macmillan, 2007.

Cordery, Leona F. "Cannibal Diplomacy: Otherness in the Middle English Text *Richard Coer de Lion.*" *Meeting the Foreign in the Middle Ages,* edited by Albrecht Classen, Routledge, 2002, pp. 153–71.

Finlayson, John. "Legendary Ancestors and the Expansion of Romance in *Richard, Coer de Lyon*." *English Studies*, vol. 79, 1998, pp. 299–308.

———. "*Richard, Coer de Lyon:* Romance, History or Something in Between?" *Studies in Philology*, vol. 87, 1990, pp. 156–80.

Heng, Geraldine: "Cannibalism, the First Crusade, and the Genesis of Medieval Romance." *Differences: A Journal of Feminist Cultural Studies*, vol. 10, no. 1, 1998, pp. 98–174.

———. *Empire of Magic: Medieval Romance and the Politics of Cultural Fantasy*. Columbia UP, 2003.

———. "The Romance of England: *Richard Coer de Lyon*, Saracens, Jews, and the Politics of Race and Nation." *The Postcolonial Middle Ages*, edited by Jeffrey Jerome Cohen, Macmillan, 2000, pp. 135–71.

Manion, Lee. *Narrating the Crusades: Loss and Recovery in Medieval and Early Modern English Literature*. Cambridge UP, 2014.

McDonald, Nicola. "Eating People and the Alimentary Logic of *Richard Coeur de Lion*." *Pulp Fictions of Medieval England: Essays in Popular Romance*, edited by Nicola McDonald, Manchester UP, 2004, pp. 124–50.

Royan, Nicola. "A Question of Truth: Barbour's *Bruce*, Hary's *Wallace*, and *Richard Coer de Lion*." *IRSS*, vol. 34, 2009, pp. 75–105.

Shutters, Lynn. "Lion Hearts, Saracen Heads, Dog Tails: The Body of the Conqueror in *Richard Coer de Lyon*." *Masculinities and Femininities in the Middle Ages and Renaissance*, edited by Frederick Kiefer, Brepols, 2009, pp. 71–100.

Turville-Petre, Thorlac. *England the Nation: Language, Literature, and National Identity, 1290–1340*. Clarendon, 1996.

Uebel, Michael. *Ecstatic Transformation: On the Uses of Alterity in the Middle Ages*. Palgrave Macmillan, 2005.

Yeager, Suzanne M. *Jerusalem in Medieval Narrative*. Cambridge UP, 2008.

Literary and Historical Contexts

Ailes, Adrian. *The Origins of the Royal Arms of England*. Graduate Centre for Medieval Studies, University of Reading, 1982.

Akbari, Suzanne Conklin. *Idols in the East: European Representations of Islam and the Orient, 1100–1450*. Cornell UP, 2009.

Brewer, Keagan. *Prester John: The Legend and Its Sources*. Crusade Texts in Translation. Ashgate, 2015.

Broughton, Bradford B. *The Legends of King Richard I, Coeur de Lion: A Study of Sources and Variations to the Year 1600*. Studies in English Literature 25. Mouton, 1966.

——, editor and translator. *Richard the Lion-Hearted and Other Medieval English Romances*. E.P. Dutton, 1966.

Calkin, Siobhain Bly. *Saracens and the Making of English Identity: The Auchinleck Manuscript*. Routledge, 2005.

Claster, Jill N. *Sacred Violence: The European Crusades to the Middle East 1095–1396*. U of Toronto P, 2009.

Evans, Michael R. *Inventing Eleanor: The Medieval and Post-Medieval Image of Eleanor of Aquitaine*. Bloomsbury, 2014.

Furrow, Melissa. *"Chanson de geste* as Romance in England." *The Exploitations of Medieval Romance*, edited by Laura Ashe, Ivana Djordjević, and Judith Weiss, D.S. Brewer, 2010, pp. 57–72.

Gillingham, John. *Richard the Lionheart*. Times Books, 1978.

——. *Richard I*. Yale UP, 1999.

Hamel, Mary. "*The Siege of Jerusalem* as a Crusading Poem," *Journeys toward God: Pilgrimage and Crusade*, edited by B.N. Sargent-Baur, U of Michigan P, 1992, pp. 177–84.

Kadar, Benjamin Z. *Crusade and Mission: European Approaches Toward the Muslims*. Princeton UP, 1984.

Lloyd, Simon. "William Longspee II: The Making of an English Crusading Hero." *Nottingham Medieval Studies*, vol. 35, 1991, pp. 41–69.

Loomis, Roger S. "*Richard Coer de Lion* and the *Pas Saladin* in Medieval Art." *PMLA*, vol. 30, 1915, pp. 509–28.

Matthew, H.C.G., and Brian Harrison, editors. *Oxford Dictionary of National Biography*. Oxford UP, 2004, www.oxfordonline.com/online/odnb.

McDonald, Nicola. "A Polemical Introduction." *Pulp Fictions of Medieval England: Essays in Popular Romance*, edited by Nicola McDonald, Manchester UP, 2004, pp. 1–21.

Middle English Dictionary. https://quod.lib.umich.edu/m/med/.

Nelson, Janet, editor. *Richard Coeur de Lion in History and Myth*. King's College London, Centre for Late Antique and Medieval Studies, 1992.

Nirenberg, David. *Neighboring Faiths: Christianity, Islam, and Judaism in the Middle Ages and Today*. U of Chicago P, 2014.

Norako, Leila. "The Crusading Imaginary of Late Medieval England." PhD dissertation, U of Rochester, 2012.

Owen, D.D.R. *Eleanor of Aquitaine: Queen and Legend*. Blackwell, 1993.

Pearsall, Derek. "Middle English Romance and Its Audiences." *Historical and Editorial Studies in Medieval and Early Modern English for Johan Gerritsen*, edited by Mary-Jo Arn and Hanneke Wirtjes, Gronigen, 1985, pp. 37–47.

Price, Merrall Llewelyn. *Consuming Passions: The Uses of Cannibalism in Late Medieval and Early Modern Europe.* Routledge, 2003.

Putter, Ad. "A Historical Introduction." *The Spirit of Middle English Popular Romance*, edited by Ad Putter and Jane Gilbert, Routledge, 2000, pp. 1–15.

———. "The Metres and Stanza Forms of Popular Romance." *A Companion to Medieval Popular Romance*, edited by Raluca Radulescu and Cory James Rushton, D.S. Brewer, 2009, pp. 111–31.

Rubenstein, Jay. "Cannibals and Crusaders." *French Historical Studies*, vol. 31, 2008, pp. 525–52.

Rubin, Miri. *Corpus Christi: The Eucharist in Late Medieval Culture.* Cambridge UP, 1991.

Tolan, John. *Saracens: Islam in the Medieval European Imagination.* Columbia UP, 2002.

———. *Sons of Ishmael: Muslims through European Eyes in the Middle Ages.* U of Florida P, 2008.

Tyerman, Christopher. *God's War: A New History of the Crusades.* Belknap, 2006.

Weston, Jessie L. *The Three Days' Tournament: A Study in Romance and Folk-Lore.* David Nutt, 1902.